Adobe® Experience Manager

A Guide to CQ5 for Marketing Professionals

CLASSROOM IN A BOOK®

The official training workbook from Adobe Systems

Adobe Press books are published by Peachpit, a division of Pearson Education located in San Francisco, California. For the latest on Adobe Press books, go to www.adobepress.com. To report errors, please send a note to errata@peachpit.com. For information on getting permission for reprints and excerpts, contact permissions@peachpit.com.

Project Editor: Nancy Peterson
Development Editor: Bob Lindstrom
Copyeditors: Darren Meiss, Eric Schumacher-Rasmussen
Proofreaders: Darren Meiss, Liz Welch
Production Coordinator: Maureen Forys, Happenstance Type-O-Rama
Compositor: Happenstance Type-O-Rama
Technical Reviewer: Rob Winkle
Indexer: Jack Lewis
Cover Designer: Eddie Yuen
Interior Designer: Mimi Heft

Printed and bound in the United States of America

ISBN-13: 978-0-321-92863-4
ISBN-10: 0-321-92863-6

9 8 7 6 5 4 3 2 1

Acknowledgments

I'd like to thank the following people for their love, support, and encouragement while I wrote this book:

- My wife, Lauren, who never let me get discouraged. Your unconditional support kept the wind in my sails through this entire project. I love you.

- My parents and family for their love and encouragement. You've never doubted me in my life, even when I've doubted myself.

- Peachpit Press for putting a lot of faith in an unproven writer. Working with everyone at your organization has been a pleasure and a privilege. I look forward to a long working relationship.

- My editors, Bob Lindstrom and Nancy Peterson, for keeping me out of a straight jacket. You guys made this project enjoyable, even on the days it was difficult.

- My copyeditors, Darren Meiss and Eric Schumacher-Rasmussen, for making me sound like a much better writer than I am.

- My tech editor and colleague, Robb Winkle, for having my back during this project. You were the last line of defense, keeping me from publishing something stupid.

- All of my colleagues at CITYTECH, Inc. who helped me with parts of this book. I had some of the smartest people I've ever worked with behind me for this undertaking.

- Matt and Janet Van Bergen for your genuine support of my career goals and of my involvement in this extracurricular endeavor.

- The MISST program faculty at Muskingum University for your enthusiasm about my graduate school learning experience and your encouragement to take on this project.

- Loni Stark, Cédric Hüsler, Vebeka Guess, Elliot Sedegah, and everyone else from Adobe who took time out of their schedules to help me with the development of this book.

There are many more people who had a part in creating this book. I'm truly grateful for everyone who made this a reality. Thank you so much!

CONTENTS

2   EVALUATING AEM

3 MANAGING CONTENT

4 DIGITAL ASSET MANAGEMENT

5 METADATA AND TAGGING

6 MULTILINGUAL CONTENT

10 MOBILE FOR MARKETERS

11 ARCHITECTURE BASICS

20 THE IMPLEMENTATION PROCESS

GETTING STARTED

If you're reading this book, you probably have a vested interest in Adobe Experience Manager (AEM). Maybe your organization just purchased it and you are preparing for your implementation. Maybe you started a new job where they are using AEM. Perhaps you are leading a team tasked with evaluating a purchase. Or maybe you're already familiar with AEM and want to supplement your experience. Whatever your reason, you should be excited about the platform. I'm excited about the discoveries you're about to make.

This book describes the value of Adobe Experience Manager for the marketing team—more specifically, the digital marketing team. It discusses technology-agnostic challenges that digital marketers face. Each chapter begins with *why* you should be concerned about a specific digital marketing challenge. Then the chapter explains how AEM helps you address that challenge.

If you've worked with Adobe technology, you're probably familiar with their *Classroom in a Book* series. This book, however, is an atypical *Classroom in a Book*. You won't find step-by-step directions that explain how to use each and every feature of Adobe Experience Manager. Instead, my goal is to help you understand the business value of AEM's features so that you can evaluate if and how you want use them.

Note: You can reference the Adobe documentation (which is available online) for step-by-step directions for many features.

I structured the book this way because every AEM implementation is unique. AEM isn't a typical software application that works the same way on every computer that runs it. It is an enterprise technology platform, and every implementation customizes it to suit the users. One marketer's methods may be very different from another's, but a customized AEM implementation can serve both. As a result, I chose to concentrate on the value of the AEM features and basic AEM patterns of use.

At the end of this book, you should be prepared for your role as a marketer overseeing an Adobe Experience Manager implementation. You should be able to assemble an actionable plan for using AEM to accomplish your digital marketing goals. You should be prepared for the technical conversations that you will have with an implementation partner. Lastly, you should be fired up about how Adobe Experience Manager will help to transform your marketing organization.

Who is this book for?

I wrote this book for the marketer. I'll generally refer to you as a marketer throughout this book. That general term may include a Chief Marketing Officer, web writer, copy editor, digital marketing manager, information architect, or any number of different job titles.

I deliberately made the assumption that you are reading this book *before* working through your first AEM implementation or making your first AEM purchase. That doesn't mean the book won't have value for marketers who are experienced with the AEM platform. Working through an implementation is the best way to learn the platform, and I believe that explaining AEM through that implementation lens is the best way to teach it.

There's also a growing, loyal community of technologists, programmers, and system administrators who are passionate about what AEM offers. Many of you may have picked up this book. If you are looking for tutorials on how to build components, how to code for Apache Sling, or how to set up JMX monitoring, you're reading the wrong book. There will be *very little* code in this book, and that little bit will be absolutely fundamental. This is not a book for the techies. It's a book for marketers.

That said, this book does hold value for technical folks who are interested in learning the platform. If you want to be great at technically implementing Adobe Experience Manager, you *need* to understand the marketing context of why you will do the things you will do. Why would you build that component? Why would you make that integration to SiteCatalyst? Why would you build a configuration page instead of a dialog? All the programming or administration tasks you might undertake are rooted in marketing needs. This book can help you to understand those needs.

CQ5 or AEM?

You may have noticed a bit of confusion about the name of the product you'll be reading about, CQ5 or AEM. Even Adobe's documentation and marketing material remains a little fuzzy about the name.

Until the most recent release of AEM (as of this writing), Adobe Experience Manager was called Adobe CQ5. The CQ5 brand dates back to Day Software, the Swiss company that created the platform. Adobe acquired Day in 2010, and Day CQ5 became Adobe CQ5. The platform also has been known by many aliases, including Day Communiqué, CQ5, Adobe Digital Enterprise Platform, and Adobe WEM. As of the version 5.6 release in 2013, the product is Adobe Experience Manager.

This book will refer to the platform as Adobe Experience Manager (AEM), although we'll make occasional reference to CQ5. AEM remains much the same product under its many aliases; many of the concepts in this book apply backward to CQ5.5

and 5.4, as well as other incarnations of AEM. The book assumes you're looking at or using AEM 5.6, but much of the content will still be applicable to earlier versions. (If you go back as far as Communiqué 4, however, this book becomes less relevant.)

As a general rule, when you see the terms CQ5 and AEM (in this book and elsewhere), you can consider them interchangeable. We'll discuss the new naming convention and how it fits into Adobe's broader digital marketing platform in the first part of this book.

The role of the solution partner

Throughout this book, I'll frequently mention your solution partner, implementation partner, and other variations of those terms. The solution partner plays a critical role in your AEM implementation. It's not the kind of software that you can buy, install, and start using. It's a platform on which you implement the tools you need to build your website. Someone with a deep understanding of AEM must build those tools, called page templates and components. That deep understanding comes from your solution partner.

The solution partner will build your page templates and components, make necessary customizations to your AEM installation, integrate with other technology platforms, and provide guidance on how and how not to use AEM. Selecting a compatible partner and working with them to implement AEM is vital if you want to justify the ROI of purchasing the platform. Therefore, throughout the book I point out when you should lean on your partner for information or support.

My "day job" is as a solution partner consultant, so I know the role well. This book is what I would want every client to read before entering into an AEM implementation with me or any solution partner. So do your homework before you dive in!

What's in the book?

This book is written to break down the digital marketing issues addressed by Adobe Experience Manager in a methodical way. It's made up of four parts and twenty chapters.

Part 1: Understanding AEM

The first section of this book will give you the context to understand why Adobe Experience Manager is important. We look at the following general topics:

* What the Adobe Marketing Cloud is

* How Adobe Experience Manager fits into Adobe's holistic digital marketing platform

- What kind of software Adobe Experience Manager is and the meaning of terms such as "web experience management"
- The basic value proposition of Adobe Experience Manager
- How you can decide if Adobe Experience Manager is right for you

If you know very little about the platform or about Adobe's vision for digital marketing technology, this section is for you. The rest of the book builds on the concepts discussed in this section.

Part 2: Executing with AEM

In Part 2, we get down to the nuts and bolts of Adobe Experience Manager. We talk about the business value of all the basic features of the platform. The section addresses the following:

- How AEM enables you to perform basic web content management functions
- The functional advantages of AEM over other types of content management systems
- The basic AEM interfaces and operations you should know
- Why you would or wouldn't want to use those interfaces or operations
- The basics of AEM's architecture and administrative requirements
- How you can use AEM to address your marketing needs

This section describes the features of AEM but won't give you step-by-step directions for using those features. After reading this section, you should understand all the basic AEM functionality and why it can be valuable to your marketing organization.

Part 3: Optimizing AEM

Part 3 looks at the Adobe Experience Manager functions that set it apart from its competition. We look at the features you can use to optimize your content to create incredible web experiences for customers. This part addresses the following issues:

- How to use dynamic content to create impressive web experiences
- How to measure the effectiveness of your content and how to optimize your content's effectiveness
- How you can use Adobe Experience Manager to deal with the content concerns of your marketing campaigns
- How to integrate AEM with other digital marketing platforms

After reading this section, you'll understand what sets AEM apart from other systems. You'll also know how to build dynamic, effective web experiences that delight your customers.

Part 4: Implementing AEM

The book closes with a few chapters that prepare you to participate in or supervise an AEM implementation. They include discussions of the following:

- The basic technical knowledge you need before working with AEM
- Implementation team concerns and how you will help address them as a marketer
- The processes an AEM implementation will entail
- How you can define and communicate your AEM implementation needs
- Issues to expect when working through an implementation

Much of the content in Part 4 isn't specifically about Adobe Experience Manager. But I promise to bring it back home so you will ultimately understand how this content will affect you.

About the screenshots

This book isn't a "how to" guide, so it isn't heavy with screenshots. However, I've included a few to provide some visual context for the text. If you're looking at an existing AEM 5.6 implementation while reading this book, you may wonder why your screens don't match those in the book. No, you didn't buy the wrong book.

Starting with AEM 5.6, the platform has begun a transition to a new user interface, casually called the "touch UI." This user interface is designed to be more compatible with touch-screen devices such as tablets. As of the 5.6 release, the touch UI is only partially implemented, so many AEM features still use the classic interface. In fact, you currently can toggle between the interfaces to use whichever one you prefer.

Adobe is gradually rolling out the new UI to test how the market receives it. They want to build a UI that delights their customers without making an abrupt change that would compromise everyone's processes and training.

Because the UI is released as kind of a "beta" feature and because all earlier versions of CQ5 lack the new UI, I've chosen to include screenshots of only the classic user interface. Still, much of what I will show in the classic UI can also be done with the new touch UI. If you can't do it yet, you'll be able to do it soon. For now, if you are trying to follow along with the text, just make sure you are doing so in the classic AEM user interface.

About Geometrixx

Throughout this book, and in the Adobe documentation, you'll see references to a company called Geometrixx. When you install Adobe Experience Manager, a few demonstration websites are included that allow you to experiment with the features. Geometrixx is the fictional company that Adobe uses to brand those sites. They are fully implemented sites that showcase the functionality of the platform. These sites are intended to give you an idea of what it would be like to work in AEM before beginning an implementation.

About Classroom in a Book

Adobe Experience Manager: Classroom in a Book is part of the official training series for Adobe digital marketing software, developed with the support of Adobe product experts. The content is designed so you can learn at your own pace. If you're new to AEM, you'll learn the fundamental concepts and features you'll need to use the program. *Classroom in a Book* also teaches many advanced features, including tips and techniques for using the latest version of this application.

Prerequisites

Before using *Adobe Experience Manager: Classroom in a Book*, you should have a working knowledge of the technology of the web, like how websites are constructed. The book assumes basic understanding of HTML-based webpages, web analysis, basic information technology concepts, and a background in marketing. This book will cover some of the technical basics in Part 4. If you've worked with digital marketing for any significant period of time, you should be good to go!

Additional resources

Adobe Experience Manager: Classroom in a Book is not meant to replace documentation available online or to be a comprehensive reference for every feature. For comprehensive information about program features and tutorials, please refer to these resources:

Official AEM documentation

http://docs.day.com

The official AEM documentation contains detailed descriptions of almost every feature in the platform. It also includes information for a variety of roles, such as programmers, marketers, system administrators, and managers. This documentation site is frequently updated and does a nice job of separating information by AEM version.

Adobe CQ5 forum

http://forums.adobe.com/community/digital_marketing_suite/cq5

The CQ5 section of the official Adobe forums is a great place to ask questions or find out additional information about AEM. The forum is moderated by members of the Adobe Experience Manager technical team and they frequently participate in discussions. Several AEM community members (including myself) pop in now and then to help one another. This is the place to ask specific questions that aren't covered by the documentation.

Experience Delivers

http://experiencedelivers.adobe.com

This is the official web experience management blog authored by members of the Adobe product team. It contains content relevant to developers, marketers, and managers, so there's a little something for everyone. Follow this blog to keep up on new features and the general direction Adobe will be taking the platform.

Daycare

http://daycare.day.com

This official support website for Adobe Experience Manager is a password-protected site, so you won't be able to access it until you've purchased an AEM license. This is the go-to portal for any issues that you or your solution partner cannot resolve.

The blogosphere

There is a *ton* of great AEM content on the web. The community of developers, marketers, and other professionals who are passionate about AEM is growing quickly. It seems that every day, new blogs and Twitter accounts are popping up. Sometimes simply Googling for the information you need is the best way to go. You may even find a few of my blog posts about AEM!

1 THE BASICS

Adobe Experience Manager (AEM), the focus of this book, is one component of a holistic digital marketing vision. It's important to understand that vision, the technologies that help marketers realize the vision, and the general concepts around which AEM is built.

In this chapter, you'll learn about:

- Web content management and web experience management
- Adobe's approach to digital marketing technology
- The Adobe Marketing Cloud
- The Adobe Creative Cloud
- The solutions of the Marketing Cloud

By the end of this chapter, you will have a better understanding why Adobe Experience Manager was created and how it can help your organization succeed. As you continue through this book, we'll dive deeper into this innovative technology to understand its features and their value to you as a marketer.

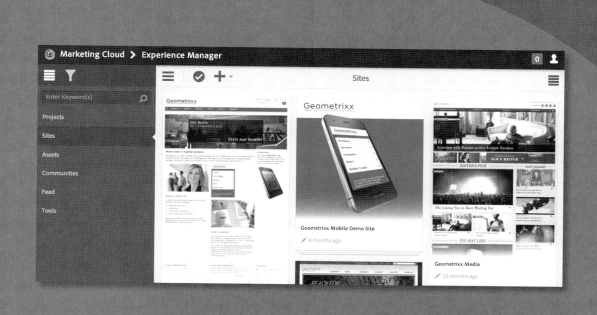

Adobe's full-featured digital marketing platform

Introduction to web content management

A **web content management system** (WCM) can be many things. There are hundreds of WCMs of all shapes and sizes. But all of these technologies serve one basic purpose: enabling nontechnical users to create, edit, and manage website content without the need to implement code changes. A WCM puts digital marketing concerns in the hands of the marketers and leaves technical concerns to the technical teams.

CQ5

The core technology in AEM comes from a web content management system platform created by Day Software, called CQ5. As constructed at the time Adobe acquired Day, the platform aligned to what basically defines a web content management system. This concept remains at the heart of AEM, which now adds an array of peripheral marketing technologies upon that WCM core.

It seems self-evident that marketers and communicators should be able to manipulate their organization's website content, but a decade or two ago that simply wasn't the case. In the early days of e-commerce and digital marketing, highly technical staff was required to make even the smallest website changes.

Changing text on the home page required a code change. Adding a link to your navigation required a code change. Updating your branding—guess what—code change. The marketer was at the mercy of the technologist, and back then these two groups had very different goals. Some of you may remember those days. Others may never have to experience that two-headed workflow. But, it's the pain point behind the creation of a WCM.

That "split personality" workflow has some pretty obvious shortcomings:

- The workflow crosses multiple, isolated business units.
- Code changes can introduce additional risk.
- The need for expensive technical staff increases the cost of content updates.
- Marketers do not have the necessary technology agility to test or adjust to changes in the world.

Overcoming the siloed organization

Some modern organizations are reorganizing to break down the silos that house marketing and information technology concerns. This was certainly less the case twenty years ago, when some of these changes had just begun to occur. Even today, many organizations are far from achieving that esoteric state of cooperation.

Digital marketing is the concern of both marketers (content creation, digital artwork, creative input) and technologists (programming, project management, architecture). When marketing wasn't digital, the two departments didn't need to mix. But today every organization is *expected* to have a web presence, and that requires cooperation between marketing and IT.

The traditional digital presence was owned by IT. They concern themselves with "nerdy" stuff like servers and code, which is important, but definitely not what concerns most marketers. Further, it creates a natural barrier between two organizations that require cooperation but see the world through very different sets of eyes. A WCM helps these departments work together toward a more effective digital presence while still working within their very specific points of view.

Avoiding risky business

The traditional model of website management required technical professionals to edit HTML files when changing the website. Depending on the site's implementation, JavaScript or other more complicated code updates could be involved. Unfortunately, the more changes made to a site, the more likely that the site might break.

In a traditional website, if a marketer spots something as simple as a missing comma, the solution is a risky change in the live site (Hint: tech guys don't like this), or slogging through an entire development iteration that could take days or weeks. For one comma.

The WCM removes the risk of making content changes: The technology team builds a "protective" framework for the marketer, a sandbox that gives the marketer the freedom to refine and update the site without introducing the potential for code problems. Supervised by the tech team, the WCM can provide as much or as little freedom as the organization requires, and high-risk changes can be limited to functionality changes and major features.

Reducing the cost of content

Many business professionals—and most people reading this book—have played some role in a technical implementation project, so you already know how complicated it is. You have developers who write code, business analysts who maintain requirements, project managers who manage budgets and timelines, business stakeholders who set the direction and write the checks, and of course, the internal and external users.

When a technical team updates content, it has to make HTML and code changes, test them, deploy them, and manage the entire process as it progresses. The man-hours required to make even the smallest content change are expensive. As a result, organizations are forced to update content in batches to reduce cost.

With a web content management system, the cost of content change is limited to the man-hours of the marketer—and that's what they are paid for. Sure, the technical team has to manage the platform from a 1's and 0's perspective, but those costs are not really altered by the marketer's communication needs. With a WCM, the marketers' time commitment is reduced as well, because necessary changes involve only their team's publishing and approval processes.

The need for speed

The three problems I just laid out can be boiled down to a more fundamental issue with the traditional website model: *marketing must move fast enough to keep up with its world.* I bet if you ask anyone in some kind of marketing function, the need for marketing agility will be a top priority. In an incredibly fast-paced world, organizations must adjust their marketing initiatives immediately.

Revenue, mindshare, and success depend on marketing agility, the speed at which marketing plans can adjust to unpredictable changes in the business environment. Although overhyped at times, that agility represents a significant shift in the way marketing departments view their jobs. A marketing agile organization will make many minor, incremental changes over the course of more traditional, long-cycle campaigns.

Web content management platforms were created for the fundamental purpose of providing nontechnical stakeholders the speed to serve customers. When managing an organization's digital presence is fast, easy, and cheap, that organization can more effectively communicate its message to the world. Time and time again, marketing agility has enabled organizations to increase revenue and better meet their goals.

Web experience management

Many argue that the basic idea of a web content management system is outdated. They once enabled a competitive advantage, but that time has passed. Today, WCM is an absolute necessity; more to the point, it's become a commodity. Simply introducing a basic WCM platform will provide only the minimum requirements for managing a modern digital presence. Basic WCM functionality doesn't help differentiate an organization from its competitors' processes and infrastructure. It only helps the organization keep up.

Web users expect more than just an updated website. As customers, we have high expectations for delightful online interaction. Just having a website is the required minimum; it won't impress anyone. Customers now demand personalized experiences on the Web, and not static "brochureware" sites. Naturally, WCM vendors have made every effort to respond to these new expectations by including resources that enable marketers to manage that kind of digital presence.

The new term for these platforms is **web experience management** (WEM or WXM). Sometimes the term **customer experience management** (CEM or CXM) is used, but it typically refers to a broader set of technologies, including some that are not customer-facing. WEM platforms are the next evolution of WCMs that enable organizations to dynamically market to customers based on data from multiple channels. That's the role of Adobe Experience Manager.

The core concepts of a WEM system start with the basics of WCM and add the following:

- Contextual content
- Multi-channel delivery
- Social engagement
- Cross-platform integration

These four elements—contextual content, multichannel delivery, social engagement, and cross-platform integration—are by no means a global definition of WEM. It's a newer concept, and to a certain degree, it's somewhat abstract. But I think those four elements would summarize the way most experts would define the term web experience management. (Also know that this book will refer to AEM as both a WCM and a WEM.) On the whole, a WEM is just a more modern version of a WCM. At their cores, they are the same thing.

Contextual content

Fundamentally, a WCM delivers content. It's better than a static website because, as you've seen, the content can be adjusted without developer intervention. A WEM platform will typically also enable marketers to create contextual (or targeted) content. It's a primary difference between a WEM system and WCM system.

Contextual content is tailored for each visitor. The platform uses whatever information is available to it (such as IP address, previous clicks, GPS information, and so on) to deliver an optimized user experience. As you can imagine, this custom content is quite a bit more complicated to manage from a marketer's perspective. But you can also imagine how much more effective that WEM-generated content could be. Instead of attempting to create one experience that delights as many people as possible, you create experiences specifically calculated to delight the targeted individual.

With a WEM, you can stop trying to be everything to everyone. You can deliver exactly what User A needs when he needs it, and provide something else, just as personalized, for User B.

Multi-channel delivery

Did you know that your computer isn't the only way to access the Web? If not, take a look around (and maybe get your eyes checked). We have phones. We have tablets. We have TV-based web browsers. We aren't far from getting the web into cars and kitchen appliances. If your website is still only optimized for a basic computer-based web browser, you are steps behind in the ways customers will visit your site.

Unlike a WCM, which is basically built for desktop-access sites, a WEM platform will allow you to adapt your web presence to multiple channels and devices. Your strategy may be as simple as one desktop and one mobile site. Or it may be quite a bit more complicated. The WEM system can help deliver the right content through the relevant channel, which enables you to interact with your customers on their terms. Don't think that matters? Tablet users spend more time online with their mobile devices than they do with their computers. Does that change your mind?

Social engagement

As part of a delivery of contextual content, customers expect a social experience on the Web. We're spoiled by the likes of Facebook and Twitter. Browsing the Internet was once a solitary behavior, done in isolation at home. Now it's virtually impossible to evade the opinions, shares, and likes of friends and strangers. Web experiences that don't include an engaging social experience are increasingly seen as outdated and irrelevant.

By definition, a WCM system pays no mind to the social inclinations of a site's visitors. They get what you give them. A WEM system, on the other hand, builds "social" into the core personality of a site. The WEM infrastructure integrates social networks and interactive features, so visitors can communicate with your brand instead of just reading and buying.

Cross-platform integration

No technology lives in isolation. The extent to which organizations can integrate their technology platforms often defines their IT success. For a web platform to deliver a personalized and true representation of a brand, that platform must integrate with other technologies, such as the following examples:

- Sales automation integration, so that the web presence integrates into the offline sales process

- Measurement platform integration (such as web analytics), so that the web presence's goals can be quantified

Generally speaking, any enterprise technology can be customized and integrated with any other technology. This is especially true of applications built on widely accepted standards and/or open technologies (AEM does both very well). But, as a characteristic of a WEM, I really mean to call out a higher level of integration. A WEM platform should integrate with related, critical technologies at the configuration level. It shouldn't require code-based customization—only a matter of setting some options. Achieving this goal requires a new level of foresight, but creates more agile integration points.

Adobe's approach to digital marketing

To understand the broad context that drives all Adobe software development decisions, let's examine their philosophy and approach to digital marketing from a macro perspective. If you make AEM a part of your marketing strategy, you will find it useful to make informed decisions that align with Adobe's view of the big picture.

At the 2013 Adobe Summit, Adobe's CEO Shantanu Narayen described their approach to digital marketing as "a mix of art and science." Adobe has long been respected for their implementation of the "art" side of that equation. The vast majority of creative organizations use Adobe tools such as Photoshop, Illustrator, and Dreamweaver.

For the past few years, Adobe has worked to establish a similarly powerful brand with enterprise customers. In 2009, they acquired a leading analytics company, Omniture. In 2011, they acquired Day Software, the creators of the WCM platform, CQ5. They've acquired PhoneGap, Scene7, and other organizations to play specific parts. These mostly technical platforms, targeted toward the enterprise, are all powerful on their own; but Adobe's vision is to integrate them into a holistic marketing platform.

What is "the cloud?"

Though "the cloud" gets mentioned quite a bit, many people simply don't understand what it means. It's an extremely important concept if you want to understand what Adobe's vision is trying to accomplish, so it deserves a baseline definition for the purpose of this book.

The cloud refers to the World Wide Web outside the walls of an organization or your home. It's really not a new concept or a new technology, but it names that external digital abyss your organization doesn't control. It's called "the cloud" because network topography diagrams typically use a cloud to symbolize the external Internet.

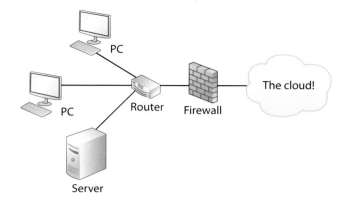

Figure 1.1
A basic networking diagram

Traditionally, information technology has always resided within the walls of an organization. Large enterprises even manage expensive, complicated data centers full of thousands of servers and switches. This technology is a necessary cost for these organizations, but the majority of it does not contribute to any competitive advantage. It's simply the infrastructure that enterprises require to operate. Over the past few years, a new model for infrastructure has been emerging, whereby enterprises outsource their technology and its management to other companies. It is fundamentally changing the way we implement technology.

This technology outsourcing "into the cloud" manifests itself in many ways, but three basic terms are used for classification:

- **Software as a Service (SaaS)** is a piece of software that does not need to be managed internally. It's hosted on someone else's network, and the enterprise simply subscribes to its use. Salesforce.com is an excellent example of a product that was once on-premises software. Now, it is offered in the cloud as a subscription-based service.

- **Infrastructure as a Service (IaaS)** is when an organization external to the enterprise actually manages and owns the information technology hardware. It means an organization doesn't have to build a data center, buy thousands of servers, pay for the utilities to run those servers, and hire teams to manage them. They simply outsource the hardware to a company such as Amazon Web Services at a subscription-based cost. IaaS providers are able to utilize hardware virtualization and economies of scale to more efficiently and more cheaply manage enterprise hardware.

- **Platform as a Service (PaaS)** is the halfway point between SaaS and IaaS. When using PaaS software, organizations control the deployment and configuration of an entire software platform—a group of technologies that make up a technology solution. PaaS doesn't offer low-level control of the hardware infrastructure (as does IaaS), but it's more flexible and configurable than a SaaS offering where you sign up and get what you get.

Each of these models fall under the definition of a "cloud application" because they all include information technology hosted and owned outside of the walls of the enterprise organization.

Defining a platform

Adobe's digital marketing software suite is designed to serve as a platform upon which organizations can build a digital marketing presence. A **platform** is software that requires customization and implementation for an enterprise to realize benefits. Most large enterprise applications, such as enterprise resource planning (ERP) and customer relationship management (CRM) software, will likely fall under the definition of a "platform." It is meant to be a set of building blocks for the organization to organize in whichever way best suits their needs.

Adobe calls their digital marketing solution a cloud because many of the components are (on their own) either SaaS or PaaS implementations. Typically, organizations that implement Adobe's technologies will have a mix of on-premises technology and cloud-hosted technology. Every company has different regulatory and security concerns, technology competencies, and general attitudes toward "the cloud." With that in mind, Adobe has intentionally built infrastructural flexibility into their digital marketing products.

The Adobe Marketing Cloud

Adobe has announced its intent to integrate the art and science of digital marketing. The art is the concern of the creative people: the copywriters, graphic artists, and pure marketers. The science is the concern of the technical people: the programmers, web analysts, and infrastructure managers.

Adobe has organized their technology into two platforms: the **Creative Cloud** and the **Marketing Cloud**. The former includes a highly integrated platform of Adobe's creative software, such as Photoshop and Dreamweaver. The latter consists of the enterprise marketing technologies for managing a digital presence. Traditionally these platforms represented separate concerns for separate parts of the organization, but Adobe has decided to pull it all together into one holistic platform.

A great deal of the Adobe Marketing Cloud was gained from various Adobe acquisitions, which briefly made it complicated to pick and choose from the multiple products Adobe offered. In some cases, functionality overlaps made that choice even more complex.

To streamline the software evaluation process and to better align their software to an overall vision, Adobe grouped their digital marketing technologies into a set of five solutions:

- Social
- Media Optimizer
- Target
- Analytics
- Experience Manager

Each one serves a fundamentally different purpose, but they can be integrated to suit the needs of every organization. These five solutions are basically groupings of once separate products, and some of those products are packaged into more than one solution. The solutions are designed to assist digital marketers with the core challenges they face in modern marketing.

Adobe Social

Social networking has become an integral part of the online world, and as a result, many organizations see it as essential to connect with customers through social channels. But the social networking world is complicated and fast-moving. Should you have a Facebook page? A Twitter account? A Pinterest presence? What about Google+? Do people actually still use MySpace? It's complicated enough for an individual to keep it straight. It gets way more complicated for an organization to sort out how to use these tools to drive revenue and/or provide customer service.

Adobe Social is intended to provide a holistic social management platform to the enterprise. It provides facilities to respond to social interactions from customers, manage a presence across multiple channels, and integrate that social presence with the other parts of the digital marketing platform. Adobe Social provides marketers with insights that have been difficult if not impossible to achieve in the past. However, organizations that cannot turn their social media presence into a revenue engine are leaving money on the table.

The separate software products that now make up this solution are:

- Social
- SiteCatalyst

Adobe Media Optimizer

If your business receives any remotely significant portion of revenue from online sales (chances are that it does), you may rely on online advertising to bring in sales. The world of online advertising is complex. How do you optimize your online ad budget? How do you increase second-chance conversions? How do you

separate concerns. Trying to use one tool to accomplish both diminishes the quality of the functionality designed for both concerns.

Adobe Experience Manager is not one of the platforms that attempts to ride the line between ECM and WCM. It is absolutely designed for websites. However, it's possible to use AEM to host your corporate portal or intranet; and I've worked on projects that nudged toward that line and were considered successful

Blogger community sites

Adobe Experience Manager does include a module, Social Communities, that includes components to implement blogs on a site. I've applied it a number of times and it can be very effective. That said, some websites are intended to be nothing *but* blogs. These sites enlist an army of bloggers to create a community of content producers. Their revenue is driven by on-site advertising, and their product is their content. These sites include Venture Beat and Mashable.

You *can* use Adobe Experience Manager to implement such a site. You can probably argue that some Adobe Marketing Platform technologies are effective for blog sites. But, AEM was not designed as a blogging platform.

If blogs are your primary channel of content, you probably will find more success using a blogging platform. With any task, you want to implement the technology that best meets your needs. With the huge variety and differentiation between WCMs, trying to turn AEM into something it's not doesn't make much sense.

Small, simple websites

I already discussed how Adobe Experience Manager is really effective when it comes to the basics of managing web content. It takes quite a bit of the complexity out of authoring complex web pages, especially those with dynamic, targeted content. Really, few website requirements are unreasonably outside the realm of AEM's capabilities, but I feel it's important to establish one thing: If you are trying to manage a very simple, standard web presence, Adobe Experience Manager is probably overkill.

The web content management industry is quite mature, with literally hundreds of options in the market. Some are designed for big companies, some for small, some for B2C companies, some for B2B companies, and the list goes on. You can probably find a WCM platform for any reasonable niche you can think of. Adobe Experience Manager is designed for enterprises. It is built (along with the rest of the Marketing Cloud) to help marketers manage the complexities of managing large amounts of content, international brands, and complicated digital marketing organizations. AEM can certainly manage a small web presence, although it isn't designed for that purpose and using it that way may be more costly than necessary.

With that in mind, it's important to understand the intent for the platform. I wouldn't advocate the purchase of AEM for absolutely every organization out there. If you are managing a smaller web presence or just don't need to solve the same problems a medium or large enterprise would have to solve, AEM is probably not your best bet.

An AEM success story (that we made up)

Features are great, but on their own, they don't mean much. Before you consider Adobe Experience Manager as a new solution or before you begin working with it, take a look at an example of how it can create success.

This example doesn't touch on all the merits of Adobe Experience Manager, but it does illustrate its value in tangible terms. The events described are all based on real implementations of past versions of AEM technology, although not based on a specific implementation. After reading this example, think about how your organization may be similar or different. How do you think you could use AEM to address your specific needs?

Game Changers Sporting Goods

Game Changers Sporting Goods is an e-commerce site that sells high quality sports equipment and apparel. It gets most of its traffic through social network referral traffic and direct web traffic. Game Changers is not the biggest sporting goods vendor on the web, but it prides itself on superior customer service and the ability to build relationships with customers through social media management practices.

The marketers at Game Changers have social media down to a science, and they've actually used Adobe's social media management tools for some time. They also use Adobe SiteCatalyst for their web analytics, but they really use it only at the fundamental level—not taking full advantage of the product. Their website, which is *the* source of revenue for the company (via product sales) is homegrown and not very flexible. It has served well through the company's initial growth stages, but the site's lack of scalability and its functionality limitations are now restricting growth and compromising long-term marketing plans.

Game Changers identified the following business problems as the priorities restricting growth:

- Inability to expand the functionality of their current website and to provide targeted content

- Difficulty translating their effective social media management practices to conversion success on their site

- Lack of visibility into the effectiveness of different sections or individual pages of their site

- No mobile-optimized web presence without implementing heavy (and expensive) customization

- Lack of marketing agility because the current technology requires a long time to roll out new landing pages and marketing campaigns

Game Changers decided it was time to invest in a marketing platform to help it reach the next stage of digital maturity, and chose the core part of the Adobe Marketing Cloud to do so: Adobe Experience Manager, Adobe Social (which they already used), and Adobe Analytics. They also migrated their e-commerce concerns from a platform designed to power small- to medium-sized businesses to Hybris, because of the integration advantages between Hybris and AEM.

The implementation was not easy, nor was it an overnight change. Game Changers worked with Adobe and a solution provider to merge its already successful marketing practices with new techniques designed to maximize the value of the platform they purchased. The largest opportunity for growth centered on effective content management and integration with the e-commerce platform, so that was where they began.

Phase 1 of their marketing platform integration introduced the following:

- A fresh, new website design with the new site launched on Adobe Experience Manager

- Responsive web design that served tablet- and mobile phone-optimized content from a single body of content

- Direct integration between AEM and Hybris, enabling authors to build content about those products as if they were part of the same system

- Direct integration between AEM and SiteCatalyst to track campaign-based analytics and effectively measure funnel conversion

- New agile marketing practices for content updates. Because of the flexible, easy content management, the content team could adopt agile practices for responding quickly to the trends identified by SiteCatalyst.

Once the company had a new web presence, it focused on optimization. Company marketers already knew what content worked. They had metrics about funnel drop-offs and conversion rates. And they now had an integrated web platform that didn't restrict change. Game Changers' marketers began to ask, "How do we upsell to return customers?" and "How do we use our social media competency to increase sales?"

In phase 2, the company implemented Adobe Target and AEM personalization to create a unique web experience for each customer, including:

- Customer segmentation based on past product purchases and social media interest (pulled in for customers who registered with Facebook accounts)
- Targeted content presentation based on that customer segmentation
- Integration with Adobe Test&Target to measure and optimize the customer segmentation, so it's not just based on educated guessing
- Integration with Adobe Search&Promote to create a personalized and optimized site search experience for customers

With the phase 2 implementation, Game Changers was not only able to personalize content for each visitor, it was able to measure how effective that personalization was, and tailor it accordingly.

After two major phases of implementation, Game Changers is already seeing benefit. The conversion rate for return customers has increased and site traffic from social referrals and organic search results has more than tripled. The new design, up-to-date content, and social network integration made products and pages easier to share on social networks and boosted the company's relevance in SEO terms, which drove this traffic increase.

Game Changers has been able to scale its infrastructure to meet these rapid traffic demands, because of AEM's flexible architecture. The best part is that the company's marketers are better able to innovate with their practices. Removing the burden of technology is the best thing you can do for a marketing person, and they did just that.

Despite Game Changers' success, it is already scoping out a third phase of implementation. It plans to expand internationally by rolling out Spanish, French, and Chinese versions of the site. This initiative will not only require translations for the page text of each site, but it will need to appropriate design and copy changes to adapt to cultural differences. Personalization campaigns will also have to target content for various parts of the world to respond to cultural differences.

All the while, the international sites must be optimized for tablet and mobile phone traffic, which Game Changers identifies respectively as their first and second most profitable channels. Fortunately, Adobe Experience Manager and the peripheral technologies implemented around it fully support this next phase of business requirements.

As mentioned, Game Changers is not a real website (nor is it intended to represent any real brand or company), and this is not a real story. But, I've borrowed concepts and parts of stories from a variety of success with Adobe Experience Manager and the Adobe Marketing Cloud. The successes of this hypothetical e-commerce company can be your success.

Considering AEM

Let's get down to the fundamental question: Is Adobe Experience Manager the best solution to solve your business problems? In an enterprise, this question is rarely easy to answer. That answer is never a binary "yes" or "no." But you still need to make a decision one way or the other. I want you to be able to make an informed choice about whether Adobe Experience Manager is right for you. In this section, let's consider the kinds of questions you should ask when working through that decision. I can't give you a definitive answer, but I can help guide you to one.

How does your organization feel about open source software?

Adobe Experience Manager is not open source software, but many of the layers of infrastructure under the hood are open source. The creators of Adobe Experience Manager have led many of the open source projects that are combined to power their commercial product. As a result, AEM licensees get the best of both worlds: innovative, community-driven open source solutions and enterprise polish and support. I have all the confidence in the world in the security and stability of these open source layers of the platform, and many extremely familiar, enormous brands trust AEM to power their content. But not everyone shares my positive opinion of open source technology.

Right or wrong (I think "wrong"), many organizations are still gun-shy about open source technology. Maybe they've previously been burned by bad open source software. Maybe their industry is bound by regulations. Maybe the CIO just has the wrong idea. But some organizations are just not comfortable allowing open source software within the enterprise. If your organization is not comfortable with it, and your management cannot be convinced to let go of that notion, Adobe Experience Manager may not be not a good fit.

On the other hand, some organizations embrace the open source concept—organizations that openly share otherwise proprietary data or that participate in industry-wide development instead of only company-specific development. This model of business is fairly modern (and unfamiliar to dinosaurs of the business world), but it does exist. These organizations would do well to consider Adobe Experience Manager, even against open source competitors like Joomla or Drupal. AEM offers the polish and support of enterprise software, while maintaining the spirit of open source.

Your organization is likely to fall somewhere between these two extremes, but it is important to recognize which pole is closer. Open source technology is built into the culture of the AEM product, so organizations must take a decisive position on it.

Who manages your marketing technology?

Distribution of technology responsibility and accountability can vary significantly from one organization to the next. Some companies manage technology through a large, command-and-control IT unit, while others outsource all of their IT. Some companies allow different business units to manage their own IT infrastructures, without much cohesion or collaboration between them. Management of enterprise technology is fragmented today, so you assume that the tech guys are the only ones worried about tech.

Understanding *who* manages your organization's marketing technology (content management, web analytics, social media tools, and so on) is important when considering Adobe Experience Manager. AEM will become the hub of your web presence. Depending on the organization, there can be a significant divide between the unit that worries about brand and messaging and the unit that worries about IT security and efficiency. AEM implementation will highlight issues that both groups will want to worry about, so it is important to assess and manage the relationship between the CMO's organization and the CIO's.

Some marketers have begun to use cloud-based technologies as a way to bypass the slowness, contention, or complexity of working with a monolithic IT department. These organizations allow digital marketing departments to "outsource" their technology to SaaS and PaaS products. This approach often results in faster time to market and simplified implementation, but it does have drawbacks. When a marketing unit outsources its technology, it can wall the unit off from the rest of the enterprise, which can complicate necessary (and desirable) integrations and can strain the relationship between marketing and IT. This approach also may be viewed as incompatible from an enterprise architecture perspective.

Adobe Experience Manager and the rest of the Marketing Cloud are very scalable and very cloud-ready, so keep that in mind during initial planning. You will need to honestly analyze who controls (and wants to control) the multiple facets of your digital marketing technology portfolio. Those internal relationships will have a significant effect on what you buy and where you put it.

How agile are your marketing plans?

Many modern marketing organizations have adopted the same agile practices that are sweeping through the software development world. With agile marketing, the marketer frequently makes small adjustments to respond to short-term market changes, instead of executing long, expensive campaigns and retroactively assessing success. Your organization's ability to be "agile" isn't a simple question, but assessing just *how* agile you are and how agile you want to be will be important.

Adobe Experience Manager was designed with marketing agility in mind. Can you execute long-duration, expensive campaigns with it? Of course! But, AEM enables marketing to make changes quickly. Integrated with other facets of the Adobe Marketing Cloud, AEM also helps to give marketers real-time feedback about the success or failure of their digital marketing initiatives. If your new landing page campaign is failing miserably, you want to know as soon as possible, so you can adjust.

If marketing agility is a challenge for your organization, or if it has been made a focus for the future, Adobe Experience Manager is definitely a content management system that can help.

How flexible are your business processes?

The Adobe Marketing Cloud is designed to help marketers turn fragmented, disorganized, and nonintegrated marketing processes into a holistic digital marketing initiative. Therefore, when implementing AEM, as any other part of the cloud strategy, it's important to assess how rigid your current business processes are and how flexible you can make them.

I've worked with many clients implementing Adobe Experience Manager. Some insist on doing things the way they've always done them. Others are very open to new processes that help them operate more efficiently with the software they've purchased. Both types of client can be successful, but they take different paths to success. With the former client, I discuss the customizations and integrations we can build into the AEM to adapt it to their process needs. With the latter client, I spend more time implementing AEM per best practices and then helping them adapt their business processes to align with those best practices.

When evaluating Adobe Experience Manager, you'll want to think about which of these scenarios you favor. You can have success in either, but you must consider the trade-offs when going with one or the other. An effective solution implementation partner should be able to guide you through whichever choice you make.

Do you currently license other Adobe products?

This may seem like an obvious question, but it warrants discussion, all the same. How much Adobe technology do you already use within your organization? How much are you considering purchasing? Adobe Experience Manager, SiteCatalyst, and Photoshop are all excellent tools on their own, but their value compounds exponentially when combined in a holistic platform.

Adobe Experience Manager turns into a much more compelling option if you already license or are seriously considering the other Adobe marketing tools. On its own, AEM may not currently seem like your best option for a WCM. But nothing lives in a vacuum. If you anticipate the opportunity to put together an integrated digital marketing system, you should use that opportunity to weigh heavily toward AEM as your content management platform.

What other systems will you want to integrate?

In addition to additional Adobe products, you may want to integrate other technologies with Adobe Experience Manager. This could include infrastructure platforms like LDAP or SSO systems. It could include another content management platform for primarily internal use. It might even include homegrown applications. Understanding what technologies will integrate with AEM is an important upfront consideration.

Because Adobe Experience Manager is built on open standards technologies, integration is typically a viable option. The decisions that might limit your ability to integrate are:

- Cloud-hosted implementations when the on-premise tools are located behind a tall firewall

- Fragmented IT ownership, where it will be difficult to settle on common interfaces between the organizations that own the technology

- Integrations that fundamentally alter the core functionality of either platform

- Integrations where best-practice approaches are not possible or not pursued

You *can* integrate Adobe Experience Manager with other enterprise technologies. The key is applying the proper planning and foresight to ensure that you are doing so effectively and for the right reasons.

What form does your content take?

What kind of content are you trying to manage? This question may be the fundamental decision point between an ECM and WCM solution, but it can also provide insight when evaluating WCMs. Also important to know is what forms that content will take during the creation process. Does content start as a Word file that is shared between copywriters? Are you extracting content from existing HTML pages? These questions will affect how simple or complicated it will be to implement Adobe Experience Manager as your central content management platform and the destination of that content.

Licensing considerations

Before moving on to discuss how AEM features can help you as a marketer, it's important to talk about licensing. Throughout this book, I discuss features without any regard to how Adobe packages and sells them. Typically, I assume an unlimited pocketbook and a fully licensed Adobe platform. (Remember, I admitted that most of my examples are only *based* on reality.) I completely understand that actual budgets and schedules are much more restrictive.

Understanding what to buy, when to buy it, and what you can/should do with it can be a real challenge. Occasionally it's not even clear which features are licensed as part of which projects. Further, even within Adobe Experience Manager different facets are licensed separately. Sorting this out can get especially tricky because Adobe allows for "partial" AEM implementations.

When you install Adobe Experience Manager, you install *everything*, meaning you install features that you may not yet own. The benefit is that you get to try out these other features before you buy them. The challenge is that if you implement a partially-licensed AEM, you need to be *very* aware of those unpurchased boundaries.

To help you through the licensing and feature evaluation process, I highly recommend enlisting the services of a solution implementation partner. They can consult with your organization and your Adobe account managers to really understand what you need to accomplish your business goals. Doing so will help you avoid purchasing software you don't need and needing software you didn't purchase. Locking up a good implementation partner can help you through these early, pre-implementation stages. Don't wait to find one until it's time to write the code.

I won't take licensing into consideration throughout the rest of this book because licensing arrangements change often, sometimes from customer to customer. Trying to anticipate and explain where those boundaries might exist would not be that helpful. As you read about the features and potential of Adobe Experience Manager, keep track of the ones you find most interesting. Then work with Adobe and/or a solution partner to make sure you license all the tools you need. It'll save you headaches (and face palms) down the road.

Summary

Adobe Experience Manager is a web experience management system, designed to make it easier for marketers to manage their web presence. AEM includes a number of core features that enable things like in-context content authoring and integration with a full digital marketing technology stack. There are many ways you could implement AEM and many use cases that the product can serve. It's important to understand which ones the platform is designed to address directly. Working with Adobe and an effective solution partner to identify what pieces of AEM and the Marketing Cloud serve your needs is the first critical step towards a successful implementation. Adobe Experience Manager is a powerful tool, when effectively used, but trying to implement it without assistance is difficult.

Review questions

1. What is content personalization?
2. Why is AEM a good fit for international websites?
3. Why would AEM not be an ideal fit for small websites?
4. What is AEM's relationship to open source technology?

Review answers

1. Personalization means targeting specific content to specific subsets of site visitors based on whatever limited information the system can derive about those users. This can be a more effective marketing tactic than presenting the same static website to all customers.

2. AEM provides the functionality to roll out multiple versions of the same site, and then make culturally sensitive changes. AEM also includes the infrastructure to help manage translations for your content, though it does not actually translate the content without integration with another system.

3. AEM is built for enterprises with large, complicated digital marketing strategies. It is perfectly capable of implementing small websites with basic features, but doing so is probably overkill in terms of budget and functionality.

4. AEM is not an open source product, but the most important layers of the underlying technology are open source projects. Some of Adobe's top engineers are key contributors to some of those projects.

3 MANAGING CONTENT

In this chapter, you'll learn the best ways to apply AEM's content management features:

- What it means to be a page-centric content management system

- The basic parts of content management in Adobe Experience Manager

- The relationship between templates, components, and pages

- How to create and manage page-centric content within Adobe Experience Manager

- Managing complex, multi-team content creation and publication

- Common patterns of content inheritance

- Basic features for managing pages

- How to create search-engine optimized content

By the end of this chapter, you'll understand the basics of content management within Adobe Experience Manager, including the different ways you can create content.

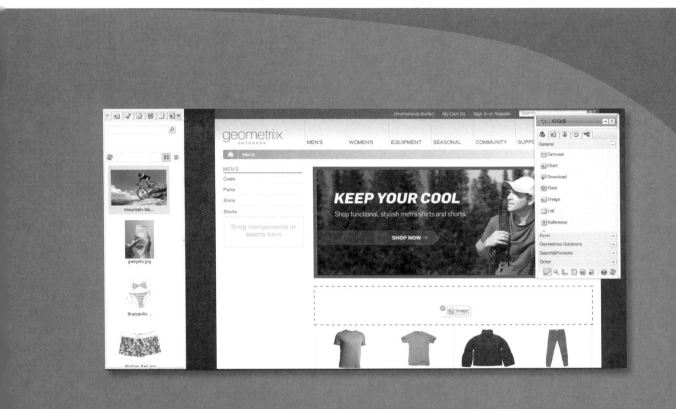

AEM's innovative in-context page authoring features

Managing content the AEM way

If you are responsible for managing your organization's web presence, you are forced to answer many questions. How do I keep my content fresh and accurate? How do I distribute the content management workload across my team? How do I reduce the time needed to author the content on my enormous website? I could go on, and I'm sure you could, too. If your success within your organization, and maybe your bonus, are dependent on deploying a successful website, these questions are ones you wrestle with daily. More importantly, if you've decided to invest in a web content management system (good decision), you expect it to answer those questions head on.

Adobe Experience Manager is designed to make it easy for those with a marketing mind, not a computer science mind, to manage their digital brand. Once the basic infrastructure is set up, your content editors, information architects, and managers can take full control of creating pages and editing the content on those pages. This marketing empowerment is the core function of any web content management system, but AEM addresses it uniquely.

The content editing experience in Adobe Experience Manager is as natural as arranging icons on your smartphone or playing with building blocks. The interface is visually appealing and organized. Content is authored within the same hierarchical structure that site visitors will experience. Marketers edit pages by looking at (and editing) those pages exactly as the site visitor will see them.

If you've worked with an older content management system, you know the frustration of filling out a form and hoping it looks good. You know how difficult it can be to find the file you need to edit. You knew there had to be something better…and there is. Through the rest of this chapter, we'll dive into the basic content management ideas available in Adobe Experience Manager and look at why they might matter to you.

Key roles

A fundamental challenge when managing the web presence for an enterprise-level organization is that a lot of people—and priorities—are involved. Managers provide oversight because they may have bonuses driven by the revenue the website generates. Copywriters want to publish creative writing that embodies the organization's brand. Different teams are responsible for different sections of the website. Before you give everyone free reign of your CMS, consider the basic roles that separate the goals of its users.

AEM and its documentation define this participation within the context of specific roles. While no one expects an organization implementing AEM to completely reorganize company structure around the roles defined in the documentation, it's important to understand them. In reality, digital marketing managers will have to identify which participants inside and outside the company correspond to roles as defined in AEM. This will also require that managers identify when the roles in AEM are not adequately granular and therefore require more specific definition (this is common).

This section defines the following key roles, as related to content creation and management:

- Administrators
- Content authors
- Content approvers
- Tag administrators
- DAM administrators
- Anonymous users

Certain individuals or groups may embody more than one of these roles. These roles are also not necessarily shipped as "groups" out of the box in AEM. These are simply abstractions of the key content management functions within the system.

Note that these roles simply define a set of functions that different groups of people perform within the system. If you need to break up team permissions by different parts of your site, you can do that, too. If you have a large site, you probably *will* do that. (We'll cover how user permissions work in Chapter 12, and it will include how to break up permissions across a site.)

Administrators

Administrators are the super-users of the system. In short, they have permission to do anything and everything. Therefore, only a select few should possess this level of authority, especially in a production environment. With the appropriate settings, administrators can also impersonate other users within the AEM authoring interface. That can be a very powerful function. Only system administrators and development team leaders will typically hold this role.

Content authors

Content author (sometimes just "author") is a catch-all title to describe the people who actually create content within the system. Generally speaking, these are people who are building pages and setting up content. Many of the AEM features are designed to optimize authoring for this group of individuals. In the simplest implementation, a content author can author all the websites in Adobe Experience Manager. Larger organizations with many content authors may restrict individual authoring abilities to certain sites or parts of sites.

Content approvers

Many organizations set up AEM so that content cannot be made public until approved by a small group of stakeholders, known as content approvers. An AEM implementation does not require content approvers, but they exist more often than not. Their job is to ensure that content meets quality and brand standards before being shown publicly. Individuals performing this function will heavily use their workflow inboxes for managing publication requests.

Tag administrators

Tag administrators are the individuals responsible for maintaining tagging taxonomies within Adobe Experience Manager. Tags add another abstraction of categorization to content that isn't limited to the hierarchy of pages. (Tag management will be discussed in Chapter 5.) It is important to limit the ability to manipulate tagging taxonomy to a select few individuals.

DAM administrators

Some organizations use AEM Digital Asset Management (the DAM), for managing digital media files, more heavily than others. They may require content authors/administrators who are specifically responsible for managing the media files within the DAM. DAM content carries quite a bit of metadata, which can get complex. When that metadata is well managed, content authors can more easily locate the media they need. The DAM administrators share a similar responsibility with tag administrators, in that they are responsible for structuring and categorizing content with AEM. DAM administrators are not required for an AEM implementation and are typically used only in implementations that use the DAM heavily.

Anonymous users

An anonymous user is anyone accessing a website within AEM without being authenticated with an AEM-managed account. During content authoring, anonymous users play no part; but they are important to mention, because they are the ultimate audience for the content. They are actually defined as a user in AEM, so that permissions can be specifically granted or revoked. But generally speaking, anonymous users are limited only to reading webpages and DAM media files.

Pages and page-centric content

Content management systems help users deal with content using a variety of paradigms. First, there are differences between systems that are built to manage web content (webpages and digital media) and enterprise content (documents, spreadsheets, diagrams.) Then, within the group of systems that manage web content, you'll find additional differences. (We'll leave enterprise content management systems off the table for this book. That's a whole other animal.)

Web content management systems, such as Adobe AEM, fall into one of two categories: page-centric and content-centric. In a page-centric system, the webpage is the basic unit of content. You create content *as* a webpage and manage it accordingly. In a content-centric system, you manage the content separately from the way it's delivered and displayed, even though it's likely to be delivered as a webpage.

A content-centric system is a little more flexible, because it keeps the information separate from its delivery format. These systems are good for serving as a central hub for information that can be fed into other systems or channels (think mobile apps, aggregators, and so on.) However, these systems aren't always totally intuitive for managing *just* web content. You have to work through an extra layer of abstraction to understand how your content turns into the webpage you deliver to a customer.

A page-centric system is specifically built for creating and delivering webpages. You can certainly integrate a page-centric system with external systems such as mobile applications; it just isn't quite as seamless as using a content-centric system. The page-centric system isn't an information hub, it's a webpage hub. However, because its focus is on web content, these systems are specifically optimized for building and managing webpages.

Adobe Experience Manager is a page-centric system. The page is the basic unit of content you will deliver to your customers. You'll create, edit, move, delete, and deliver webpages. You *can* deliver content in other formats like XML or JSON. You can aggregate your content into RSS feeds. But, the most natural and common way you will deliver content is via a webpage. Keep that in mind as we discuss the ways you can use AEM to create web content.

Content editing tools

Adobe Experience Manager provides a set of conceptual tools to enable marketers to build webpages. These are the building blocks that a marketer assembles to actually create a website. This section may get a little technical, but hang with me. The point of going through all of these concepts is to better prepare you to define your AEM requirements when you get to that point.

AEM is not the kind of software you can simply turn on and use. You *must* work with a solution implementation team (usually an Adobe solution partner) to develop the templates and components you'll need for building your website(s). AEM does include a few components out of the box, but it's not a best practice to use them. They are mostly provided as examples or foundations on which to build. However, they are helpful for playing around and for getting the feel of authoring content in AEM.

As a marketer, you will have to work through the process of defining your needs for your development team, so they can build the pages and components that allow you to meet those needs. This section breaks down the basic building blocks you'll have to define to set up an AEM implementation.

Site administration interface

The site administration (site admin) will be your home if you are a content author, primarily working on webpages. It's the interface for building and managing a hierarchy of webpages. From this interface you can drill down through that hierarchy, add or edit pages, delete pages, and hook into other page management features. The site admin is identified by links within AEM labeled "Websites," even though there is not really a *thing* called a website.

The site admin is the easiest place to view the names and titles of your pages. These terms sound synonymous, but in AEM they are not. The name is the part of a URL that a page represents. The title is the reader-friendly description of the page, usually shown in the top of the web browser. Consider the following site structure:

- Game Changers (/gamechangers)
    - Products (/products)
        - Football (/football)
    - About Us (/about-us)

If you were to access the About Us page, your URL would be /gamechangers/about-us.html. The name is *about-us* and the title is *About Us*. The pages from which another descends define that page's URL. So, the URL for the Football page is actually /gamechangers/products/football. Your page's titles and names are best managed in the site administration interface along with other features.

The AEM documentation talks through all the different features available in the site admin UI. However, most of the site admin features are just shortcuts to other features that will be discussed in this chapter and beyond.

Understanding components

While the page is the primary AEM unit of content, it's not the lowest common denominator. Components are the building blocks of pages, and really, the entire AEM platform. A component is an individual piece of functionality that renders as a piece of a webpage. Some components are extremely simple, such as a Title component that simply outputs a line of text. Some components are quite a bit more complex, such as a dynamic Calendar component that displays events in several different visual formats. After a page is created, content authors will spend most of their time adding, removing, arranging, and configuring AEM components.

Essentially, *everything* in AEM is a component, including pages. That may sound confusing, so let's dig into components a little deeper. They are conceptually quite simple.

Because Adobe Experience Manager is page-centric, every interface within the platform, and basically every application built on top of the platform (usually websites) is made up of webpages. HTML (HyperText Markup Language) describes content so that web browsers can universally interpret and display that content. An AEM component is simply a piece of code that outputs part of the HTML that makes up the page.

There are two kinds of components: page components and content components. Page components create the page-level HTML elements that are necessary for a browser to interpret the page. These are the HTML elements that only appear once on every page, like <head> and <body>. Naturally, there will only be one page component per webpage. Content components make up the individual pieces of the page, and they are usually reusable on many webpages. A content component cannot exist on its own, because without a page component, it doesn't contain the necessary top-level HTML elements for the browser to display it. A single webpage will contain many content components.

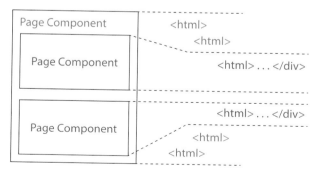

Figure 3.1
Page and content components

Components can (and often do) extend from other components. Programmers on an implementation team do this as a way to reduce code, but component structure also has important implications for content authors. This concept of extension allows for families of components that share similar functionality. For example, a Title component may simply output one line of text, configured by the author. Developers could also create a component called Advanced Title, which outputs that same title line of text, but also outputs an author-configured subtitle below it. All of the properties and functionality for Title would exist in Advanced Title, but the latter would add additional functionality.

This sounds like kind of a technical concept (and to a point, it is). So, why would I discuss it in a book about the value of AEM to a marketer? As you develop the requirements of your AEM implementation, you'll want to think upfront about your authors' experience in editing pages. Identifying which components share related functionality, and are therefore candidates for extension, helps you find ways to streamline the authoring experience.

Working through these relationships early will enable you to discuss them with your solution implementation partner, so that they aren't making their own assumptions about how components relate. If you are having trouble identifying how components may be related, work with your solution partner and an information architect to talk through the requirements. Let's look a bit closer at what makes up a page or content component.

Page components

Page components define the overall structure of a page and include the required page-level HTML markup. Every page is backed by a single page component. Page components almost always extend from another page component.

Generally speaking, all webpages in a website tend to share a few very similar layouts. They likely share a header and footer. They likely use the same fonts and colors. Therefore, a site will generally start with a "global" or "base" page component that defines all those basics. Then all other page components will extend from that page component, adding functionality. Theoretically, you can extend levels of components forever, but with page components extending beyond three or four levels generally isn't practical.

Page components are generally invisible to a content author because they are presented to AEM users behind the façade, called a template. If you've used other content management systems, the term *template* is probably familiar. When you tell AEM to create a page, you will select a template. The template will tell AEM which page component to use to render the page. As a marketer, you can generally consider *template* and *page component* to be synonymous.

Work with your information architect to draw out the templates you'll want to build so that you can create content in whatever form you need. The information architect and your solution partner can help you lay out a pattern of page component inheritance. (See "Content inheritance" later in this chapter.)

Content components

Content components make up the individual pieces of functionality on a webpage. They can be extremely simple or extremely complicated. Some content components may be added to a page by a content author, and others are statically included in a page component. Statically included components cannot be removed or rearranged, but otherwise function exactly the same as those added by an author.

Unlike a page component, a content component cannot exist by itself, because it doesn't output the required page-level HTML. A browser wouldn't be able to interpret a lone component as a valid webpage. Therefore, components have a dependency that they be included inside a page. When you think about the relationship between page and content components, remember this: Page components can render on their own as webpages, but typically don't have much business value. Content components cannot render on their own as pages, but when added to or statically included in a page, they add value to the page by displaying information or providing some kind of interactivity.

As an author, the content component will become quite familiar to you. After creating a new page (or choosing one to edit), you'll be presented with a webpage that includes some built-in components. Those statically included components cannot be removed, but can and should be configured. You'll also probably have some free content areas into which you can drag additional content components. These content areas, called paragraph systems, join content components as the tools for building out a webpage that accurately communicates your brand.

Dialogs

All page components and almost all content components are configured using a dialog. The dialog is a window that appears when a content author selects a component and clicks Edit. Dialogs are just tabbed forms that prompt the content author for a set of required and optional configurations for the component.

For example, a dialog for a Title component has a single text field in which the content author specifies the text that the component outputs to the page. Generally, page components use a standardized Page Properties dialog, but this is more a convention than a requirement. I've occasionally customized the Page Properties dialog for clients. Sometimes components do not require a dialog, because they have no configuration options.

Figure 3.2
An example of a dialog

List	Descendant pages		
Build list using	Descendant pages		∨
Display as	product		∨
Order by	jcr:title		∨
	Enter a property like 'jcr:created'		
Limit			
	Maximum number of items displayed in list		
Enable Feed	☐		
Paginate after			

Help   OK   Cancel

Paragraph system

The paragraph system (sometimes shortened to *parsys*, pronounced PAR-siss) is a component that acts as a container for other content components. Technically speaking, the paragraph system is a content component itself, but it is only statically included with pages. A content author will never add a paragraph system to a page, and this makes sense. It is a special component, and its only purpose is as a container for other configurable components. It also has no dialog.

The paragraph system is the free-form area on a page where content authors can add components. Most page components will have at least one, where the content author defines the content that makes this page unique from the others. Without a paragraph system, all pages in a website would have to be individually built, which defeats the purpose of using a content management system altogether; or the page would have to be defined only with dialogs, which would be pretty complicated for authors. The paragraph system is identifiable by the following box, defining where components can be added:

Figure 3.3
The indicator of a paragraph system

Drag components or assets here

When you work with designers and information architects to design your website, you'll have to think about which parts of the page should be empty content areas. Remember, you aren't building the entire site. You are building the pieces that will be assembled to create the site. As you design templates and determine which components will be statically included, you should also consider which areas should be paragraph systems.

The site design

Depending on the page, certain components will be allowed or restricted from use in different paragraph systems. Marketers are granted the freedom to manage their content as they wish, but they must do so within a framework of predefined rules that enforce the brand value. These rules are defined by an entity called the site design (or just *design*), a page configuration that defines visual style and other page-agnostic configurations. This includes the rules about which components are allowed in what paragraph systems; or the global settings for components, such as the font size used for text in all Title components.

The site design is important to the marketer, especially at a management level. Carefully consider how much power you want to give different team members to edit different pages on your site. If you have a smaller team or one you are comfortable granting liberal access, you can pretty much make all your components available everywhere. On the other hand, if you have a large or novice team, you may want to consider locking things down a bit. Enforcing stricter rules via the site design, about what components can go where, is one strategy for doing so.

Templates

Pages are built from page components, but this is rarely visible to content authors. Page components are hidden behind a façade, called a template. Templates are sets of configuration that define how page components can be used to build pages. In and of itself, a template cannot do anything. It is literally just metadata about the type of page it creates. Generally speaking, a template will have a one-to-one relationship with a page component, but that's not a hard and fast rule. In fact, when that is not the case, it's even more important for a content author to be aware of what page components (not templates) build each webpage.

A template defines some standard data about the starting point of the page it will help a content author create. Its name defines the type of content and often includes a brief description of the type of page it will create. Occasionally templates also include default preloaded content to be placed on a page. Behind the scenes, a template contains a pointer to a specific page component. When you create a page by selecting a given template, the template tells AEM to use that page component to build the page.

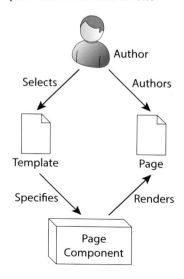

Figure 3.4
The relationship of pages, templates, and components

Content inheritance

If you had 1,000 pages in your website, would you really want to configure the logo image in the header 1,000 different times? What if it changes in six months? Do you want to go back and do it all again? Of course not! With content inheritance you can set your logo image at the top-most page, and then allow that configuration to inherit down to the other 999 pages.

Content inheritance is when a component's configuration is pulled from another component somewhere else within the AEM platform. Content reuse, powered by inheritance, allows you to manage huge websites without digging through a disorganized pile of repetitive content.

There are two categories of inheritance: hierarchical and referential. Both do the same thing, but accomplish it in different ways. You *will* use content inheritance in some form when authoring your site, because it significantly improves the content authoring experience.

Hierarchical inheritance

Hierarchical inheritance is the easier of the two types of inheritance to understand, because it aligns nicely with the tree-based content structure of your website. It's also more commonly used.

Hierarchical inheritance is a pattern by which components inherit their configuration from the same component from a page higher in the page content tree. (Remember, all pages in AEM are part of a big hierarchy, with the content root at the top.) This inheritance pattern is commonly used to reduce the effort required to create large numbers of pages. It also helps to reduce content entry errors by setting content in one place and automatically reusing it. For example, most websites use a consistent header and footer for the entire site. The consistency is important, because it ties the entire site together and ensures that the user doesn't get lost.

Headers and footers are typically built into your page components, but they usually require some kind of configuration. Without inheritance, content authors would have to open every page and configure the same header and footer components. It would be tedious and error-prone, and quite frankly just a waste of time and money.

Fortunately, your solution partner can build hierarchical inheritance into the header and footer components so that the content author need only configure both components at the top-most page in your page tree. At each lower level, the component will first determine if it has a configuration specifically set. If not, it continues up to its parent page, grandparent, and so on, until it finds a configuration for the same component. Then it just reuses that configuration, meaning that you configure the component once, and never again. It also lets you override the configuration at some lower level in the site—as in a microsite or special landing page that requires a change.

Hierarchical inheritance maximizes content authoring efficiency without sacrificing flexibility. It's a pattern you will use in a number of places in your website. Just be sure not to overdo it, because *too much* automatic content can become confusing for content authors.

Referential inheritance

Referential inheritance is another method for content reuse, where a component inherits its configuration from another component specifically selected from anywhere in the site structure. Referential inheritance is a little more complex and a little less common than hierarchical inheritance, but given the right scenario, it can be a very effective way to reuse content.

With referential inheritance, you aren't limited to the structure of your site, so you can make horizontal associations of components. Some AEM functionality (such as Multi Site Manager [MSM], discussed in Chapters 6 and 10) uses the concept of referential inheritance. AEM also provides a Reference component that exclusively pulls configuration from any other content component in the site.

For example, when using MSM to create a separate mobile website that shares some content, you can "roll out" a set of pages to another site (in this case, the mobile site). When pages are rolled out as what is called a live copy, the rolled-out pages and all included content components maintain a reference to the originals. Whenever the originals are updated, so are all the copies that refer to them. Authors have the choice to break inheritance on any of the components that are part of the live copy, so they can be very granular about what inherits and what doesn't.

The benefit with MSM live copies is that each page component points to an original and inherits the original's configuration. The same is true for each content component on the page. This relationship isn't limited to the child-parent relationship, so it allows content authors to be more flexible about reusing content. It's also quite a bit more complex to manage, because you have to be very aware of which components inherit from the one you are changing. AEM does provide some of that information to the authors, but be strategic about deciding what content should be inherited and where.

Creating content

The ability to create content is obviously a pretty important feature in a content management system. The facilities for creating content in Adobe Experience Manager are intuitive and unique. Many would argue that the content creation experience is one of the most important differentiators for the product. AEM allows authors to create content using a "what you see is what you get" (WYSIWYG, pronounced WIZ-ee-wig) paradigm, which enables authors to simply drag components onto a page and configure them within the same context that the user will see them.

● **Note:** If you will be authoring content or managing content authors, this is an important section. It's not a detailed "how-to" guide, but it explores the basics of how page-centric content is created in AEM, which will better prepare you to discuss how you want to help architect your content authoring experience.

This is the primary means of content creation and authoring, but AEM also provides a few others.

Basic page creation

The vast majority of content that marketers create in Adobe Experience Manager will fall under a category I'll call "basic page creation." It just means that authors use the standard WYSIWYG paradigm to build content. The author selects where he wants to create a page, selects a page template (remember, this technically points to a page component), and then adds components to that page as allowed by the page's paragraph system(s). Voilà! A webpage. But let's break that down a little further though.

First, a content author selects where, within the tree structure of pages, he wants to build a new page.

Figure 3.5
Creating a new page

In Adobe Experience Manager, all pages live below a single location, known as the content root. There isn't really an entity called a "website" in AEM. You build a website by starting at a certain point in the hierarchy, below the root. Consider the following example's page hierarchy:

- Content (/content)
    - Geometrixx (/content/geometrixx)
        - English (/content/geometrixx/en)
            - …
        - Spanish (/content/geometrixx/es)
            - …
    - Geometrixx Mobile (/content/geometrixx-mobile)
        - English (/content/geometrixx-mobile/en)
            - …

This hierarchy adheres to a generally accepted best practice in which your websites are organized by application, and then by language. Each node in the hierarchy is technically a page. However, /content, /content/geometrixx, and /content/geometrixx-mobile are pages that do not have any content. Each of the three language nodes are considered the homepages of three websites: Geometrixx English, Spanish, and Mobile. Again, nothing about these pages establishes that they are "the website" or "the application." This is all based on convention. Your web server is what directs browser requests to http://www.geometrixx.com to a specific page node (/content/geometrixx/en) in that hierarchy. Configuring the web server is a task for a system administrator, so don't worry much about it.

Next, the content author creates the new page, by selecting a template.

Figure 3.6
Selecting a template

Depending upon where the author is placing the page in the hierarchy, different templates may be available. Templates can be limited to specific areas in the hierarchy, such as /content/geometrixx/es only. Template availability can also be limited to locations where they are children or parents of pages defined by other templates. When developing requirements, consider this a tool to define rules about how authors can build content. Generally speaking, keep the rules about templates as simple as possible, so it's not too difficult to keep straight.

Once the page is created, you can configure any of the content components that are statically included on the page (but you can't remove them). You will also likely add additional components to whatever paragraph systems are available on the page.

Note: See the AEM documentation to learn how to edit components in both the classic desktop authoring experience and the new touch experience.

Two key functions are available in the authoring experience: the sidekick and the content finder.

The sidekick is the main control for editing pages within the page itself. From the sidekick, authors can pick from the library of available components, open the page properties dialog, perform page management actions, launch the client context for testing personalization, and access other important functions.

The most common function for the sidekick is as a toolbox. The sidekick contains all the content components your implementation team developed. They can be dragged from the sidekick into any valid paragraph system visible on the page.

Authors can also enter Preview mode, which hides the sidekick and all the content management–based UI elements, so that the author sees exactly what a site visitor will see. The sidekick is one of the differentiating elements of AEM's webpage authoring experience. It enables authors to build pages as they will appear to users, because it provides a lot of functionality in a small, floating control.

The content finder brings digital asset management into the page authoring experience. It is a searchable tab along the left of the screen that gives authors access to images, videos, and other media files. Content authors can drag media assets from the content finder window into appropriately configured areas in the page and to components within the page. This seamless integration with AEM's Digital Asset Management system makes it easy to add media files managed in the DAM to your website.

Configuration pages

Not all pages you author are public pages a site visitor will see. In many situations content authors need to set configuration information or create content that is referred to by other pages. Configuration pages are designed to allow the content author to expose some type of functionality that is otherwise unavailable. They enable the author to take advantage of the AEM authoring experience (sidekick, content finder, drag and drop, and so on) to set up aspects of the site that aren't necessarily a public page.

A good place to find configuration pages is within the Tools utility in AEM. This interface is where Adobe put all the miscellaneous features that didn't fit anywhere else. Many of these features will be discussed in later chapters; but for now, note that many would be considered configuration pages. Identifying a configuration page within the default AEM features is easy. Any time you open a page to configure something and you see the sidekick available (and it's obviously not a page on your site), it's considered a configuration page.

You aren't likely to change any of the standard AEM features, but when evaluating how you will build your application on AEM, you should consider whether configuration pages would be a good idea. The key question is: Do they provide the most convenient experience for authors? Here are some situations in which you might consider using a configuration page:

- For authoring content that makes sense to an author in one place, but is then pulled into many different places throughout your site(s)

- For implementing customizations to the AEM platform such as new reports or utilities

- For access to configuration information (such as server URL and credentials) that is necessary to connect AEM with other enterprise systems

- For authoring content that is too complicated to author in a dialog (the most overlooked use case for configuration pages, in my experience)

On the other hand, here are some situations in which you probably shouldn't consider using configuration pages, even though they may sound like tempting use cases:

- For authoring content in forms that output webpages (which is what scaffolding is for—see the upcoming "Scaffolding" section)

- For bypassing any standard features of the platform, such as providing an alternative interface for user management

- For running scripts that perform bulk changes to content (which can work, but there are better ways)

As with many issues discussed in this book, a good solution implementation partner should be able to guide you through these decisions regarding configuration pages. My general guideline is to not use them unless you have to, but don't be afraid to consider them. Sometimes, they are indeed the best solution.

Scaffolding

Many popular content management platforms provide a form-based authoring experience, which differs substantially from AEM's in-context authoring experience. They present you with a web form in which you submit the content for the page. The CMS then knows how each of the pieces of content you provide (such as a page title or a header image) map to various pieces of the template. This is a vastly different experience from AEM's authoring experience, where you literally point, click, drag, and drop what you want where you want it. But, that's not to say a form-based WCM platform is a bad thing.

Some websites have a lot of content structured in exactly the same way. Blog sites or news media sites are both very good examples of this. On a news site, you'll probably have thousands and thousands of stories that all share the same basic structure: a headline, a byline, copy, and maybe a media file such as an image.

For these websites, the in-context authoring experience can break down. Imagine that you are building hundreds of articles for a news site. What if every time you had to create a news story page, you had to add a headline component and configure it. Then you had to add a byline and configure it. Then a copy component. Then an image or a video. You can imagine that it would be a very monotonous, error-prone, and just generally inefficient process.

Websites for authors that crank out tons of structured content are actually a better use case for a form-based WCM than an in-context one like AEM. But, wait! Adobe built an AEM feature called scaffolding to account for this.

A scaffold is a preconfigured form for outputting a specific type of webpage in AEM. Scaffolds provide form-based user interfaces for creating webpages, assuming a specific content structure. News articles are a very good use case for scaffolding, and in fact, the Geometrixx demo site included in AEM comes with some scaffolds set up already.

Scaffold pages are actually a special kind of configuration page, and they actually look and work a lot like component dialogs. Scaffold pages are preconfigured (by a developer) to include specific form fields that output content onto a page. The content author can select which page template will be used to output the given content and where in the website those pages will be created. When the content author has all the content she wants in the form, she clicks Create to generate the page with all the content baked into it. The page can later be changed (using the regular authoring features), activated, and managed just as any other page.

You definitely don't want to overuse scaffolding. Choosing to output content by using forms makes sense for some use cases, but it bypasses the content authoring experience, which is one of the most significant features in AEM. Scaffolding also is not built for websites that have many different forms available. If the list of potential scaffolds gets too big, the authoring experience diminishes significantly. There just isn't a great way for an author to fumble through 100 scaffolds to figure out how to build the right content in the right place.

Use scaffolding sparingly, but understand that sometimes you need to create a lot of content, structured the same way. Scaffolding is a tool that can significantly improve the authoring experience for doing so.

Content launches

All this content authoring functionality sounds great, but it assumes that you will have one content team with a linear path of content creation. All changes to a page are activated at the same time. Everyone has to coordinate to make sure no one steps on anyone's toes.

It's not a problem if you are authoring content by yourself or even with a small group. But, what happens when you have 50 people on your content team? What happens when multiple subgroups need to manage different versions of pages for launch? After all, isn't it a little naïve to think that everything can just be authored and activated on demand?

These questions are common in enterprise marketing organizations. Websites can be enormous and made up of subsites serving many different purposes. When various parts of a site accomplish different things, they tend to be managed by different people. When you have many people, management quickly gets confusing. Here's a fairly common example (we'll use Game Changers Sporting Goods again):

It's wintertime and the marketing team at Game Changers is planning for a new Christmas marketing campaign. A task force of three content authors was assembled to plan and author the content for that campaign. It'll involve new home page content, many new landing pages, and some minor, contextual content changes on the site's most visited product line pages.

The task force has all the content planned out, but there's a problem: They can't enter it into AEM because it'll put a stop to the regular schedule of content updates that happen every few days. As soon as the campaign content is added to all these pages (some of which are extremely important), those pages cannot be made public until the campaign actually launches.

For this exact use case, AEM provides the concept of a content launch: a branched version of content that can be authored and updated separate from the primary line of content authoring. When you create a content launch, you copy a set of content pages that can be authored without affecting the copied pages (the *real* content). Your content launch maintains a connection to the original content and can be updated to reflect changes made over time, so you don't get too far away from the main content. When you are ready to make the content launch public, you simply "promote" it, which copies your launch back to the main content. It then becomes the live content.

This very powerful new feature (as of version 5.6) in AEM enables content teams to work in parallel on different sets of content. It is a complicated feature, though. Before deciding to use a content launch, be sure to work with your solution implementation partner to ensure that it's the correct solution. Implementing content launches requires that your content team complicates its processes and learns how to branch. Software engineers understand branching, but it's not something a marketer typically has to learn.

Marketers are more than capable. Just make sure you really *need* to go down that path before you do. But, also know content launch is there, in case you find yourself looking for a solution to enable parallel content development.

Versioning

Adobe Experience Manager provides content authors with an Undo feature to remedy mistakes. However, managing mistakes one change at a time is tedious and unstable. What happens if you spend a week making many content changes to a page, only to have your manager change his mind? How do you roll *that* back? What about a change you made a week ago? The Undo function maintains past changes for just a short time. Things change quickly and unexpectedly in business. AEM provides a content versioning feature to help address these challenges for content authors.

A version is simply a snapshot of a page at a specific point in time. As you develop content, you can roll back to any previous version with no problems. Versions can be created manually, via the sidekick, and are also created automatically every time a page is activated (made public). Versions can also be referenced by date. If you don't remember which version number was active on last January 15, you can use the timewarp feature to retrieve that version based on a point in time.

The most powerful versioning feature is version comparison. It displays the differential between two past versions of content. You can select two versions (maybe the current one and one three versions old) and compare them side-by-side. AEM will add annotations that help to call out the differences in the content, which allows content authors to analyze those changes and make relevant alterations.

Versioning is not a replacement for server backup, but that should be the concern of system administrators. It is a good way track content snapshots over several points in time. It allows marketers to undo what they've done. Let's face it. Sometimes, you just need to do that.

Annotations

When managing content as a team, especially if the team is not co-located, communicating content changes can sometimes be difficult. Team-based content creation requires conversation and iterations of changes. It's rare that someone puts content in the system and everything remains hunky dory. You need a solution that helps you collaborate asynchronously on content changes. Otherwise you and your team will spend lots of time waiting for answers to emails.

You can take that conversation out of AEM (into another piece of software like email) and copy in the final content at the end. Or, you can keep your content creation processes in the AEM system, where it belongs, using a feature called annotations to help facilitate that conversation.

Annotations are types of markup that content authors can add to pages as they are developed. They are not intended to be visible on the public site, but are simply a means to communicate about the content asynchronously.

AEM provides two ways to annotate content. The first is simply a sticky note. All you have to do is select a component and add an annotation. A sticky note will appear for a comment and also show who left the comment. When other authors view that in-process content, they'll see the sticky note. AEM also provides a sketch feature in which you can annotate content using a rudimentary drawing tool. This is nice when you want to circle part of an image or underline some text. It also opens a sticky note to describe the sketch.

Annotations aren't a feature I see used very often, but sometimes being able to mark up the content in a page comes in handy. As the work of digital marketers continues to move from the PC to the tablet (a huge focus for AEM), using these annotations becomes easier. I expect them to be a more common part of the authoring experience in the not-so-distant future.

Manuscripts

Adobe Experience Manager is mostly a page-centric system, but the manuscripts feature pushes that boundary. Manuscripts are text files of content—written in markdown syntax—that are stored in the DAM, completely separate from their eventual presentation. Markdown syntax is a way to augment text to describe attributes such as emphasis and headlines. It's used to create raw copy in a very basic way.

The manuscript editor interface is very streamlined. It looks very similar to a text editor on your computer. The simplicity is by design because it's intended for a special kind of content author, often called copywriters, who are literally concerned only with their copy. They don't care about webpage layout, browser compatibility, or responsive design. They just care about the words. This interface allows copywriters to write content without any distraction. That copy then becomes an asset in the DAM that can be consumed by other components, such as an AEM component that displays manuscripts in a magazine-style layout.

As with scaffolding, using manuscripts complicates the content authoring process by removing the fundamental in-context editing paradigm. If you overuse it, it'll just make the whole system more difficult to interact with.

It's important to understand the fundamental use case for manuscripts: to create content that needs to be presented through more channels than just the website. A good example is the one that inspired the creation of this feature. Manuscripts are part of the Adobe Digital Publishing Suite, which is a platform for creating tablet-based e-magazines. Manuscripts can be used to save article copy in a single place (the DAM), and then output it in different formats on the website and from within a tablet magazine. These two channels are very different in terms of implementation, but because the copy is saved in such a simple format, it can be reused.

It may be tempting to use manuscripts to manage content that will be pulled into both your mobile and nonmobile websites; and in some cases, this application may be valid. But, for cases where you have a mobile site completely separate from your desktop site (but needs to share some content), think hard about implementing inheritance via the Multi Site Manager.

Basics of page management

A number of important features in AEM are used only after the page is created. These are typically administrator or content approver functions because they tend to be more powerful than authoring tools.

In small AEM implementations, everyone commonly has full power; but in larger implementations, these functions should be restricted for most content authors. The powerful features described in this section will help you manage the content after it is created.

Activation/deactivation

Simply adding components to a page, configuring them, and making everything look nice doesn't actually make the webpage public. You wouldn't want that anyway, because you would have no way to author content, check for errors, send through an approval workflow, and so on. Changes would all be visible to users as you made them. As you can imagine, that would create a pretty poor user experience.

To control when content is made public, AEM uses activation and deactivation, the processes of pushing content changes to and pulling content from (respectively) public view. Other terms that are sometimes used in place of *activate* are *publish* and *replicate*. These terms are very often used synonymously, if not entirely accurately. If you hear any one of the three, consider them the same thing.

You have quite a few ways to activate content in AEM. Pages can be activated from the sidekick or the site admin interface. Configuration pages can be activated from the Tools interface if that is where they live. DAM assets can (and must) be activated from within the DAM interface.

AEM also makes sure to remind you when related content must be activated. For example, if you activate a page that has images pulled from the DAM, AEM will ask if you also want to activate all of those DAM assets. This ensures that you won't activate your page without the images and display a bunch of broken image icons to site visitors. AEM also provides the Bulk Activation tool to activate large chunks of content at once. It's a very powerful tool, but only administrators should have access to it.

You can also schedule activations and deactivations. In fact, AEM provides redundant features for doing so. From the site admin interface, you can choose Activate Later and enter a date and time in the prompt. For already activated pages, a Deactivate Later feature is also provided. The other function for timed activation is within the page properties dialog. The On/Off Time properties do the same thing. (On is activation, and Off is deactivation.)

It's worth noting that you can only activate or deactivate pages. Individual content components on a page cannot be activated on their own.

Moving/copying/deleting

You may not always initially create a page exactly where it needs to go. Sometimes managers change their minds. Sometimes, especially with new sites, the content taxonomy is in flux. Or you just make a mistake. Naturally, Adobe Experience Manager allows content authors (with appropriate permissions) to move, copy, and delete webpages. These features enhance the content authoring experience by keeping pages from being set in stone.

Copying a page in the site admin interface works just as you would expect it to work: Select the page you want to copy, and then paste it in the new location. Copying does not maintain any kind of referential inheritance (that would be a *live copy*). It simply rubber-stamps the page and content into a different location in your site. This feature can be useful for creating multiple similar pages; but if this were a frequent occurrence, you would be well served to consider using a template with preloaded content, or building a scaffold.

Deleting a page is also fairly simple. Page deletion completely removes the page and all its content. As long as previous versions of the page have been saved (either manually or automatically with an activation), you can restore the deleted page. However, AEM does not have any concept of a Recycle Bin as do many PC operating systems. When you delete a page that is already activated, AEM will automatically deactivate the page first (remove it from public view) because when you delete the authorable page, you have no way of controlling the public view version. Sometimes only managing level content authors or administrators are given delete permissions on pages.

Moving pages is a combination of deleting and copying. When moving a page, you are simply picking a new location for a page that already exists. AEM will inform you of all the other components that refer to that page (such as a link component), and ask if you want to update those links. Typically you will want to update those links. AEM will also ask if you want to automatically republish (reactivate) the page in its new location. However, be aware that regardless of your "republish" selection, AEM will automatically deactivate the page at the old location, just as it would for a deletion.

You might notice that AEM doesn't have a "rename" feature, even though the name of a page is extremely important. It is pretty easy to rename a page using the "move" feature. It also gives you the option to rename the page. When you only want to rename a page, but leave it in the same place, you "move" it to the same location and change the name.

References

When you move a page, AEM asks whether to update any references to that page. As long as the references are implemented properly, AEM does a great job tracking linked pages, so that you don't inadvertently break things when you move or delete a page. This is especially helpful in very large sites where an individual content author is not familiar with the content on every page of the site. Content authors can specifically view a page's references using the sidekick, so that before they perform an action they'll know what they are potentially affecting.

Auditing

Adobe Experience Manager maintains a rudimentary audit log of the actions are performed on a page. This log isn't the same thing as versioning, because audit log records cannot be used to restore a previous version. However, auditing is more aggressive about when a record is added. Every time someone modifies a component on a page, a Modify record is added. These records don't explain much, but do provide a timestamp and a record of who made the modification. This feature isn't often used, but it can be helpful when you're trying to figure out who made a content change.

Locking/unlocking

No feature in Adobe Experience Manager allows content authors to make concurrent modifications (though I hope we'll see that some day). So, if person A opens up a page and starts to make some changes, and person B does the same at the same time, whichever user saves changes second will overwrite whomever saved first.

To prevent this situation from happening, AEM provides a locking and unlocking mechanism for content authors. When a content author opens a page and then locks it, other users are prevented from making changes until the first author completes her work and unlocks the page. The feature isn't used much by small content teams, but it can be critical for larger teams who have to manage important content such as landing pages or a homepage.

SEO considerations

● **Note:** If you are interested in reading more about content strategy (which includes some SEO information), I highly recommend *Content Strategy for the Web* (New Riders, 2012) by Kristina Halvorson.

Search engine optimization (SEO) refers to strategies for making your site content appear higher in search results pages. This book isn't about SEO best practices, but certain features of Adobe Experience Manager can have very direct SEO implications. This section briefly touches on them and explains how the way you author pages can positively or negatively affect your site's SEO.

Name and title

Two of the biggest influencers of SEO optimization within AEM are a page's title and name. At first glance, these might seem like redundant terms for the same thing, but in AEM, name and title are two very different, equally important concepts.

Remember, the title is the reader-friendly title of the page, which is output in the <title> HTML tags. The name is the page's location in AEM and representation in the page URL. In fact, each level of a URI in AEM is the name of a different page. For example, given the URI /content/geometrixx/en/products.html, *products* is the name of the current page. Its parent page's name is *en*.

These titles are important for SEO optimization because most search engines highly weigh the content in the <title> tag and the words in the URL. Therefore, make sure your title and name describe the content on the page accurately and succinctly.

For example, if you are building a page that contains gardening tips, a page name (and URI) of /outdoors/gardening/tips-and-tricks.html and title of "Gardening Tips and Tricks" will be more SEO effective than /categories/1434/index. php?type=gardening and "Tips and Tricks." The former is more descriptive and keyword-heavy than the latter, and therefore better SEO optimized. For content authors, work with your SEO specialist to make sure you are effectively naming and titling pages.

URLs and redirects

Depending on the implementation, content authors can have a lot of control over the URLs of different pages because they control the page hierarchy. As described in the previous section, this can have significant impact on pages' search engine visibility.

We already noted how page naming affects SEO, but what happens when you move pages around or delete them? Search engines only periodically index websites, so it may take days or weeks before Google or Bing realize that you've moved or renamed a page. That lag could mean your page is appearing in search results with an incorrect link. Guess what? You don't want that to happen.

This is typically remedied by redirecting requests for the old URL to the new URL, so the user isn't just shown a "Page Not Found" message. For some environments, the system administrators will handle this at the web server layer. You need to make sure they are informed of the change so that they can make the appropriate configuration alterations. That can be a complex process, though, because you have to coordinate two usually separate teams.

An easier strategy may be to manage redirects from within AEM. With this approach, when a content author wants to "move" a page, she actually makes a copy in the new location. Then in the original page's properties dialog, the author sets the Redirect URL to the new location and activates the page (along with activating the page at the new location). Whenever someone hits the old URL from an out-of-date search engine index or a browser bookmark, he will automatically be transferred to the new location. You can take the same approach when deleting pages, only you redirect to a similar location such as the deleted page's parent or the home page.

As a matter of policy, content authors will probably want to agree that whenever a page is moved or deleted, the old location remains as a redirect page for some period of time. A length of 90 days is probably sufficient, but that's up to your team to decide, based on your specific needs and concerns. You could set a timed deactivation to ensure that no one forgets to remove the redirect page.

Metadata

By convention, some of the other options in the page properties dialog are printed in HTML tags that affect SEO. Metadata and tagging are discussed in Chapter 5, but I'll touch on them here.

The page description property will be output in the metadata tag that tells the search engine the description of the page. (You'll see this in search results.) AEM will also output the selected tags as keywords metadata, which some search engines also weigh for consideration.

When working with an SEO specialist, know what you are changing and how it could affect your search engine optimization. Even more critical, understand the implications of ignoring these properties—a failing I see far too often.

Page content

Naturally, the content within a page will have significant SEO implications because search engines are concerned first and foremost with directing people to relevant content. Make sure your content is rich with relevant keywords, but don't overload it to the point you lose readability. Quality content should always be priority number one.

When using Title components or styles in a rich text editor, make sure to accurately follow the H1, H2, H3 hierarchy. You want only a single <h1> HTML tag on a page, and the rest should break that down further. Effective use of heading tags can positively affect SEO, so content authors need to be aware of what they are creating. You'll want to work with your implementation team to understand what components output which header tags. To the extent that you can, you should also try to implement rules that reinforce best practices of header use.

Summary

In this chapter, I went over the basics of content creation, one of the most central features in Adobe Experience Manager. AEM is a page-centric content management system, meaning that the webpage is the primary unit of content.

Authors create a page by selecting a template, which points to a page component that renders the page. Once the page is created, content authors add components and configure them. Components create the page content and derive business value.

AEM provides a number of features, such as page locking and content launches, for large-scale content teams. It also provides the facilities to enable content authors to manage their search engine optimization by configuring certain properties and configurations.

Review questions

1. What is the difference between a page-centric and a content-centric content management system?

2. What is the primary function of the content approver role?

3. When would you want to use a configuration page?

4. What is content branching?

5. What term describes content inheritance based on the page's content tree?

6. How can content authors prevent Google from sending people to pages that have been moved?

Review answers

1. In a page-centric content management system, the webpage is the primary unit of content. Authors create and edit pages, and their primary use is specifically for websites. In a content-centric system, content is created and edited abstractly and separately. The content may be pulled into a webpage, but may also be pulled into other applications. The content is completely decoupled from its placement in a webpage.

2. The content approver is typically a managing level content author who is responsible for approving all content changes before they are made public. This is usually enforced by limiting content authors' permissions to activate and by using an approval workflow.

3. You would use a configuration page when you have content you need to centrally locate. Often configuration pages are used for content author–specified configurations that aren't directly reflected as pages in the website.

4. Content branching is the concept of making a copy of the content for parallel work. One team works on the original content, while another works on the copy, making sure to periodically pull in changes from the original. When the time comes to make the copy public, it is promoted back as the original. Branching enables a team to make content changes for large campaigns without interrupting the normal content process.

5. Hierarchical inheritance

6. Instead of simply deleting or moving a page (which would create a dead URL), content authors can set a to-be-moved-or-deleted page's Redirect property to a new location. Then, if a search engine still has that link indexed, it will automatically transfer the visitor instead of displaying an error.

4 DIGITAL ASSET MANAGEMENT

In this chapter, you'll learn about AEM's Digital Asset Management (DAM) system, including:

- The basics of digital asset management as a business domain
- How Adobe's DAM system addresses that domain
- The kinds of digital assets that can be managed within the DAM
- How those assets are processed
- How to integrate the DAM with other Adobe tools such as Scene7

By the end of this chapter, you'll understand why a DAM system is such a critical part of the Adobe Experience Manager platform, as well as how to use it to meet your needs.

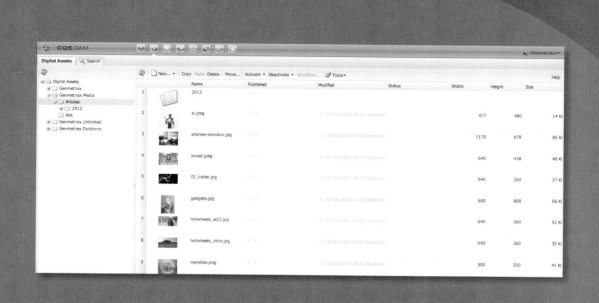

Managing DAM assets with Adobe
Experience Manager

Business domain of DAM

One of Adobe Experience Manager's core features is its Digital Asset Management System, commonly referred to as "the DAM." Digital asset management as a domain isn't unique to AEM. Rather, Adobe has implemented an enterprise class DAM system that can actually serve as a stand-alone solution, apart from all the WCM features. However, what makes Adobe's DAM solution particularly valuable is how deeply integrated it is with the rest of the AEM platform. The DAM is a key piece within AEM for integrating the creative concerns of designers and artists and the digital marketing concerns of content managers and web-driven revenue generation.

Before digging into the DAM's capabilities within Adobe Experience Manager, I want to step back and discuss the general business concept of DAM.

What is digital asset management?

Your organization's brand is embodied in a sea of media files. Some of them remain within the organization's walls, such as graphics used as letterheads or design files for creating print advertisements. Some are made public and shared, such as video demonstrations and white papers.

Many of these media files actually toe the line between internal and external assets. Some may become public and go viral, even if they weren't intended for that use. Others that were intended to be public simply waste away.

The thread tying them all together is the difficulty that virtually all organizations face attempting to keep track of these media files. Digital asset management is the domain of managing a variety of rich media files so that they can be effectively used to support the organization's brand.

Digital asset management is not really the same thing as document management or records management, although they do have some similarities. Some organizations find that a document management solution is adequate for their digital asset management needs. Document management is really about cataloging *mostly* text-based content. You often see document management systems in place for managing forms, reports, structured content such as XML, and the many Microsoft Office document types. Document management is usually a key component of enterprise content management (see Chapter 1).

When trying to manage media files, however, you face some unique, complex challenges compared to simply managing documents:

- How do you catalog files of completely different formats?
- How do you search files that cannot be indexed textually?
- How do you deal with the huge amounts of data created by media files?
- How do you make it easy to adapt those media files to changing business needs?

You'll still face some of the same problems as with document management, including how to provide permission-appropriate access to files and how to distribute those files to the appropriate channels. But, I want to dig a little deeper into these issues to really hone in on the benefits of a dedicated DAM.

Catalog diverse media

Digital media files can be vastly different from one another, to a much greater extent than documents and records. The former tends to be less structured and richer, whereas the latter tends to be more structured and text-based. Media can include video files of different formats, image files of different formats, PDFs, or design assets like InDesign files. These formats are all so different that cataloging them in a common way becomes difficult. Imagine trying to sort a bunch of photographs, CDs, receipts, and videotapes (yeah, remember those?). There's not a particularly good way to sort them...at least not obviously. Digital asset management uses software to address that very problem. It enables you to catalog diverse media in such a way that it becomes ubiquitous.

Optimize searchability

Search engines use indexing to determine how relevant a resource is to a search term you enter. The search engine "crawls" all the available resources making records (an index) of how it is categorized, what it contains, and other properties of those resources. The search engine internally organizes and optimizes that information to create a fast search experience. Then, when you enter a search term, the search engine can poll its index of resources and immediately return the resources relevant to your search terms.

Most enterprise platforms that manage data or content include search features, including document management and digital asset management systems. In a document management system, where most of the content is text-based, the crawling approach is fairly straightforward. It's easy to understand how a machine can "read" the text in a document and make an index of keywords.

But how to interpret the content of videos, images, and other rich media files? Most of them don't have text to "read." Those that do contain text would probably require some kind of optical character recognition technology to read it. That's why digital asset management systems enable those managing the resources to apply rich metadata describing the media assets. The system will also make sure that metadata taxonomy is similar enough that it can be indexed effectively, making for an efficient search experience that doesn't care whether the media is a picture or a video.

Manage file size

Remember when Napster—the first mainstream platform for downloading music in MP3 format—became available? It took half an hour or more just to download a single song. God help me if my dad picked up the phone and kicked me off the modem-based connection, or I finally got the entire song and it downloaded incorrectly. It was frustrating because rich media files, like audio and video, are enormous compared to text-based files. Images are bigger than text. Audio is bigger than images. Video is bigger still.

As a result, a digital asset management system must manage huge amounts of data—for enterprise organizations, gigabytes (or terabytes) of content. The sheer scope of managing potentially vast amounts of digital media means the system has to maximize speed and performance. As cloud-based architectures continue to become the norm rather than the exception, a DAM must also consider how to optimize that design.

Adapt media

In case you haven't noticed, I'll break the news to you that requirements change fast. Customers will change their minds on a dime. Managers trying to stay ahead of customers will do the same. That means rapid change. It also means that inflexible systems will become a burden rather than a benefit.

Digital assets are often multiple file formats, sizes, variations of color, and so on. Without a system to manage these nearly identical versions of a media file, it can be cumbersome to keep track of all these variations. A digital asset management system does this. It allows those responsible for the media to retain the element that should remain consistent while also organizing each variation created for special uses. And while doing this, the system also maintains the fundamental relationship between these multiple media file variations.

What are your needs?

I find that many clients for whom I implement management solutions overlook the relevance of digital asset management in their overall digital strategy. Digital asset management is less generally understood than basic web content management, and it's not as easy to see how effective digital asset management contributes to revenue.

However, I can assure you that effective digital asset management processes and implementation are a key piece in the digital marketing puzzle. If implemented well, it will increase the value of your overall platform by simplifying the integration of rich media into your digital brand experience.

If you don't truly understand what you need from a digital asset management system, you could end up with a catch-all media repository. I see it time and time again. Content managers throw all their website images into a single folder, just so they can be added to a webpage. No one manages the metadata. No one organizes a logical taxonomy of media files. The repository gets bigger and bigger until it's no more organized than whatever system was previously in place.

I'm not going to insist that everyone's digital asset management needs are complex or dynamic. Some organizations' needs are complicated and some are simple. I'm only advocating that you go through the exercise of truly understanding your needs before you start using a DAM system like a storage closet.

To assess what you need in a digital asset management system, ask the following questions:

- What kinds of media assets do I need to manage?
- How do I plan to distribute them to the public?
- What is the volume of my media files as a whole?
- What are our key workflows when creating and managing digital assets?
- How are those workflows effective? How could they be improved?
- Where are the opportunities to automate parts of those workflows?
- What creative development tools do I use to edit digital assets?
- How are our media files organized? How do we want them to be organized?

Answering these questions won't guarantee that you'll have an effective digital asset management or content management implementation. But, if you can build consensus about the answers to these questions, you will be in a better position to execute your digital asset management strategy.

Basic digital asset management

Armed with the fundamental concepts of the digital asset management and being somewhat in tune with what you'll need out of a DAM solution, you're ready to dig into the Adobe Experience Manager DAM. Adobe's digital asset management system is a top-of-the-line product on its own. Consider that it's completely integrated within a full-stack digital marketing platform and you've got one heck of a solution. After reading the rest of this chapter, you'll have a better idea of just what the AEM DAM is and how you can use it to meet your specific needs. In some ways, the rest of the chapter details the first part, focused specifically on the actual functionality of the DAM.

Basic DAM functions

The user experience for DAM administrators is similar to that of content authors. The DAM is presented in a similar way, and actually shares quite a few of the interface elements of the website administration interface. Often I find that the lines between the DAM administrators and content authors are quite blurry, so the similar user interfaces are definitely a plus. Let's dive into some of the basic functions of the DAM at a business-value level.

Organizing assets

The DAM allows you to organize your digital assets in the same way you organize pages in the site admin interface. It uses the same hierarchical file structure approach, which allows DAM administrators to create an easy-to-understand taxonomy of assets. The DAM provides very nice features for searching assets, but DAM administrators should still take care to design and enforce a logical organizational structure. Your structure will also be very important if you choose to granularly define user permissions to different parts of your DAM (as you'll learn in Chapter 12).

Figure 4.1
Managing a DAM hierarchy

Editing assets

One of the key parts of the DAM is the interface provided for editing assets. However, unlike editing text-based assets, you are actually editing the representation of a digital media file as it is stored in the DAM. You are not really editing the file itself, although you can perform some really basic tasks such as cropping or rotating images.

That said, we'll still get into some ways that the DAM and some peripheral technologies make editing media files within the DAM extremely easy. When editing an asset, you have control over most of the asset properties and enhancements, such as metadata, dynamic renditions, tags, and so on.

When editing an asset, the most useful tool is the set of metadata fields that remains almost completely consistent across all assets, regardless of file format. This metadata represents a common abstraction of media assets that makes them searchable, usable, and organizable on a consistent basis. Think about the previous example of organizing photographs, video cassettes, receipts, and CDs. Imagine how much easier the organizing process would be if each one were placed in the same size box, with the same kind of label. That's the idea behind the "asset" abstraction of these media files.

Editing the asset also lets you view the renditions and versions of the asset. Renditions are a set of instances of the media file that are automatically generated by AEM as the asset is created or dramatically changed. For example, changing images will automatically generate renditions of different sizes that represent various thumbnails.

Editing videos will generate renditions that are actually image files representing the video itself. Renditions are preconfigured to generate via a workflow, but they can be customized.

Versions are stored snapshots in time of the changes made to a DAM asset. One really easy way to see how snapshots are used is by editing an image in the DAM and rotating it. This edit actually changes the underlying image and rebuilds all the renditions, but it also creates a new version to represent the significant change. Versions can be restored much like restoring page versions.

Figure 4.2
Editing DAM metadata

Finding assets

The DAM makes searching for assets stored within it extremely easy. If you have only 30 or 40 assets, the search function isn't that useful. But, when you have 15,000 assets, manually drilling down through folders is not a realistic way to locate a specific file. A faceted search feature allows you to find assets based on metadata, general location, tags, and file type. The search also can be extended and customized, with help from your solution partner.

Also helpful is the ability to view an asset's references. Remember that a page's references are a list of other pages that link to it, and would be affected if that page were moved or deleted. The DAM applies the same approach to digital assets. It identifies every location within the platform where that asset is used. Therefore, as you edit or remove the asset, you can know every webpage you are potentially affecting.

Figure 4.3
Searching for DAM
assets

Digital Assets	🔍 Search	Norfolk.jpg ×

Fulltext

Path

☐ Do not search in sub folders

Modified after/
before

Filter expired assets ☐

☐ **File Types** ▲
☐ Images ▼
☐ Documents ▼
☐ Multimedia ▼
☐ Archives ▼
☐ Other ▼

☐ **Tags** ▲
☐ Business ▼
☐ Industry ▼
☐ Lifestyle ▼
☐ Nature ▼
☐ Illustrations/Vectors ▼

Content finder

The content finder (the frame along the left edge of the screen) enables content authors to bring DAM assets into the webpage. The content finder is organized by file type, but also has a view in which the author can drill down into the DAM's hierarchy to locate an asset. The content finder also accesses the DAM search to help authors find assets faster. As a content author, you will spend quite a bit of time with the content finder.

Figure 4.4
The content finder

Other basic features

The DAM also provides DAM administrators some other basic features for managing websites. Assets can be activated and deactivated in the same way as pages. Consider an asset's references when deactivating, though, to ensure that you aren't removing images being used on a live site. In addition to the automatic rendition workflows, DAM administrators can also apply workflows to assets as desired, which is helpful for approvals and external integrations.

DAM metadata

The Adobe Experience Manager DAM uses the extensible metadata platform (XMP) standard for encoding metadata within digital media files, a standard originally spearheaded by Adobe. It provides a common way to define metadata regardless of file type, without restricting the metadata to any specific taxonomy, which means the metadata can be universally understood, but the properties of a particular file type needn't completely align with the properties of another. All Adobe products use the XMP standard when applying metadata to assets.

In practice, the DAM becomes a nice interface for configuring the metadata of digital media assets regardless of format. In fact, under the hood, when setting the metadata of a DAM asset, AEM actually changes the metadata of the original binary file that was used to create that DAM asset (remember, a DAM asset is just an abstraction of that file). So, when using the DAM as a tool for web content management, your assets are more searchable and more semantically cataloged. However, because the metadata applied is based on a standard, if the DAM is used to distribute assets for more than web content concerns, the metadata can be used by any system that consumes the asset.

When a DAM administrator edits an asset in the DAM, the Title, Description, Creator, and other fields are all used to set the metadata of that asset. Those fields are generally standardized for all types of DAM assets you can work with. XMP does support extending the metadata vocabulary for specific file types, but this is not something DAM administrators can just do at will. Maintaining a consistent, well-thought-out taxonomy is critical if the metadata is to provide any value. Therefore, the extensibility of DAM metadata is limited to a specific process that must be implemented by a developer. If you think you need additional metadata, work with your solution partner to understand whether you really need this capability and then determine the best way to implement it.

DAM components

Two DAM-related content components can be added to webpages: Asset Share and the Asset Editor. These components provide specific functionality for exposing the DAM to the public. Like many components in AEM, these are largely intended as a starting points or examples, although they are fully functional and can be used on live sites.

It's a use case for the DAM that is a little less common than web content management support, but the DAM can be used as a central repository for assets that are provided to external parties. Along with the explanation of both of these components, I provide a high-level example use case that describes why you might use it.

Asset Share

The Asset Share is a set of components used for authoring an easy-to-use faceted search for digital assets. Internally, AEM provides robust functionality for searching for DAM assets, but what if you want to expose that functionality to people who won't have access to the AEM interface? The Asset Share consists of a few parts:

- Asset Share page component, which can be extended to create your own custom page component and template
- Query builder component, which allows users to create search queries for DAM assets
- A set of search facet components for filtering results by specific attributes
- A set of "lens" components for a content author to specify views that define the search results

The Asset Share also contains a set of components, called actions, that can be added to the page to define what an end user can do to interact with the DAM. The Adobe documentation describes how to configure the parts of an Asset Share. It also describes how content authors can define a complex search interface without any developer intervention (after the page component and styling are defined).

The Asset Share component exposes facets of the DAM to the public—for example, if you were building a portal in which your organization's partners could access the creative assets that represent your brand.

As a large organization, you may work with dozens of marketing agencies, advertising partners, or media organizations. You could have a team responsible for working with those external stakeholders to organize and retrieve the media as necessary, but that would be expensive and labor intensive. You could give those people access to the AEM DAM, but with obvious security challenges.

Or, you could build a portal where those external stakeholders can independently search for and retrieve media assets. Permissions for that portal can define what outsiders can and cannot do, and enables you to build a fully branded user experience. The Asset Share would be at the core of such a solution.

Asset Editor

The Asset Editor, like the Asset Share, is a set of components that exposes the DAM asset editing functionality to public users. It enables site visitors to edit metadata, tag assets, customize thumbnails, and manipulate other aspects of digital assets. The Asset Editor can also be used to display a detailed, non-editable view of assets to provide more info to site visitors before they download assets. Once a page component is defined and styled, this experience is completely configurable by a content author. She can make changes that would otherwise require a programmer. The Asset Editor contains the following components:

- Asset Editor page component, which can be extended to create your own custom page component and template

- Metadata form components for viewing or editing the metadata of a DAM asset

- Components for viewing sub-assets and thumbnails of a DAM asset

Like the Asset Share, it also contains a set of Actions components that display no user interface element, but define which tasks can be performed by end users.

If your content team is relatively small, providing and managing their access to the DAM interface within AEM isn't a big deal. But, what if you have hundreds of people who may be editing DAM assets? What if DAM asset manipulation is just one of many tasks those people perform that may not necessarily be part of logging into AEM?

You could use AEM to build a portal application that exposes DAM asset editing via the Asset Editor. It would enable your content team to author a web experience for interacting with the DAM without actually providing login access to the DAM. This is especially useful when you need to provide access to external stakeholders who may not have direct access to your internal AEM servers.

Beyond web content management

The Adobe Experience Manager DAM is most often used to support web content management by providing the foundation for managing digital media files to be used within the web experience. But the DAM was originally designed as a stand-alone digital asset management solution that can be used independently of the content management parts of the platform. It truly is a full-featured DAM that can be applied to a variety of use cases.

This book is primarily about AEM's web experience management features, so I don't dig into this any further. But, if you are using the DAM according to best practice to empower your web experience, you are already positioned to expose the DAM's functionality for other uses. You can discuss those options with a solution implementation partner.

Advanced digital asset management

We've gone over the basics of why the Adobe Experience Manager DAM is valuable and how you can use it. That set of basic concepts is mostly universal to AEM implementations, but the DAM goes beyond the "happy path" use cases. AEM includes more advanced features designed to enable marketers and their associates to unlock very specific pieces of value. These features may not be relevant to you at present, but it's helpful to know that they exist and why. You may need them someday.

Integration with Scene7

One of the most compelling features of Adobe's DAM solution is the out-of-the-box integration with Scene7, a cloud-hosted solution for editing and publishing media files. With Scene7 you can make ordinary digital media files interactive and customized.

For example, Scene7 can generate on-the-fly images on landing pages, such as "Welcome from Ohio!" if the system detects that state as the user's location. Scene7 is a full-featured solution for managing digital media files in the cloud.

Wait…doesn't that sound a lot like the Adobe Experience Manager DAM?

Truthfully, AEM DAM and Scene7 have some functional overlap, because of the way both of those products came to Adobe. The AEM DAM was part of CQ5, acquired with Day Software in in 2010. Scene7 was acquired by Adobe in 2007. In the most recent releases of AEM, Adobe has begun to integrate these two asset management platforms to take advantage of each of their strong points. The eventual goal is to completely turn them into a single integrated solution. So, let's explore how Scene7 integration can help take your digital asset management to a whole new level.

Simple integration

The first thing to point out with Adobe's DAM–Scene7 integration is how easy it is to configure. Unlike with many enterprise software integrations, you do not need programmers to build integration. One of the most valuable aspects of Adobe's Marketing Cloud is its seamless integration between products. Adobe continues to build upon those integrations, and this is a newer, but very powerful example.

Integrating an AEM instance with a Scene7 instance is all configuration-based, so you should be able to do it with an administrator or even a power user. If you have to involve a programmer, you are either doing something interesting (that I want to hear about) or something wrong. You'll see this simple integration between Adobe products as a recurring theme throughout this book, and we'll discuss cloud services configurations, like the Scene7 integration, in Chapter 16.

Asset synchronization

After you have your AEM instance configured to connect with your Scene7 account, you can set up asset synchronization between the two platforms. This synchronization is especially helpful if you've been using both products separately for some time and have different categories of digital assets in each. You can configure automatic synchronization or trigger it manually, but you should be aware of how much you are synchronizing. Within AEM, it's all workflow-based processing, which can be pretty resource-intensive. If you have hundreds or thousands of DAM assets you want to synchronize in either direction, you should work with a solution partner to make sure you put together an appropriate plan for doing so.

Scene7 components

Scene7 integration includes some content components that allow you to add Scene7-specific functionality to your websites. Doing so can enable powerful ways to improve the user experience of your site, and stand as a great example of how Adobe is integrating Scene7 benefits into the rest of the AEM platform. The following components are included:

- Basic zoom—Allows you to add simple zoom in/out features to images
- Flyout zoom—Allows you to add "magnifying glass" zooming to images (such as on a clothing retailer's site)
- Flash flyout zoom—A Flash-based flyout zoom, for sites that don't support the DHTML code needed for the standard flyout zoom
- Flash template—A component for configuring dynamic content in Flash movies
- Image template—A component for configuring dynamic content in images
- Video—A universal video player that detects which video format is optimal for the site visitor

Templates are a core feature of Scene7 that allow you to dynamically change media files on the fly. They integrate into AEM nicely, because they open up your options when creating dynamic content or performing multivariate testing.

Content finder integration

The Scene7 integration is also seamless for content authors because it includes content finder integration. Basically it extends the content finder and interface into Scene7 so that a content author can utilize Scene7 assets without leaving the context of AEM. The author sees the same digital asset browsing experience, but can search and drill down through a tree of assets that are actually hosted in Scene7 and not within AEM DAM. This is very handy when you have a combination of DAM assets and Scene7 assets.

Long-term vision

Adobe Experience Manager's integration with Scene7 is fairly new, but already extremely compelling. Adobe is obviously working toward a fully integrated platform that accommodates all aspects of the digital asset creation and delivery workflow. You'll probably still find some holes in the form of things you want to do but cannot… yet. But, you can expect this integration to continue to improve. Adobe has made a commitment to the complete integration of AEM and Scene7, and you can already see how compelling that vision is.

Integration through Adobe Drive

While the AEM DAM and Scene7 provide certain aspects of digital asset manipulation from within the platform, it's sometimes just not enough. The changes you can make to assets using Adobe Creative Suite products such as Photoshop or Illustrator far exceed what you can do with the DAM or Scene7. But, downloading and uploading DAM to those Creative Suite products is kind of a pain. Fortunately, Adobe built a solution to this problem called Adobe Drive.

Adobe Drive is a free software product that provides direct integration between local instances of Creative Suite products and a digital asset management platform. Obviously, the AEM DAM is one of the platforms with which Drive can integrate. Drive works with Photoshop, Illustrator, InDesign, and InCopy by exposing the DAM to those products just as if it were a local file store. It uses a protocol called WebDAV, which allows you to browse the data structure of Adobe Experience Manager as you would a file system. (There are other examples of how WebDAV is used in AEM, too.)

Adobe Drive doesn't expose only the DAM to Creative Suite products. It also unlocks additional features that are otherwise not easy to utilize. You can manage check in/out of digital assets for editing, view and edit metadata in a more sophisticated interface, and view version history.

Furthermore, Drive is a desktop application, so it also allows offline editing, so you aren't restricted to editing DAM assets only while connected to the DAM.

Ultimately, Adobe Drive just makes treating the DAM as a repository for creative assets a little simpler, even while your creative team continues to work on them. It's not for everyone, and for some organizations, it's overkill. But, if your creative team needs direct access to the DAM, it's a great way to provide it.

Dynamic image servlet

The DAM allows you to create renditions of an image that include different sizes and versions of the same asset. You can use those renditions in the content of your website, and that can be helpful when you need to create thumbnails or smaller views of large, high-resolution images. When you are creating multi-device websites where Internet bandwidth is a varying concern, this feature becomes even more important. After all, you want to minimize the size of any files a site visitor has to download to view your site. Making your site load faster improves your search engine optimization and the user experience.

Although not really a DAM function, you have another option in AEM for dynamically generating optimized images. The image servlet allows you to request images using a special URL that dynamically changes them on the fly. Out of the box, it doesn't allow you to do much in terms of image manipulation, but with the help of a solution implementation partner, the image servlet's functionality can be expanded. You can create image servlets that resize images, add dynamic text, or rotate and crop. If an available Java library lets you do what you want to your asset, anything is technically possible.

Implementing an image servlet is not something a content author or even an administrator can do. It requires foresight and implementation and programming. Much of what you can do with the image servlet can be accomplished using Scene7, so going through the process of implementation may not always be necessary. But, if you aren't planning to use Scene7, have other reasons to keep this functionality within AEM, or just want to customize the heck out of it, the dynamic image servlet is a good option to consider.

Video

The trickiest type of digital asset to work with is video. The files are huge. The encoding requirements are complicated. The debates about best practices are rampant. In AEM, you have a number of options for managing and delivering video within your web experience. It's a complicated topic that has filled entire books. I just touch on a few high-level points here, related to what AEM offers. If you are planning to implement websites with a lot of video, I highly recommend you work with the Adobe documentation, a solution partner, and additional video-specific resources to put together a detailed plan for managing your videos.

DAM video

You can host, encode, and deliver video in your websites directly from the Adobe Experience Manager DAM. Video files uploaded to the DAM can be transcoded into a number of formats, so that you can implement a fallback approach to delivering the optimized video format to a site visitor.

AEM then has a video component that allows you to choose videos to display from the content finder, just as any other digital asset. It typically requires some upfront configuration to make sure you are transcoding videos into the right formats and have the correct logic in place to choose which version to play. But once that is set up, it makes adding video to your web experiences pretty simple.

That said, be cautious when deciding to stream video from the AEM DAM. Video requires significant computing resources to deliver, much more than the images and text that make up the majority of your websites. Videos cannot be cached in the same regard, either. Therefore, delivering lots of high-quality videos out of the DAM is probably not the best solution because some significant hardware challenges may arise. You'll need to beef up the servers on which your AEM instances run, and even still it'll be difficult.

Organizations implementing video on AEM very commonly utilize external, cloud-hosted platforms as their video solution. Then all they have to do is implement that platform's video player on their site and let someone else's hardware manage their video.

Fortunately, Scene7 (a cloud-based solution) is one of those viable options for hosting video to be delivered via Adobe Experience Manager.

Scene7 video

Using Scene7 to host your video lets you take advantage of a cloud-hosted video platform option without sacrificing the content management integration you have with DAM video. Videos can be uploaded to the DAM, Scene7, or both. They can be transcoded as necessary. Conveniently, those video assets are available in the content finder for easy access when authoring content.

AEM's Scene7 integration also includes a special video player that takes advantage of Scene7's ability to dynamically decide which rendition of a video to play. It considers the device, the bandwidth available, and the screen size to optimize the user's video experience. Scene7 video is a great option for cloud-hosting video, especially when you have a lot of videos to deliver through many different channels.

Summary

Digital asset management is a critical part of delivering high-quality web experiences that contribute to the achievement of business goals. It involves cataloging and managing digital media files, including images, video, audio, and certain kinds of documents. It's a complicated domain on its own, for which there are a number of solutions on the market.

Adobe Experience Manager includes a digital asset management solution that unlocks these features within the context of a web experience management platform. Integrated with peripheral technologies such as Scene7 or Adobe Drive, the AEM DAM is designed to serve as the central repository for managing and delivering an organization's digital media, and to reduce the complexity of managing that media.

Review questions

1. What are the four key functions of a digital asset management solution?

2. What are DAM renditions?

3. What standard does the AEM DAM use to manage the metadata of assets?

4. What content components are specifically designed to unlock DAM functionality to site visitors?

5. What is the main advantage to using Scene7 video over another cloud-hosted video solution?

Review answers

1. Managing multiple file formats in a single interface, finding assets effectively, handling high-quality media files that consume significant hardware resources, and allowing adaptation of digital media files

2. DAM renditions are automatically generated versions of DAM assets. They are generated by AEM upon asset upload.

3. Extensible metadata platform (XMP)

4. Asset Share and Asset Editor

5. Scene7 video enables a deep level of integration with the web content management functions of AEM, specifically with the content finder. In the long-term vision, the proprietary Scene7–AEM integration is likely to continue to become more robust and valuable.

5
METADATA AND TAGGING

Content management is the art of managing the data that makes up a digital representation of your brand. Metadata is one of the most powerful tools at your disposal for doing so.

In this chapter, you'll learn:

- What metadata is and why it is important

- What tagging is and how it can be used

- The standards and protocols that define *how* to use metadata

- How you can build a vocabulary that represents your business domain

By the end of this chapter, you'll understand the fundamental concepts of metadata and tagging. You'll also know how to use the tools provided with Adobe Experience Manager to manage metadata.

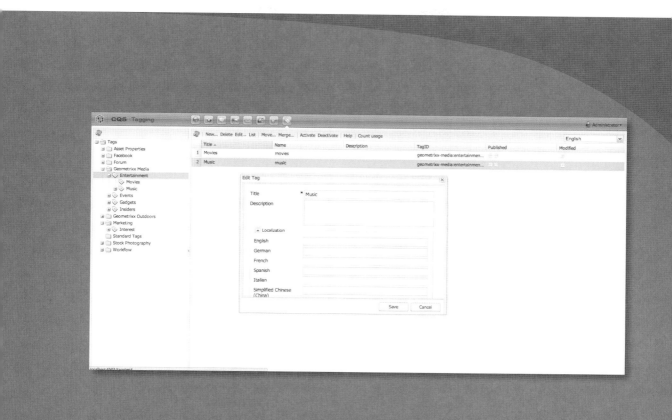

The AEM Tagging Administration Interface

Data about data

As you can imagine, or maybe have already experienced, managing the data that makes up an organization's digital presence is complex. You have a lot of data to deal with. Some of that data is binary files, such as images and videos. Some of it is text and markup (HTML and XML). Some of it is abstract, like your content or branding. Those examples are abstract because they exist, but neither represents a tangible *thing*.

Metadata can describe and organize data by adding a structured layer of abstraction. Simply put, metadata is data about data. It helps to categorize and catalog your data so that it can be located or organized in a way that enables data consumers to achieve goals. Metadata is a critical part of society, technology, and government and takes many different forms.

Whether or not you realize it, you are already familiar with some kind of metadata. Think about a library. The data a library patron seeks is the information within the books, periodicals, and media. Even the smallest libraries have a ton of data. Just a single book contains enough data that you can't even absorb it all in one reading. Books are written in different languages, formats, and vernaculars. Other media in the library has information that isn't text based. How could you possibly find answers in this mountain of data?

Metadata

Libraries use metadata to organize their content and enable librarians or patrons to locate the desired information. At the very least, it helps them narrow the search so they need only examine 50 books instead of 15,000. The Dewey Decimal System is one form of metadata. It classifies books into multiple topics. That way, when you go into a library looking for cooking advice, you don't have to filter through books on computer science or U.S. history. You determine which classification is relevant (641 – Food and Drink), and you search for your information within the cookbooks. The metadata about the books describes the data within the books, which makes finding and using that data easy.

Modern libraries now use metadata well beyond classic organizational structures like the Dewey Decimal System. Electronic databases currently track where a book resides, who has checked it out, who wrote it, and what it's about. Library patrons can use computer terminals to search that database and find what they are looking for. These systems are able to operate only because the database stores metadata about the library's books.

These library search systems use a common metadata structure so that author, title, and publication date always means the same thing, regardless of media type. This common metadata vocabulary enables you to locate information in a largely media-agnostic way. The metadata about the data adds value by classifying the data it describes.

Two important aspects of metadata make it work. If either or both of these aren't present, the metadata doesn't do anything but add complexity:

1. The metadata must adhere to a common vocabulary.

2. The metadata must be maintained and complete.

I'll explain some strategies for addressing #1, specifically within the context of web content. Addressing #2 is a matter of implementing the appropriate processes and policies for ensuring that the metadata is kept accurate. I touch on this at the end of the chapter, when I discuss some best practices.

More examples

Metadata is an essential concept in web content management, yet it is far too often misunderstood. To drive home the point, I want to look at two more real-world examples of metadata. Before you can understand how to deal with metadata in Adobe Experience Manager, you need to truly and completely understand what it is and how it's used.

Data about groceries

When you grocery shop, you probably care what you buy. There are thousands of items you could put in your cart, but you want what tastes good, is healthy, and satisfies your family's basic needs for nutrition. If everything came in the same black box, shopping would be impossible. You'd just be guessing about what you purchase. But that's not how you grocery shop, because metadata describes the groceries (the data).

Food producers must follow a standard for reporting nutrition facts and ingredients on all food and beverage items (requirement #1) so that no matter what item you're looking at, you can find the fat content or whether it contains peanuts.

The labels also describe a standardized set of classifications (such as calories, total carbohydrates, and calcium). In the United States, the Food and Drug Administration requires that manufacturers adhere to the standards for nutrition information to ensure that the data on the box is always correct and complete (requirement #2).

Data about television shows

I use a satellite dish for my television service, so I have a *lot* of choices when I sit down to watch TV. Flipping through hundreds of channels to find something I will enjoy is difficult at best. I may end up recognizing a scene from a movie I like. I may happen to find a documentary about a topic that interests me. But what about shows and movies I've never seen? How can I decide if I might enjoy them? What if I miss something I would like because I happened to click past it during a commercial break? Fortunately, my satellite dish company uses metadata to describe what's on TV (the data).

My satellite receiver will tell me when and where to find shows and movies. It will tell me how long a show is, what parental guidance rating it has, and when it originally aired. It will even tell me what the show or movie is about by classifying it as "comedy" or "documentary" and providing a brief description. Though occasionally incomplete, this data is almost always an accurate description of the broadcast (requirement #2). The data about what's on is also consistent across every channel. That way, I can compare television options in a consistent manner (requirement #1). The metadata about television shows enables me to make informed decisions about how I spend my viewing time.

Web metadata standards and protocols

The importance and value of metadata certainly hold true for the web. In fact, metadata is largely responsible for enabling the Internet as we know it today. Google and other search engines would not be able to provide real-time search results without metadata. Websites could not be accurately shared on Facebook or Twitter without metadata. The Internet as a holistic system wouldn't function at all without metadata.

Because metadata is so critical when dealing with web technologies, looking at some of the metadata standards relevant to managing web content is useful. When using Adobe Experience Manager (or any web content management tool), you need to understand these standards, at least fundamentally. You will probably use most or all of them.

Although many different metadata standards may be relevant, I cover just a few that are particularly important. However, the same practical concepts should apply regardless of the standard you use.

Resource description framework

The Resource Description Framework (RDFa) is a set of attributes that can be used within HTML and XML documents to help describe them. Combined with the Dublin Core (see "Dublin Core Metadata Initiative" later in this chapter), RDFa enables the metadata-based classification required for accurately describing the resources of the web. This metadata is added to the code of your website, as part of the HTML.

Here's an example:

```
<meta property="dc:creator" content="Ryan Lunka" />
```

This HTML tag could be placed in a webpage to establish that I created it. The `meta` tag is part of the HTML standard that can be placed within a webpage to add metadata that isn't visible to the user. The `property` attribute specifies what metadata property will be set. In the example, the `creator` metadata property is used. The `dc:` is a namespace that establishes "this property called `creator` is part of Dublin

Core." In the `content` attribute, "Ryan Lunka" establishes the value that is set to the metadata property specified in `property`.

In summary, this tag specifies structured metadata that says this webpage was created by Ryan Lunka. The `property` and `content` attributes are specified by RDFa and implemented by the HTML standard, which is why this tag can be universally used to identify the creator of a webpage.

Dublin Core Metadata Initiative

In 1995, web professionals met in Dublin, Ohio (right down the street from me) to develop a standard vocabulary to describe a variety of web elements. They settled on a standard of terms that describe web resources such as images and webpages, physical media, artwork, and more. The Dublin Core Metadata Initiative (DCMI) has become the foundation for many important metadata standards on the web. DCMI maintains standards about syntax, vocabulary, and guidelines for use, to ensure the effectiveness of metadata that implements the Dublin Core.

This simplest part of the Dublin Core is the Dublin Core Metadata Element Set. It contains 15 attributes that can universally classify content:

- Title
- Creator
- Subject
- Description
- Publisher
- Contributor
- Date
- Type
- Format
- Identifier
- Source
- Language
- Relation
- Coverage
- Rights

As you look over those terms, think about how you use them to classify objects. The goal is that they use a common generic vocabulary to classify dissimilar *things*. These terms are typically used, in conjunction with RDFa, to describe webpages. This classification enables programs (such as search engine crawlers) to understand webpage content and determine what to do with the page.

Open Graph

The Open Graph protocol is another metadata initiative, inspired by Dublin Core, intended to describe resources in a way that specifically makes them shareable on social networking sites. The initiative was started by Facebook but has since been adopted by other social networks. Though the purpose of Open Graph metadata is similar to the Dublin Core metadata (describing webpages), it is used in a more specific way.

Open Graph metadata becomes part of the Social Graph concept Facebook is building into its platform. When you share content that is described with Open Graph metadata, it becomes part of your social representation, just as if you "liked" Kurt Vonnegut books or soccer.

Open Graph data is used in webpages as is Dublin Core data (using RDFa):

```
<meta property="og:title" content="Ryan's Web Page" />
```

The preceding tag uses the Open Graph (`og:`) property `title` to tell social networks the name of the webpage. It uses almost the same format as the first example because it takes advantage of the HTML `meta` tag and the RDFa attributes `property` and `content`.

Social networks don't require Open Graph tags, and most have automatic fallbacks when basic properties such as `title` and `url` aren't specified. But you need to think about how you want your web content to be shared, and to specify metadata that describes your content for that particular purpose. Social sharing is every bit as important as search engine optimization in the modern web era.

Schema.org

The Schema.org initiative is a collaborative effort by Google, Bing, and Yahoo! to establish a robust set of metadata to make webpages more findable. Classically, search engines use basic metadata and the content of a webpage to guess what the page contains. But with Schema.org metadata, content creators can specify more details about their webpage content. Doing so enables a search engine to provide a better search experience because it can know whether a page is about a store's hours of operation or about a medical condition. Applying Schema.org enables search engines to be more intelligent about connecting users with the information they seek.

The Schema.org taxonomies are described on its website. This metadata is implemented similarly to the first two examples using HTML attributes:

```
<div itemtype="http://schema.org/Movie">
        <h1 itemprop="title">Star Wars</h1>
</div>
```

The `h1` tag would be the main heading on a page about the movie Star Wars, whether or not you were implementing any metadata. Search engines could make an assumption that the term in the `h1` is the most important term on the page, and that the term is "Star Wars." But how can the search engine know what that means? In the example, the `itemtype` property in the `div` containing the `h1` describes that everything in this `div` is about a movie because it points to the specific Schema.org metadata taxonomy for describing movies. Then the `itemprop` attribute in the `h1` specifies that the content in this `h1` element is the title of the movie.

Translator

For managing multilingual content, AEM provides the translator interface. It's a fairly simple concept: a web interface in which specialized authors can manage a big table of translations used throughout the site. I single out "specialized authors" because I'm guessing that most of your content authors do not have the expertise required to manage multilingual content. The translator allows you to manage each individual phrase based on a root language (typically English) and specify the translation for each language you want.

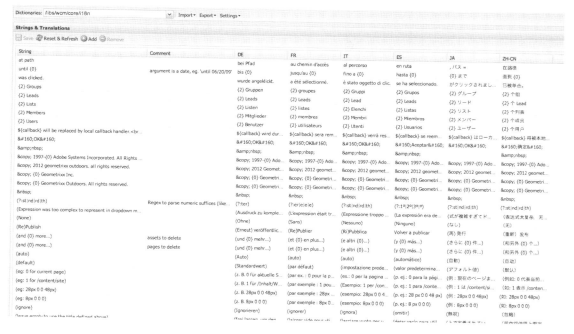

Each row in the translator interface represents a single phrase or word you will translate to different languages. Sometimes individual words are sufficient, but typically these are phrases. After all, you can't just translate sentences word for word. Each column represents a different target language, but you don't need to translate every phrase into every language. Anything that isn't translated will simply be displayed as the default language.

Figure 6.1
The translator

Dictionaries organize the content available in the translator. A dictionary is a group of phrases that will be translated, but by organizing them into groups you get quite a bit more flexibility. If you have multiple applications (totally separate websites) built on a single instance of AEM, you'll generally place each one's translations into separate dictionaries. When you have a big website, you might also want to consider splitting it up into logical dictionaries, which makes your translations more organized and more flexible. A good solution implementation partner can help identify how you'll want to group translations.

The translator also gives you controls for importing or exporting content so that you can use other systems to manage your translations. Translations can be transferred between systems as XLIFF files. XLIFF format is just an XML file that adheres to the XLIFF schema. (It's basically an XML representation of what you see in the translator interface.) XLIFF is designed specifically for interoperability of content translations and will allow you to send your "to be translated" content off to a translation service organization. They return an XLIFF file with all the translations filled out, and you can just import that file into the translator.

But how the heck do you do anything with the translated content? Serving up the translator interface to customers certainly isn't going to sell any products. Don't worry; there's more to it.

Translated content is referred to throughout the code that implements your website. The copy built into your components is flagged so that AEM knows it is eligible for translation. Generally, all built-in copy will be flagged because you are typically going to translate entire pages, not just parts of a page. AEM has a few mechanisms for determining which language the current page should be in, and uses that information to look for translations for all flagged copy on the page. If the translations are available, it displays them. Remember, this process is performed on a per-phrase basis, so it is possible to partially translate whatever content you see fit.

For example, let's say I have a website to be translated from English to Dutch. I have a home page signup widget for my email list, and under the signup button is a message that reads, "Sign up for future sales." Assume that text, which is built into the component, is flagged for translation (which I'll explain shortly). When I create the Dutch copy of my website, I set the Language page property on my home page to Dutch. AEM loads the page, sees the flagged copy, and notes that the page language should be Dutch. AEM goes to your dictionary looking for the phrase "Sign up for future sales." If it finds a Dutch translation, it'll display that instead of the English default. If the translation doesn't yet exist, English will be displayed until an author adds the translation.

One key thing to remember with translations is the difference between built-in copy and authored content. This translation function is not intended to translate authorable content. When you enter text in a dialog to set up a component, that is authorable content. The translator will not be set up to translate it. Trying to manage *authorable* content in the translator would be difficult. You'd have to add authored content, add that copy as a single phrase to the translator, and then translate it. This method is inflexible, complex to manage, and not recommended.

You don't have the same problem with built-in copy, because the only person who can change it is a programmer. All a content author can do is change the translations. Again, the only phrases you can translate are the ones that have been defined by the development team. Let's see how it works.

Bear with me while I get a little technical as a way to help you more clearly understand this issue. The programmer who works on your implementation team is the person who flags copy for translation. If I'm the developer building that email signup widget, instead of simply printing out the text in the HTML, I wrap that text in a special translation function that looks something like this:

```
i18n.get("Sign up for future sales.")
```

That function wrapper tells AEM that it should translate the content if an appropriate language translation is available. The resulting output will either be the original English text or the translation. If you're wondering what "i18n" means, it's shorthand for the word "internationalization."

The implication of the developer's role in this is that you'll need to put some foresight into your content internationalization plans. Building your page and content components with translation in mind the first time around is far easier (and cheaper) than later reworking components to make them translation friendly. If early on you work with your implementation team to identify which pieces of text will need to be translated and what the "phrases" are, you'll be able to build an application that supports translation. Even if you don't plan on rolling out non-English sites until much later, you should still put this plumbing in place upfront.

● **Note:** You might be asking what you can do about translating authorable content. Although AEM doesn't support this directly out of the box, you have some options that I explain shortly.

Multi Site Manager

The AEM Multi Site Manager (MSM) helps you create and manage multiple versions of your website, although it's technically not a function specific to managing multilingual sites. In fact, you can also use it to manage mobile and tablet versions of your site. But the most common use for the MSM is for creating and managing multiple versions of a site in different languages.

At a 10,000-foot view, the MSM allows you to copy your website into different locations of the content hierarchy. Then it uses referential inheritance to maintain a connection to the original. The idea is that the duplicate site can inherit as much or as little content as is needed from the original site. You can replace the authored content in the copied site, perhaps with content in Spanish or Japanese. You can copy the content but convert it into a different presentation, perhaps to produce a mobile version of the site. The MSM is a flexible tool for creating several kinds of rubber-stamped content. It means you don't have to go through the mind-numbing and error-prone process of manually copying pages and making minor changes, and manually keeping everything in sync.

The MSM isn't the easiest function in AEM to understand or configure, so you'll want to work with your solution implementation partner. However, as a marketer, you need to understand two fundamental parts: live copy and blueprinting. These two functions are the core of the MSM and allow you to manage duplicated content. As we look into these, I also go over the Language Copy function, which is a specialized version of blueprinting.

Multinational vs. multilingual

You can build two categories of international sites with Adobe Experience Manager: *multinational* and *multilingual*. They sound like the same thing, but they aren't. The distinction is subtle yet important to identify.

Multinational refers to sites that are targeted toward specific geographies. For example, you may have a site created specifically for your Chinese market. Building a multinational site doesn't require language translation, just cultural relevance. In a multinational site, you need to worry about holidays, phrasing of copy, and cultural context clues. You should also consider technology differences.

Multilingual refers to sites that are targeted toward speakers of specific languages and aren't necessarily constrained by any regional geography. For example, even though the majority of your customers (and web traffic) may be from the United States, you may find it appropriate to provide an English and Spanish version of your content. With a multilingual site, you need only correctly translate content from one language to another. Strictly speaking, cultural relevance isn't that important.

In practice, with an international web presence, you will most likely implement a multinational-multilingual site and consider both scenarios. Your sites are targeted toward specific geographies, and some or all of them are translated into the native languages.

Live copy

A live copy is a copied version of another site that maintains links to the original for referential inheritance. When you create a live copy of a site (remember, a site is just part of your content hierarchy), AEM duplicates the pages. But when it makes that duplicate, behind the scenes it adds a link to the original content. A content author with the appropriate permissions can break that link, an action typically referred to as *breaking inheritance*. Live copy duplicates maintain updates to the original; you don't have to manage the duplicate manually.

Creating a live copy doesn't just magically happen out of the box. It requires a very specific configuration. You'll have to work with an implementation team to build that configuration. Essentially, the live copy configuration tells AEM *how* to copy the content. In its simplest form, the configuration does a direct copy. However, the configuration also includes directives for translating the content properties. For example, if you are making a live copy for your mobile site, your live copy configuration can tell AEM to change each of your pages to a page component and template optimized to display mobile content. Without live copy, this change would be tedious and risky, and it would require a programmer who could perform the change via script.

When authoring a live copy page, the experience is basically the same as authoring a normal page. But the major exception is the locking mechanism displayed in all component dialogs. When you open the dialog for a component and see the "locked" icon, it indicates that this instance of the component is inheriting from elsewhere in the content hierarchy using referential inheritance. If you have the appropriate permissions, you can break that inheritance by clicking the lock icon. Then you can edit that copied version of the component without altering the original. Changes to the original will no longer be pushed down to the unlocked component instance, at least until you click the lock again to reassign it to inheritance.

You'll want to consider using a live copy when you have a one- or two-off version of a website. That's what makes the live copy feature a good candidate for mobile and tablet sites. However, live copy is not used on its own that often because it's typically used in conjunction with a blueprint.

Blueprint

A blueprint is basically a rubber stamp for creating entire site structures on the fly. It defines the structure of the new site which, when created, will be a live copy of another. Once the copies are created from a blueprint, content authors are provided with a nice interface for managing which blueprints are rolled out where. "Rolling out" a page that is defined by a blueprint means pushing content updates down to all corresponding components that haven't broken inheritance.

The blueprint configuration interface allows you to manage these rollouts at an administrative level. Rollouts can also be performed on a page-by-page, tree-based, or component-by-component basis from the Sidekick while authoring a page. In short, creating and managing your live copy through a blueprint gives you more control over when what content is inherited. You'll have to work with a solution implementation team to set it up, but they will be able to help you work through the requirements.

Language copy

Adobe Experience Manager provides a function called a language copy, which makes rolling out multilingual copies of your sites easier. Once you have your language options preconfigured by an administrator, you can tell AEM to create a copy of your site in a different language. This function will not translate your content, but it will create a copy of the site that is set up to be translated. You have to create the language root page manually, but then language copy gives you a nice interface for creating the rest of the pages. You simply tell it which pages you want to copy and from what language.

Tag translation

The AEM tagging interface, discussed in Chapter 5, allows you to translate tags into multiple languages. The underlying ID of the tag will remain the same, but an end user never sees it, anyway. When a multilingual site has a tag applied to it, it'll look for a relevant language translation for its display term. This is especially important if you expose the tags to the public, as you would in blog components, for instance. Tag translations can be set in the same dialog in which you define the tag itself.

A set of tools

I'm going to guess that you're still a little confused about these different translation features and what they can do for you. It's a complicated problem to solve, and there isn't a single way to solve it. My intent with this chapter is not to provide a prescriptive approach to managing content translation, but to introduce the available tools to give you some context for additional conversations with your solution implementation partner.

Applying the concepts

When you want to create a new website in a different language, you have to deal with two primary concerns: translating built-in copy and translating authored content. I explained the translator and how it enables you to manage translations of built-in content. I explained the Multi Site Manager and some of the tools it provides for creating copies of content in location-specific websites. But nothing discussed so far actually translates the authored content. To wrap up this chapter, I discuss some of the approaches to authored content translation.

Manual content translation

The simplest way to translate authored content is to do so manually. AEM provides some features to ease this process, but you'll ultimately have to provide the translations yourself. While authoring each page, you can switch to a view in the Sidekick for creating page translations. You should implement those translations on the language-specific page, not the original. If you've used something like language copy, the language-specific page will be flagged as that new language but with the English content copied into it. Using the Translations tab of the Sidekick, you can kick off a special "translation" workflow to start the process.

The translation workflow sends the page to a designated human translator, who is a multilingual content author. That person opens that page (from their workflow inbox) and manually changes all the authored content to whatever language is required. When finished, she passes the page on and it is marked as translated. The Sidekick tab for translations then gives you a side-by-side view of translation versions, if you need to compare past versions.

<!-- marginal note -->● **Note:** I explained this scenario to break down the concept into the raw basics. However, this manual process is rarely used for content translation.

This is a manual translation process, but it's one over which you have complete control. If you have the in-house resources to translate content, this process might be a good one for you. As long as the translators can be trained to use the AEM authoring features, they can translate copy in context, emulating original English where appropriate. That is, they can immediately see whether a translation is too long or too short. They can view exactly how the translations look in the styled fonts. However, most companies don't have the budget to employ 10 translators, which generally makes this process out of reach.

Using a translation service

If you don't want to manually translate content in-house, you can use an external translation service. Yes, doing so costs money, but you have access to experts in as many languages as they offer. You send them your content for translation, and they send it back. This process allows you to focus your time and resources on building your digital brand and not have to worry as much about language nuances.

When you use a translation service, you'll have to export the content and get it to them in a format they can use. Adobe Experience Manager doesn't provide for doing that out of the box, so you'll have to spec something out to be built by your implementation team. You'll also probably create a custom version of a translation workflow that sends content to the external translation service. Doing so will require customization and extra work, but I've seen quite good custom interfaces built to handle this problem. It's definitely something you should consider if quickly translating authored content would serve as an advantage to your marketing team.

Some translation services and other vendors have created AEM add-ons to facilitate the process of exporting content for translation. The way they work depends on the solution, but I've seen some handy implementations for managing translation. If budget is not an issue for you, a suitable add-on can be a fine way to manage your translation logistics.

Work with your solution partner to figure out what you should consider for your translation implementation. Every AEM project is different. The partner should be able to explain your options and suggest translation service integrations you might consider.

Summary

If you're going to manage an international digital presence, you need to show the people of other countries that you are connected to them. Targeting your content (specifically, your copy) to different areas of the world by translating the text and making culture-sensitive adjustments demonstrates that you are just as concerned about your international markets as your domestic market. In an increasingly global economy, these are concerns that even small companies must deal with.

Adobe Experience Manager provides a set of tools for helping marketers manage multiple-language versions of their websites. The primary functions are parts of the Multi Site Manager: live copy and blueprints. AEM also provides a language translation feature for creating language-specific copies of websites. These features are designed for slightly different purposes, but offer some overlap in functionality that can make it confusing to choose one over the other. My goal with this chapter was to present the tools to you in an implementation-agnostic way. Everyone's internationalization requirements are different, so it would be difficult (or long) to talk through how to address all those differing challenges.

Think about the features presented in this chapter. Review the documentation about them on the Adobe website. Then work with your solution implementation partner to attempt to translate your business requirements into an executable solution using Adobe Experience Manager. The thought put into how you'll manage translations will be worth the time investment.

Review questions

1. What are the three primary issues you have to deal with when creating an international web presence?

2. What kind of content can you translate using the translator interface?

3. What is a live copy?

4. Can Adobe Experience Manager automatically translate content?

Review answers

1. Language, cultural context, and technology differences

2. The translator is an interface for helping marketers manage the translations for built-in copy. It is *not* used to manage translation of authored content.

3. A live copy is a duplication of part of the page hierarchy that maintains a referential inheritance connection to the original content. Authors with appropriate permission can break inheritance on a per-component basis as needed.

4. No. Adobe Experience Manager does not translate your content for you. However, it includes a number of features to facilitate the translation process.

7 WORKFLOWS

Workflows enable automation of some processes that involve humans and others that do not. They are an important part of the process efficiencies realized by using a content management system. Adobe Experience Manager's workflow engine is a more technical concept than many covered in this book, but you need to understand what workflows are and why you would use them.

In this chapter, I'll answer the following questions:

- What is a workflow engine and why is it an important part of content management?

- What features does Adobe Experience Manager include, in terms of workflow functionality?

- For what use cases would you want to consider implementing workflows?

By the end of this chapter you'll be able to intelligently discuss the reasons you would or would not use workflows in Adobe Experience Manager. You'll also start to understand *how* to use them. This will help you develop a plan for using workflows in your AEM implementation.

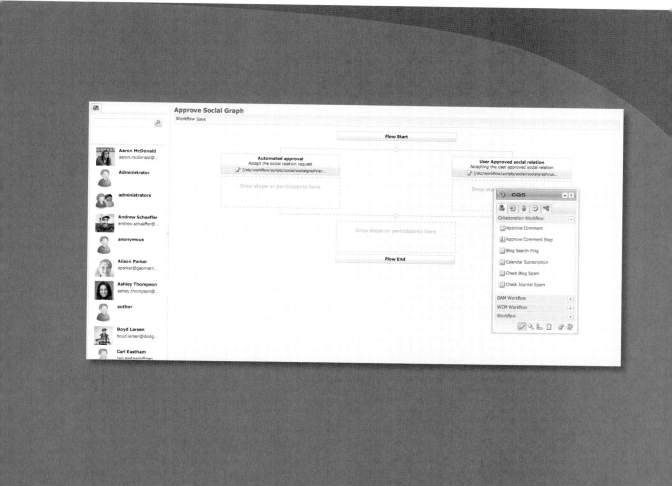

Designing a workflow model

Workflow basics

Workflows are a critical part of business, even if you take technology out of the picture. A workflow is a business process whereby information or data is transferred through various channels to provide additional value. In less jargony terms, a workflow is simply a process of transferring information. Workflows happen every day in any organization that has more than one person, regardless of technology. Let's look at an example.

Let's say you are in charge of acquiring enterprise software for your marketing department. You've settled on Adobe Experience Manager (good choice) as a web content management solution, but you don't have the authority to write the check on the spot. You fill out a purchase order for the software, then pass it on to your finance department. The CFO reviews the request's financial feasibility and, if she approves it, passes it on to the CMO. The CMO reviews whether the acquisition will add worthy business value, and if he approves it, passes the request back to you.

At each step of the workflow, a person or group adds business value and then passes the information to the next party. What started as a simple request to purchase software became a full and proper review by management, helping to audit the value of the purchase.

If you keep technology out of the equation, you can imagine the manual steps involved with the process. You have to fill out the paper form for the purchase order. You then have to walk or (eek!) mail it to the CFO for review. She has to read the form and cross-reference the other documents that will provide the information to approve. Then the form goes to the CMO, who does the same thing.

This process is extremely simple, and you can already see the justification for automating parts of it using technology. Imagine the complex business problems you work on every day. How crazy would they be if they were completely manual? Maybe they are! We'll get into how technology helps solve these problems soon, but first, let's look at the basic elements of a workflow.

The anatomy of a workflow

There are numerous ways to define workflows. Organizations have created standards and certifications for doing so. Consulting companies make all their money by implementing best practices for workflows. I'm going to boil it down to some fundamental basics, just to go over the general parts. I won't use any specific framework, just some generalizations based on my experience. However, these concepts are important, because later in the chapter you'll learn how the AEM workflow terminology maps to these workflow elements.

Actor

An actor is a human being who interacts with the workflow in some way. In the previous example, the CFO, CMO, and you are all actors. Some workflows have many actors and some have none. Oftentimes when workflows (or business processes) are modeled, the actors are illustrated by using swim lanes into which fall any processes that actor is responsible for. Remember that the actor is a person who is part of the flow.

Data

Data is the *thing* passed through the workflow. Often, the data is simply a document, but it can be many other things. Without data passed between parties, a workflow doesn't have much of a point. Just remember that sometimes data can be an abstract concept—it doesn't have to be a physical form. However, in the previous example, the data is the purchase order itself.

Process step

A process step defines a single action that must occur in the sequence of events that makes up the workflow. It might be a human action. It might be some kind of calculation. It may be an interaction with a piece of software. Sometimes a process step can even kick off another workflow. If you imagine drawing your workflow onto a piece of paper, the process step is each point in the flow where something happens.

There are two kinds of process steps: synchronous and asynchronous. A synchronous process step is one that stops workflow progress until it is completed. Typically, any process step that involves some kind of calculation will be synchronous. In our previous example, each approval step was synchronous because the flow couldn't move on without a "yes" or "no."

Asynchronous process steps do not halt the workflow. If a process step initiated a different workflow, it could be asynchronous. A process step that sends out email notifications of some event—and doesn't require a response—is asynchronous. The difference is that the workflow requires no output from the step from calculation or actor decision, so the step is kicked off and the workflow just keeps going.

Process flow

The process flow is the roadmap that links all the process steps. Once again, imagine drawing out your workflow. Without a process flow, you would randomly list the things that would happen. To make a workflow, you have to link those process steps in a sequential order that respects the business rules of your organization. The process flow is simply the abstraction of that sequence of events that defines when each must happen.

Decision points

Few business processes are linear; that is, one thing happens, then another, and another down a prescribed path. Among the most common complexities of business processes and workflows are the decision points. A decision point is a break in the process flow, where some logic determines that the flow will continue down one of two or more different routes. The decision points are key to implementing business rules in your workflows. Without them, your workflow would be static and, therefore, pretty useless.

Think about the purchase order example. Between the CFO and CMO, you have a decision point because there are two potential routes to take. If the CFO approves the purchase order, it is routed to the CMO for additional approval. If the CFO does not approve it, the purchase order is routed back to you, informing you of its denial.

You could also have a decision point prior to the CFO approval process step. Maybe your organization has implemented a business rule to alleviate the paperwork for your CFO that states, "All purchase orders for less than $100,000 can simply be routed to the CMO for approval." If this is the case, your workflow would start with a decision point whereby the purchase order is only routed to the CFO if the data specifies a request of $100,000 or more.

Parallel process flow

The inverse of a decision point is a parallel process flow. This is effectively a split in the process flow that uses AND logic instead of OR logic. Even with decision points in place, workflows would be terribly inefficient if they required only one thing to happen at a time. Parallel process flows allow multiple things to happen at once by splitting the flow into two or more simultaneous paths. Ultimately, at some point, those paths usually have to recombine to continue, so one flow may have to wait on completion of the others.

The previous example didn't have a parallel process flow, but we can add one. Let's say that after the CMO approves the purchase order, we implemented a parallel flow that (1) sent the approved P.O. back to you for notification of approval and (2) sends a copy to the purchasing department to begin the paperwork for acquiring the software. The flow has split into two parallel flows.

Workflows in content management

The marriage of computers and business has always been about creating process efficiencies. Sure, we've gone through several generations in *how* that is accomplished. But ultimately increased efficiency has always been the goal. Business is a human system that often requires meticulous, redundant, and/or time-consuming work. By implementing technology to automate parts of that work, we free ourselves up to devote our limited energy and attention to tasks that create more value than the tasks we automate.

Content management systems absolutely fall into this strategy. A workflow engine is pretty much a required piece in an enterprise-class content management system. The business processes required to execute within a web content management system are common and don't differ that much from organization to organization. Therefore, WCMs tend to have workflow engines specifically designed to automate those common tasks such as:

- Content approval and publishing

- User-generated content moderation

- Content auditing

- Automated processing, sometimes interfacing with other systems

This certainly isn't an exhaustive or complete list of the workflows a web content management platform can manage. But, as a generalization, it covers the vast majority of workflow needs in content management.

Organizations possess quite a variance in how well they understand workflow. Sometimes it depends on whether the IT department or the marketing department is in charge of the WCM. Sometimes organizations are just more mature in terms of enterprise architecture. Regardless of where your organization is, you need to learn to use workflows to make your WCM hum. They can save you quite a bit of time and money. They can save you some headaches, too (or create them if you skip this chapter). That's why Adobe Experience Manager includes a workflow engine specifically designed to enable marketers to accomplish their most common tasks.

Workflows in AEM

The workflow engine built into Adobe Experience Manager is specifically built to address web content management needs. If you're looking for a robust workflow engine to serve all your enterprise workflow needs, you're not going to find it here. You will find a workflow engine that does exactly what it needs to do and includes the appropriate extension points for proper integration with the rest of your enterprise software.

AEM workflow terminology

As a marketer you may or may not be administering workflows. It depends on your tech savvy and what roles your company will support with Adobe Experience Manager. You will have to use workflows and their requirements with your administrator and/or solution implementation team. Therefore, you need to understand some core concepts in AEM's workflow engine and what they accomplish.

Model

A workflow model is a definition of a specific workflow. If you imagine drawing out your workflow on a piece of paper, this drawing is effectively the model. However, the AEM workflow engine is more than just a picture, because it is the definition of a process for the engine to execute. It's made up of executable code that will make that workflow happen.

If you have the appropriate permissions, you can view and edit workflow models in the workflow administration interface. It looks similar to the site manager interface, except that workflow models have no hierarchy. (They are stored in a flat structure.) When you open a model for editing, it uses the same authoring paradigm as any other page. You can add workflow elements from the Sidekick to paragraph systems. In fact, workflow editing pages are simply a specialized type of configuration page (see Chapter 3).

Step

In AEM terms, a workflow step equates to a "process step" as described in generalized workflow terms. It's one part of the workflow model that represents a required action from an actor or some kind of code execution. Workflow steps in AEM are almost always synchronous, unless the step calls into an external system that manages its own workflow concept. Workflow steps that don't require human action are usually just code that makes a calculation or performs an action within the AEM system. In these cases, the step is executed in milliseconds.

Transition

A transition is the link between two process steps. It defines the path that a workflow must take and equates to the "process flow" described earlier. In the AEM workflow engine, the "decision point" doesn't exist as a specific entity. However, that doesn't mean the function doesn't exist. In your workflow definition, you add metadata logic to your transitions to establish a decision point. When a workflow leaves a step that has multiple transitions, it will evaluate each one and take the first path defined as "true." Therefore, the concept of a decision point exists, but not as a discrete element you add to your workflow model.

Work item

A work item is a task that represents a workflow step requiring human interaction. When, for example, a publish approval is assigned to you, a work item is created and added to your inbox. The work item tells you which workflow created it (so you know why you're receiving it), what piece of content it's relative to (see the "Payload" section that follows), and what transitions are available to continue this workflow. Then you choose which transition path the workflow should continue along.

Payload

In AEM a workflow payload is the resource (piece of content) passed through the workflow. It equates to the term *data* defined earlier. Usually the payload will be a webpage or a DAM asset, but it can be any resource in AEM. If you are viewing a work item, it will identify the payload, so that you can open and evaluate whatever resource it is. A workflow instance (a single execution of a workflow) can have only one payload resource, which begs the question, "How do I send multiple pages through a workflow at once?"

Workflow package

The rule about passing a single resource is a technical limitation of the AEM workflow engine. But, to allow multiple resources through a workflow at once, Adobe Experience Manager includes the "workflow package." You can think of it as a folder in which you can place multiple resources. Then, when you execute a workflow, you do so using a workflow package that becomes your single resource payload. Problem solved!

Interacting with workflows

As a marketer you may not be involved with developing workflows in Adobe Experience Manager—at least not beyond defining your workflow requirements. But whether you're a more technical administrator who configures workflows or just a content creator, you will probably have to interact with workflows at some point. Therefore, it's important to understand a couple of marketer-oriented features in AEM that enable you to do so.

Workflow inbox

The workflow inbox is an interface in which you can view and respond to your assigned workflow tasks. The inbox lists the tasks, identifies the workflow they are part of, and describes the attached payload. These tasks are technically "work items," and they allow you to create workflows that involve human interaction. Within the inbox, you can view the payload of a work item and select which of the available transitions you would like the workflow to continue down.

The most common use case you may want to implement is for content approvers who must review pages before they are made public. Those in a supervisory content authoring role will receive "ready to go" activation requests in their inboxes. They can then easily check the page in question and approve or deny its activation.

Kicking off workflows

Obviously, to send content through workflows, a workflow must be started. In Adobe Experience Manager, there are two ways to start workflows: manually by a user, and automatically based on a listener. Both of these options serve their different purposes well. You need to understand them so that you can define your workflow requirements precisely.

Figure 7.1
The dialog presented to anyone who wants to kick off a workflow

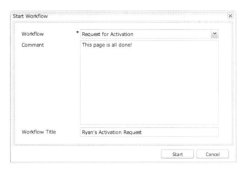

▶ **Tip:** You can also kick off and respond to work items from within the Sidekick. This makes it easy for you to do so as you're editing a page, because you don't have to switch context back to the site administration interface or inbox.

Throughout AEM's authoring interface, authors have access to a Workflow option. Choosing it displays a prompt to select which workflow you want to execute and any comment you choose to send with it. When you trigger a workflow manually, it is always while having selected a single resource (usually a page), so you don't need to do anything specific to pick the payload. If the workflow you started contains a step for your review, you'll eventually see a work item in your inbox.

The site administration interface will indicate whether a page is currently in a workflow by indicating which workflow and on which step of that workflow. Of course, this indication appears only if you kick off a workflow that involves human interaction. If no interaction is required, the entire workflow execution will be completed in a matter of seconds (or faster).

Workflows can also be configured to kick off automatically. In this setup, a workflow administrator creates a *launcher* to trigger a specific workflow. A launcher is basically a listener with a set of instructions that define exactly what it's listening for. The launcher can be configured to scan a subset of the content hierarchy for new nodes added, nodes modified, or nodes deleted. It could also detect additional information such as a node type and even some of the properties of that node. As an example, you may instruct a launcher to trigger a workflow when a new page is created under /content/geometrixx/en/services with the word *Consulting* in the title property.

Setting up workflow launchers is not typically the kind of thing a marketer will be doing. It's more of an administrator or developer task because the launcher interface requires some technical knowledge of AEM's underlying content repository. However, it is important to understand how automatic workflows are wired up so that you can talk intelligently with those administrators to meet your marketing needs.

Preconfigured workflows

Adobe Experience Manager ships with some workflows preconfigured. Some are used as examples or starting points to demonstrate what is possible with workflows.

Others are critical parts of AEM as an application and should be altered only with the guidance of an expert. Like most aspects of AEM, these workflow definitions are very open to pick apart and analyze. Here are a few of them.

Publishing

A common use case for workflows is to create a supervisory approval before content is made public. AEM ships with a workflow called Publish Example to show how that can be done. Obviously, this is one of those examples intended for instruction or extension. It's a simple workflow that asks for approval from the administrator's group; if approved, it activates a page to public view. Though this is an example workflow, it is fully functional and could be used if that basic approval is all you need.

AEM also ships with a workflow called Request For Activation (and the associated Request For Deactivation). There's a bit of redundancy because this workflow does almost the same thing. The difference is it enforces a two-step approval process for administrators in which you approve the content and then approve the activation. It's a nitpicky difference, though. Again, you can use this fully functioning, albeit simple, workflow if it meets your needs.

User-generated content

We'll examine user-generated content (UGC) in more detail in Chapter 8, but the concept has some relevance in this workflow discussion. UGC describes any content created by external site visitors—your customers. It might include comments on a blog post, questions asked in a forum, and so on. Many marketing departments like the idea of soliciting feedback or questions from customers in a public forum but are not necessarily comfortable doing so in an unmonitored fashion. Therefore, AEM includes workflows to support UGC moderation basically requiring activation approval for comments.

The Comment Moderation workflow is set up to send all user comments to the UGC moderation interface. The content components that enable user-generated content will have an author setting to specify whether to moderate comments. Applying a comprehensive "all the time" rule will require a small customization that an implementation team would have to add. The workflow works similarly to the content approval workflows, with one exception: Comments are not moderated in the workflow inbox. A special user interface exists specifically for UGC moderation.

Digital asset management

When you upload media files into the digital asset management interface, AEM does quite a bit of work behind the scenes. This work is triggered as a workflow whenever a DAM asset is created, which is what happens when you upload content to the DAM. The processing that occurs in this workflow is what makes all the magic happen in the DAM. Other workflows are also included for behind-the-scenes processing of already existing DAM assets.

Most of the workflow functionality around the DAM is involved with one of two processes: creating or modifying asset renditions, or updating or extracting XMP metadata. DAM workflows are sort of the connector between the functionality of the platform and the metadata standards used by other systems. So, when you upload a new DAM asset, workflows create the multiple renditions and then extract the XMP metadata so that it can be applied as normal AEM metadata.

There are two fairly technical things you should know about the DAM workflows: First, your requirements may require customization. I see this a lot when clients want to automatically generate rendition sizes other than the defaults. I recommend having a technical administrator or your solution implementation partner make those changes. If the appropriate care is not taken, the DAM will not work properly.

Second, pay close attention to what actions occur when. For example, the default configuration for rendition creation happens only when a new DAM asset is added. If you add 5000 assets, and then change your rendition configuration, you'll have to rerun that workflow. You may not want it to run automatically because of the computing resources it would hog.

● **Note:** I picked the number 5000 arbitrarily. The actual performance limit for DAM workflows will depend on many circumstances, like your hardware specs and whether you are using clustering.

Which brings me the last point: DAM workflows are computing resource intensive; dropping 5000 new DAM assets into your AEM platform at the same time could create temporary performance issues. AEM will require a lot of computing power to analyze each asset and perform the necessary actions. Definitely consider batching your DAM asset creation and be sure to schedule it around the schedules of your content authors and other AEM users.

Creating custom workflows

In all likelihood, you will implement a custom workflow as part of your Adobe Experience Manager solution. It may be as simple as a customized approval workflow, but it could be quite a bit more complicated. I'll brief you on the basics that a marketer should know to intelligently communicate with the techie folks on your workflow needs.

Have a plan

Don't be unprepared when you talk about workflow. The longer you wait to identify your needs, the riskier and more expensive it gets to meet those needs. As you are figuring out who will do what in AEM (your content authors, approvers, administrators, and so on), draw out the business processes you anticipate as the interaction between those groups. Use a standard business process modeling notation to define the workflow in technology-agnostic terms to establish a common language. Don't try to draw processes in terms of "what you think AEM can do." These processes should be applicable regardless of the content management system.

Having your business processes identified and documented gives you a context to take to your implementation team. That business process diagram will effectively serve as a blueprint (not the Multi Site Manager term) for your workflow model. You can start by attempting to implement that plan exactly, and then make strategic adjustments as necessary due to technical reasons. I don't recommend going it alone, though. Custom workflows often require customized workflow steps written in the Java programming language. They almost always include some scripting to configure the decision point logic. Your job as the marketer is to identify the needs and effectively communicate them to your solution partner. They'll guide you the rest of the way.

Don't create dependencies

You never want to design yourself into a hole when determining what you need. A lot of responsibility for avoiding this falls on the implementation team because decoupling functionality is largely a coding best practice. However, the same caution applies when identifying business requirements. You don't want to make business decisions such as these:

- Requiring your content structure to fit a certain format for a workflow to function

- Assuming the presence of an offline business process that affects the AEM workflow

- Designing workflow steps that cram a lot of functions into a single box (separate them!)

- Making demands that don't fit the designed paradigm of how AEM's workflow features are built

- Altering the workflow interfaces or functionality

Some of these errors are difficult to identify until it's too late, but a solution partner can help avoid them. You should give all of your workflow discussions a smell test: If your rules totally changed tomorrow, would it break what we're talking about designing? If the answer is yes, it's probably because a dependency should be eliminated.

Identify customization early

The out-of-the-box workflow steps in Adobe Experience Manager include all the basics, but any significant workflow will likely require some new steps developed by a programmer. As a result, you will need to identify those early enough that their development can be properly estimated, prioritized, and executed. The sooner you have conversations about these changes, the better. If you wait, you'll end up with extra surprise work. No one can afford to push back deadlines. No manager likes a last-minute budget increase. Figure it out earlier, not later.

Don't overdo it

You have to go into these conversations understanding what AEM's workflow engine really is. It's a relatively lightweight workflow engine designed to implement specific web content management functions. It's not a full-blown workflow solution, so if you are familiar with more developed workflow platforms, some concepts familiar to you may not be present in AEM. I'm not trying to knock AEM's workflow engine. It just is what it is.

If you get into discussions about workflow and determine that you will need a lot of customization, you may need to look at your situation a different way. Instead of customizing the heck out of a workflow engine with a ceiling, consider integrating with a more workflow-specific platform. I've seen some good implementations using external task management platforms that allow AEM to do what it does best and permit other technologies to do what they do best. With this approach, your AEM customization is about creating a seamless interface into another system. A solution partner can help you identify whether this is something you should consider.

Summary

Workflows are a key piece of the web content management puzzle. They allow you to implement critical business processes in a digital platform. They can create huge opportunities for automation and time savings.

Adobe Experience Manager includes a lightweight, albeit adequate workflow engine for addressing approval workflows and certain types of automated content processing. You, as a marketer, must take the time upfront to define how you want to use that workflow engine. With the help of a solution partner, you can determine which workflow models will need to be configured, which custom steps will need to be developed, and whether you should consider interfacing with a more robust workflow solution external to AEM.

Review questions

1. Explain the difference between a parallel process flow and a decision point.

2. What is a workflow package?

3. How are the user-generated content workflows different from those that require human interaction?

4. Why would you consider interfacing with a workflow solution external to AEM?

Review answers

1. A parallel process flow effectively splits a business process implemented as a workflow into multiple paths that execute simultaneously. Parallel process flows add AND logic to a workflow. Decisions points are the opposite. They represent a fork in the workflow, where work must continue on one of two or more paths. Decision points add OR logic to a workflow.

2. AEM's workflow engine only supports a payload that represents one single resource. To send multiple resources (such as a group of pages) through a workflow as a single payload, you must create a workflow package. Add all the resources to that workflow package, and then send the package through the workflow as the single payload resource.

3. User-generated content is routed to a special moderation interface, and not to the standard workflow inbox.

4. If your discussions about workflow requirements identify heavy development of workflow steps or customization of the platform, you should consider interfacing AEM's workflow with another system. This allows you to let AEM do what it does best, and outsources heavy workflow requirements to a system better designed to handle them.

8 SOCIAL COMMUNITIES

In the modern web era, the lines are blurred between customers and contributors. Anyone can create web content by posting comments on pages, writing their own blogs, or participating in community forums. Adobe Experience Manager includes a social communities module that provides marketers with many tools to develop a social web presence and build integrated social experiences. In this chapter, you'll learn:

- What the social web is and why it is important

- How you can leverage social media and modern social strategies to enhance the effectiveness of your web content

- Which Adobe Experience Manager tools get you started with creating social web experiences

- The parts of Adobe Experience Manager social communities that are ready to use out of the box and which parts require customization or configuration

By the end of this chapter, you should have a holistic view of what it takes to deliver a modern, social web experience using Adobe Experience Manager.

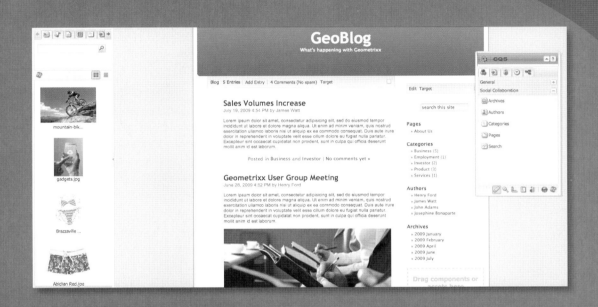

Using AEM to create a blog

The impact of social marketing

The web was once a static encyclopedia of information, but it has become a dynamic community of social connection. The web was once authored by a few with the resources or knowledge to create content, but now it has exploded because those resources are no longer restricted to scientists and engineers.

This evolution over the past decades has had a fundamental impact on the way companies interact with their customers. You no longer have even the slightest bit of control over what the Internet says about you.

Opinions and feedback about your organization are flying around on social networks such as Twitter and Facebook. Communities are forming around the products you sell, quite possibly without any facilitation from your organization. Customers are self-organizing and brutally honest about what you do. This is the nature of today's social web.

Should any of this matter to you? Should you worry about the comments on Twitter or the recommendations on blogs? Should you care what others publish about your products and services? Absolutely! You can harness and benefit from your customers' willingness to publish opinions about your organization—even the bad ones. You can facilitate a community of fans and improve your operation based on the feedback of non-fans. You can become a better organization by making use of the information that customers (past, present, and future) provide.

Think about the best salespeople in your organization. Why are they so good at what they do? How do they convert the most unlikely of consumers into long-term clients? They listen, so they can understand what problems need solutions. Then they solve them. Successful salespeople are that way because they build a trusting relationship with business partners.

It's why an account manager will take a client out to lunch when she's in town, even though they haven't done business for months. It's why a car salesman lets you take a test drive in a $100,000 car, even though he is pretty sure you can't afford it. It's why a restaurant manager calls you a few days later just to ask you how dinner was. None of those actions directly creates revenue (in fact, they cost money), but taking them builds the social currency that makes up a relationship.

It's always been tough to scale that kind of relationship to the masses because you typically can't afford to hire millions of salespeople. But today's social web has become a channel for facilitating that scalability. Customers can now contribute their end of the conversation digitally. You can respond, aided by technology that makes it more efficient to do so. You can also analyze feedback from a macro perspective to discover trends and insights about public opinion of your organization. This is an entirely new domain at the center of data science and marketing, and it's something you should be paying attention to.

Embracing the social web

Maybe I've convinced you that using the web can facilitate a relationship with your customers. Maybe you were already convinced. It's tough to build a social community that's integrated with your web presence, but it can be done, if you consider the following points:

- Go where your customers are. If your customers are on Facebook and you're trying to pull them into Twitter or some proprietary community, you're not going to get much traction.

- Make it seamless for customers to interact socially with your web content. That means implementing the common paradigms they are already used to, such as "Like" buttons or standard blog post commenting.

- Embrace your social community. You will get lots of positive and negative feedback. Both are helpful.

- Don't abuse your social community. Collecting Facebook accounts so that you can spam them with advertisements is not "being social." It's being annoying.

- Make sure your content is shareable and that it is incredibly easy for site visitors to share your content.

Building a social marketing strategy is a tall order, taller than I can completely cover in this book. Many authors have written many books on the topic. Adobe has even built Adobe Social, a software platform entirely dedicated to social digital marketing. For now, I'll focus on what you can do in Adobe Experience Manager to start moving your digital web presence in the right direction.

AEM social features

Adobe Experience Manager provides a set of components and a general framework for building social functionality into your website. It's unlikely that you'll use every one of them on the same site. In fact, that would probably be overwhelming for site visitors. But you can view the AEM social communities features as a toolbox from which you can pick specific aspects of modern social web strategy.

Before I describe AEM's social components, I want to define the term "user-generated content." We started to discuss it in previous chapters, but it's especially important here.

User-generated content (UGC) is any content that is submitted by an external site visitor. Sometimes it's created by an authenticated user (think about logging into a portal site), but UGC often is created by completely anonymous users. It's specifically called out as a separate term, because as we've discussed, managing user-generated content adds an extra layer of complexity compared to managing conventional, internally created web content. Some of the components described in this section enable your site's visitors to create user-generated content.

Social components

Some of the social features in AEM are components that you can use in your own websites with little or no customization. Sometimes they will require styling changes from your implementation team, but for the most part they can be used as is. It's important to understand how and why they should be used so that you can assess whether they meet your needs. If they don't, you should consider working with your implementation team to create custom components from scratch to address your specific needs.

Comments and ratings

Comments and Ratings are two separate components, but I've lumped them together because they are similar.

The Comments component allows site visitors to participate in a threaded discussion about a page's contents. You're probably already familiar with commenting functionality on websites; blog posts are the classic example of webpages that allow commenting. The AEM Comments component can be placed on any page but should be the only instance of it on the page. Authors have the option to specify that comments left using this component should be moderated before published. They also have the ability to disable comments, so at any point (perhaps after content becomes outdated), you can close a conversation from accepting additional comments.

The Ratings component is similar to Comments, but its mechanism for creating user-generated content is more structured. Site visitors can provide quantitative feedback about a page in the form of 0 through 5 ratings. For example, when you buy a product on an e-commerce website, products are typically displayed with an average rating as submitted by purchasers of that product. The Ratings component uses the same concept, allowing site visitors to rate your content so you have specific feedback about what is favored and what isn't.

Comments and/or ratings seem like easy elements to add to a page, but I'll warn you against making this assumption. Although these components are simple to use, you must perform some configuration along with your implementation partner. Important questions to ask include the following:

- Is it to your advantage to manage all user-generated content centrally within AEM?

- Are there any functional or technical limitations with Comments or Ratings that you can't deal with?

- What kind of volume of user-generated content do you expect?

- How do you plan to utilize the user-generated content contributed to your website?

I would start by assuming that adding comments and/or ratings is the right solution, and then work backwards from there. There are external solutions that can take the place of either component, but why sacrifice the integrated UGC management for no reason? Your solution implementation partner should be able to help you identify whether these components are appropriate for you and, if not, what other solutions are available.

Forum

The Forum components allow content authors to create threaded message boards to build communities of site visitors. The Forum consists of a few components that make up its full functionality. With the Forum, visitors can start and contribute to conversations, grouped as topics. Those topics serve as micro-content that accepts comments from other site visitors. A nice aggregated view keeps the most active conversations near the top of the list to encourage additional contributions.

The Forum components are similar to the Comments component. The key difference is that the *thing* on which people leave comments is a topic contributed by a community member and not an entire webpage. Unlike Comments and Ratings, the Forum provides value to site visitors only if many other site visitors add to the conversation. Therefore, it's essential that you put in place moderation processes. That moderation may not necessarily require reviewing every post, but you definitely want to enable someone to facilitate conversations. The good news is that implementing the Forum component doesn't cost much (you only need a designer to style it), so if no one uses your forum, the majority of the damage is to your ego.

You should think ahead of time about whether a forum is right for your website. This functionality can be extremely valuable for customer service or interaction, but only when used effectively. If you have the resources to monitor the forum and you want to use your website as a channel for customer service, the forum can be ideal. If you slap one into your site with the hope it'll magically generate conversation, you'll be disappointed.

Blog

Most people are familiar with blogs, and they are among the most common social features on websites. A blog is a website (or when used in an AEM implementation, part of a site) made up of time-stamped articles (or posts) that tend to be shorter and less formal, and are often time-sensitive. A blog is sort of like your own digital news publication. Blogging has grown into a huge industry and has given a powerful international voice to men and women who otherwise never would have been heard. If you keep the content fresh and interesting, blogs can enhance your digital marketing strategy by increasing traffic to your site.

Blogs are made up of a specific set of functions that are universal to blogs, which is part of why the format has become so popular. Visitors who read a blog know what they can expect. The AEM Blog component adheres to accepted blog norms, so it's important to understand them, at least at a high level. Let's look at some of the parts:

- Blog—This is the entire site, or at the very least, the entire section of the site dedicated to the blog. I specify this because the terms "blog" and "blog post" are often and incorrectly used interchangibly. Generally, a blog will focus on a specific topic like vintage guitars, Java programming, or the Cleveland Browns. "Blog" can also be used as a verb, meaning "to write a blog post."

- Blog Post—This is a single article posted in a blog. One of the key concepts of a blog is that it's made up of time-stamped articles (like a news site). Posts typically have a title, author, and full text. They sometimes include an excerpt summarizing the post.

- Tags and Categorization—Blog posts are not only time-stamped, but are also categorized using various metadata taxonomies. Sometimes these can be unstructured tags. Sometimes they can be predefined categories. They help define what a blog post is about, without requiring that you read it.

- Filters—Most of the time blogs offer several ways to filter blog posts. These are typically found in a sidebar next to the main content, but not always. The filters are specifically useful when someone enjoys a post and wants to see what else that author has written about the topic. Filters are effectively a faceted search for narrowing down which blog posts are displayed, to focus on what is relevant to the user.

- Comments—A key difference between blog posts and general web content is that blog posts almost always allow user commenting. The comment threads at the end of blog posts are often highly visible and useful. In fact, I've gained incredible insights from the comments on some of my favorite blogs.

- RSS Feed—Most of the time a blog will provide an RSS (really simple syndication) feed or an Atom feed. This is a link that can be used to subscribe to the blog via an RSS reader. RSS also allows other websites to curate or reuse your content. Blogs sometimes also include an email subscription function as a complement or an alternative to an RSS feed.

The Adobe Experience Manager Blog component allows marketers to start up blogs with almost no effort. Unlike the other social components we've discussed, the Blog is a page component, not a content component. Technically, it's a page component that includes many specific content components. Once you have your Blog component styled and customized as necessary, marketers can create a completely new blog by simply creating a page out of the Blog template. When authors open that page, they can fill out a form to create posts. AEM does all the work of building a date-specific URL structure and outputting the post as its own webpage. Without the blog component, all of that would be manual and time consuming. No one wants that.

Blogs are a great content medium to have on your website, so I strongly encourage you to consider implementing one. They do require some extra work to maintain because you don't want a blog with posts at six-month intervals. But a well-kept blog can bring measurable benefits to your site. For example, blogs with properly keyword-rich posts can help boost your average search engine ranking, making it more likely that search engine users will end up on your site. A blog also provides a quick, informal way to keep your content fresh, interesting, and time-sensitive. Customers generally like that.

You should consider some reasons not to use blogs, too. If you know you aren't going to manage the blog, don't do it. Blogs that are unkempt are unprofessional and not useful. You also should be careful about using many different blogs within your site. Multiple blogs are sometimes acceptable, but they make moderation and management quite a bit more difficult. Consider organizing blog posts into separate categories before deciding you must create multiple blogs with distinct focuses.

Event Calendar

The Event Calendar component provides content authors with an interface for displaying events to site visitors. It has a couple of options for displaying those events, and content authors can separately configure each instance of the component. The Event Calendar allows you to assist in linking your web presence to offline engagement by advertising seminars, meet-ups, or anything else you may have to share with your site visitors.

The Event Calendar is a feature-rich component once you add it to a page as you would any other content component. Instead of writing a chapter on a component you may never use, I've included the high points of what you can do with it:

* Authors can create/edit/delete events that are displayed to end users.

* An individual event can be imported into a component by ICS file.

* Site visitors can filter which events are displayed to them using a targeted calendar search feature.

* Authors can import calendar content from another AEM Event Calendar or from an external data source.

* Authors can integrate with workflow to push events to specific calendars.

Event Calendar components are used for a specific use case that the majority of websites don't need to accommodate. However, if you need to distribute event information to your site visitors, and specifically want to make it easy for them to consume that information, the Event Calendar might be a good option for you to consider.

User profile

If you intend to use your website to build a community of users who specifically authenticate into the site, you can create an online user profile. The user profile isn't a single component. AEM provides a set of components for creating a page that can be used as a user profile page. The user profile can also be connected to a form for letting users self-manage their profiles. When you want to target content to individual users, having information that they provide about themselves via their profile is invaluable. We'll discuss why in Chapters 14 and 15.

You should be aware of certain aspects of the user profile. You have to commit to using the AEM user management features for your end users (not just for internal users), which we'll touch on in Chapter 12. You also have to consider the significant security and privacy concerns when end users provide you with information. You probably don't need a user profile if you are only using comments on pages or within a blog. But if you use a highly engaged community function such as a forum, a user profile may be a good complement.

Community administration

Imagine that you had a product support forum but you never responded to anyone's posted product issues. What if you published compelling blog posts, but didn't participate in the engaging conversation that ensues in the comments? What if your customers gave you direct feedback about what they liked, didn't like, and wanted from your products, but you weren't listening? These are all examples of missed opportunities due to lack of community administration.

The components that encourage site visitors to contribute content are useful, but when you put any level of content creation in your users' hands, you *have* to monitor that content. I'm not necessarily saying that you need to remove negative comments about your product or filter messages with which you don't agree. However, you do need a way to digest the content that your site visitors create so that you can learn from it and possibly respond to it. You need a way to convert that customer-provided information into insight and engagement.

● **Note:** Most of the time, the functions AEM provides are sufficient to meet your goals; however, if you expect hundreds of thousands or millions of pieces of UGC daily, you might want to consider external solutions. AEM does a good job of helping you manage user-generated content, but dealing with a "big data" quantity of UGC requires special technology.

Adobe Experience Manager helps you manage your digital communities with tools such as the Community console for consuming and managing user-generated content and spam filtering for blocking malicious UGC.

Community console

The Community console is your go-to interface for managing user-generated content. It's also a key interface when considering the future of AEM and its developing integrations with the rest of the Marketing Cloud. In this interface, community managers are able to filter, digest, and respond to user-generated content. At present, this is a handy interface; in the future, I expect it to evolve into one of the most important interfaces in Adobe Experience Manager as more integration is built into the Marketing Cloud.

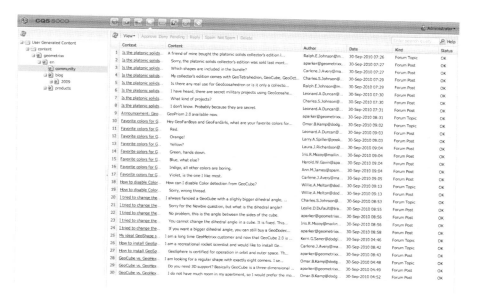

Figure 8.1

The Community console

Adobe Experience Manager is preconfigured (or at least mostly configured) to send all user-generated content to this interface using workflows. If you have your social components configured to require moderation, a community manager will use this interface to review and approve or deny all comments. The interface does a nice job of breaking down content according to the page it was created on (see the left of Figure 8.1). It keeps you from having to search through your entire site to respond to your site visitors.

Spam filtering

Adobe Experience Manager provides two spam filtering functions so that you can filter out malicious content submitted to your site. The first function is manual. In the Community console, you can mark content as spam, which will prevent it from public view but won't delete it. You can use this feature if you want to quarantine spam messages and later delete them.

The more robust feature that AEM provides is integration with the Akismet spam filtering service. This is a third-party spam filtering service used by popular blog sites like WordPress. It programatically scans user-generated content and determines whether it is malicious. It does a pretty good job, too. You can work with an administrator to configure your AEM instance to integrate with Akismet so that you needn't do much manual work to filter spam. Of course, you will need to have an Akismet account.

Social network integration

One option for building a community with your AEM website is to manage accounts yourself. Users register with you, provide you with profile information, and you manage the whole thing. A decade ago this was basically the only option for managing an online community, but times have changed.

Today, modern social networks like Twitter and Facebook have evolved into more than isolated social sites. Your social networking account is now used as a representation of your digital self. They can enable you to automatically log into sites all over the web. Usually this means you also share your social profile data with those sites so they can personalize the experience. Adobe Experience Manager provides tools to enable this social network integration on the site(s) that you manage.

AEM's social networking integration is made up of two parts: a set of social content components, and a framework for integrating social networking profiles into your site. Though complementary, these two functions serve different purposes related to the social web.

Social components

AEM Social Collaboration includes a set of Facebook and Twitter content components that can be used right out of the box. These components aren't that complicated, especially if you are already familiar with the common kinds of on-site social network integrations. They can be configured, via their dialogs, to connect to relevant Facebook pages or Twitter handles—probably the ones for your organizations.

I'm not going to go deeply into each component because they support common social concepts (just created as AEM components). Instead, I'll list them with a quick description of each:

- Facebook Activity Feed—Display the activity feed for a specific Facebook page.
- Facebook Comments—A comments component (similar to AEM Comments) where users comment with their Facebook accounts and optionally cross-post to their own Facebook walls.
- Facebook Facepile—A widget that displays the names and faces of everyone who has liked the page on Facebook.
- Facebook Like Button—Allows site visitors to "Like" a webpage, assuming they are logged into Facebook.
- Facebook Live Stream—A feed that shows live updates from Facebook about a page or topic.
- Facebook Send Button—A standard Facebook sharing button. A "Like" is for saving a page to your own Facebook wall. With this component you can share with another Facebook friend.
- Twitter Follow Button—Allows visitors to follow the configured Twitter handle.

- Twitter Search—Displays a feed from Twitter based on a configured search. For example, it could show all tweets with the #AEM hashtag.

- Twitter Share Button—A button for sharing the current page on Twitter.

Many of these components require that the user already be logged into Facebook or Twitter. But these days that's a common expectation. Even if users are not logged into those social networks, the responses from the networks themselves make it easy for them to log in. You aren't required to build any of that in.

The thing to remember is that much of the implementation for these components is *not* Adobe Experience Manager code. These are just an AEM component face on the functionality that Facebook and Twitter expose for people who build websites. That means there isn't much you can do to customize them. It also means that you wouldn't want to customize them, because doing so would break the interface paradigms that Facebook and Twitter users are familiar with. Still, these AEM components make it much easier to add these social elements to your website.

Social network login

Another social feature that many people are used to seeing on websites is the ability to "Log In With Facebook" (or Twitter). That feature makes it almost immediate to create a new account or log into a current account, because it's all tied to an existing social networking account. Users don't have to fill out another registration form and they don't have to remember another password. Social networking login removes barriers to someone joining your social community, making it an effective way to engage with customers.

Social networking login is provided out of the box for Facebook and Twitter, but you can work with a solution implementation partner to add additional account logins such as Google or Yahoo!. Social network authentication is possible because of a protocal called OAuth. To avoid getting too technical, OAuth is just a common contract that you can use to log into any social network. Because all major social networks are compatible with OAuth, those who build websites can integrate their platforms in a common way. In other words, it's not that complicated to have your solution partner expand your social networking login to enable additional networks.

If you plan to facilitate a social community on your website, I highly recommend you launch with social networking login functionality. It will encourage more registration and more participation, because it will make it much easier for users. The best part is that you will be able to target content based on users' Facebook interests. That means you can target specific variations of webpages based on the information your site visitors volunteer in their Facebook profiles. Think about how powerful that can be (and get psyched for Chapter 15 on content targeting). The upside of using the social networking login is huge. The downside is minimal (just a little configuration). You should definitely consider using it for your social community.

Summary

Today's web users expect websites to be social. They want to share, comment, like, and rate anything and everything. The Internet has become a community of people providing information to one another and, more relevantly, providing information to organizations who want to sell products. Your website, built on Adobe Experience Manager, can and probably should be part of this social web so that you can participate in the community and elicit feedback directly from customers.

AEM provides a set of components and frameworks that make it easier for marketers to build social functions into their sites. You can build a social website with little or no software development and minimal configuration. The question you ask probably shouldn't be *whether* you make your website social. It should be *how social* do you want to be?

Review questions

1. What does the term "social web" mean?
2. How are comments and ratings different?
3. How can you manage the content that site visitors contribute to your site?
4. What two social networks does AEM integrate with directly out of the box?

Review answers

1. The social web is an abstract term that refers to the modern generation of websites built to collect feedback from and encourage interaction among web users. This contrasts to the first generation of the web, which was mostly static websites. The social web is not any official technology, era, or protocol. It's simply a general term to describe a more modern concept of the Internet.

2. Comments are small pieces of text that site visitors can post to a webpage or piece of content. Ratings are a quantitative (such as 0 through 5) about the content. The comment is more flexible and freeform, but more difficult to analyze on a large scale. The rating is inflexible, but easy to quantify.

3. The AEM Community console is the hub where all user-generated content is managed. You can reply to, delete, or flag all incoming UGC from within that interface.

4. Twitter and Facebook—but it's possible to build integrations into other social networks. You will need to work with a solution implementation partner to do so.

9 E-COMMERCE

E-commerce is one of the most significant aspects of the modern economy. Many companies depend completely on e-commerce to generate revenue. Recognizing the close relationship between e-commerce and digital web presence, Adobe Experience Manager includes a framework for helping marketers build commerce-driven web experiences. But this framework is just a starting point; it's not a solution in and of itself. In this chapter, I'll answer the following questions:

- What is e-commerce and why is it important?

- What are the basic pieces of the AEM e-commerce framework?

- What vocabulary is used throughout the AEM e-commerce framework?

- What AEM components are available to enable marketers to build commerce-driven web experiences?

By the end of this chapter, you should have a marketing-level understanding of the Adobe Experience Manager e-commerce framework to prepare you for the necessary conversations with a solution implementation team.

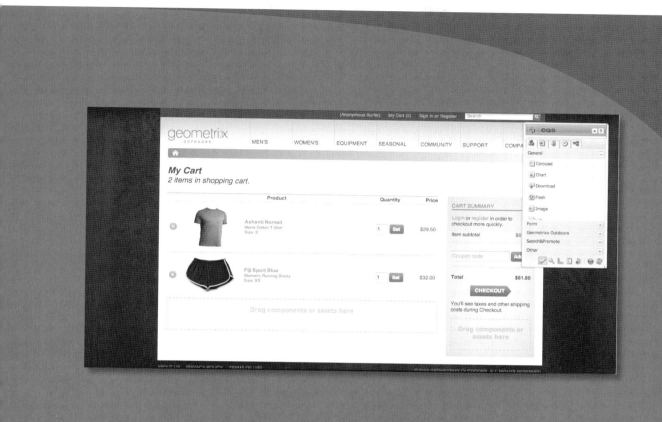

The AEM e-commerce framework's
Checkout component

Basics of e-commerce

Electronic commerce (e-commerce) is just the business of selling products over the Internet, instead of in person, in a store, in a print catalog, or by any other "traditional" selling method. It's an important strategy, because the world continues to integrate the web into its daily life. E-commerce makes selling more efficient because many (sometimes all) of the processes involved are completely computer automated. You don't need a salesperson. You don't require someone at checkout.

E-commerce doesn't just create efficiencies only for the seller. It also allows buyers to purchase what they want when they want it. When a customer wants to buy items online, she doesn't worry about store hours, traffic jams, rude fellow customers, or any of the other inconveniences of shopping in the "real world." She logs onto a website to browse products at will, adds them to a virtual shopping cart, and buys when she sees fit.

For the seller, however, this efficiency in the buying and selling experience doesn't come easy. Making shopping simple for customers takes the effort of a number of software platforms and, of course, the staff who implement and manage them.

An e-commerce platform is software that enables organizations to manage product inventory, set and track pricing, distribute coupons, and sell products online. It's a catch-all term for several technologies that are similar, but not necessarily the same. Some e-commerce platforms are very alike and some are completely unique. Many have features that overlap with other technologies, like web content management systems. Many are part of a larger integrated technology stack. Some are on premises and some are hosted in the cloud. But, despite the variety, e-commerce platforms are fundamentally designed to enable organizations to sell their goods online.

The online shopping experience

Many people are familiar with the online process, but let's examine that experience in detail. The following is a hypothetical story, explaining what a good e-commerce experience could look like.

Mary has decided to take up running with the hope that one day she'll be able to complete a marathon. Before she can get started, she needs the right equipment. The first thing she does is searches the web for running shoes. She clicks on a search result that brings her to a landing page for Game Changers Sporting Goods. That page is all about running equipment and is advertising a 10 percent discount by using the code "run to the hills." It also shows some neon pink running shoes that pique her interest.

Mary clicks the link that takes her to a page displaying Game Changers' running equipment. She finds the pair of shoes she saw in the landing page and clicks on them. On the page for those shoes she reads a detailed description, as well as a bevy of positive comments from other customers. Mary notices the 4.5 out of 5 average rating from those other customers. Wouldn't you know it? They have them in her size, so she clicks to add them to her cart.

She notices a banner at the bottom of the screen advertising women's running tank tops. She didn't intend to buy any, but with a 10 percent discount and enthusiasm for her new hobby, she adds two of them to her cart. Time to get out of here before she buys anything else. She clicks "Check Out."

Mary is taken to her shopping cart page, where she is reminded of the items she intends to buy. She notices that she accidentally added the wrong-sized tank tops to her cart, so she makes a quick adjustment right on that page. She is instructed that she can check out anonymously or create a new account. If she creates a new account, she'll receive notice of future discounts in her email. Who doesn't like more discounts? She clicks the button indicating that she can create a new account.

She steps through the process of entering her account information. Then she enters her shipping information and her credit card number. During the process, she's also able to enter the discount code that she saw on the landing page. She's informed of her final cost and she confirms her purchase. On the confirmation page, she is shown a pair of running shorts that would nicely match her new tank tops. Maybe next time. She clicks to add them to her wish list and they are saved to her newly-created account for future consideration.

This example demonstrates one ideal online shopping experience. Creating this online store made it easy for Mary to purchase what she wanted. It also enabled Game Changers to sell her more useful products that she didn't initially intend to buy. Everybody wins.

The integration challenge

When you want to sell something online, you create a website, probably using a web content management system. The problem is that a web content management system is *not* built to handle all the requirements of e-commerce, like discounts, shopping carts, and wish lists. WCMs are about page templates and components, CSS styling, content targeting, and multiscreen design. So if you want to sell online, you'll need to integrate a web content management system with an e-commerce platform.

To a customer, being on your website and buying on your website are no different. But to a technologist, they present two different problems, solved with two different solutions (WCM and e-commerce systems, respectively). The challenge for you is to align and integrate these two isolated technologies. You want it to appear to your customer that it's all one big happy website. You want the data collected from one to enhance the other. You want both technologies to be working in the same direction.

E-commerce framework

The Adobe Experience Manager e-commerce Framework is a starting point for seamlessly integrating AEM and virtually any e-commerce platform. The framework abstracts the concepts of e-commerce so that, to the marketer, the technology driving e-commerce functions is of little concern. The framework also includes a set of practices and components that can be customized to build the e-commerce functions on your website. The best part is that this e-commerce framework allows you to integrate "selling online" with all the other bells and whistles that AEM offers.

Taking advantage of the e-commerce platform is not something a marketer can just start doing. It requires an implementation team to set up all the pieces, and unless you plan to use Hybris as your e-commerce platform, it will require custom development. As a result, you might wonder what the point of this framework is. Why bother with it if you have to do a bunch of custom development anyway?

Why you should care

Think about a few scenarios that occur when you try to sell products online. What if you want to advertise gloves to a site visitor who just added a hat to her cart? What if you want to provide a 10% discount to anyone who spends $100? What about displaying a landing page that advertises skis to site visitors from Utah but advertises running shoes to visitors from North Carolina? None of these situations are uncommon or unreasonable when you're trying to maximize online sale revenue. But these problems become difficult if your e-commerce platform and web content management system aren't appropriately integrated.

The AEM e-commerce framework basically puts an AEM face on the parts of the e-commerce platform that digital marketers will work with. Adobe has abstracted basic functions, such as product catalogs and vouchers, into elements that can be consumed and used in AEM. Most of the time, these are just components that allow digital marketers to manage how products are displayed, advertised, and distributed through digital channels without worrying about the e-commerce tech behind the scenes.

The e-commerce framework is made up of two parts: a set of practices and components for using e-commerce elements within AEM, and an e-commerce API (application programing interface). An API is just a mask on top of a technical implementation that exposes what it can do without explaining how it does it. Using the e-commerce API, the programmers can integrate any e-commerce platform in the background while keeping the familiar AEM interface. Marketers need only understand the AEM e-commerce concepts. If the technical folks switch e-commerce platforms behind the scenes or implement multiple platforms for different sets of products, theoretically the marketer in AEM should see no difference on her end.

If you've ever worked through a WCM integration with an e-commerce platform without using this kind of framework, this feature should excite you. It means that for much of your requirements-gathering process, you don't have to reinvent the wheel. You don't have to make sure everyone is on the same page about the basic functions of e-commerce. The framework does that for you. Yes, you will have to go through the process of programming the integration to your e-commerce platform. But the framework puts a definitive stake in the ground to dictate what the AEM interface should look like to the marketer.

Hybris

If you look through Adobe's documentation or any of their marketing materials about the e-commerce platform, you'll see several mentions of Hybris, an enterprise e-commerce platform. Adobe partnered with Hybris to develop AEM's e-commerce framework. Because of that partnership, you can download (from Adobe) a full implementation of the e-commerce framework to integrate with Hybris, and you don't have to develop it yourself. If you're in a position to consider Hybris as an e-commerce platform, or you already use it, the AEM e-commerce integration becomes much faster and easier.

● **Note:** The Hybris e-commerce implementation is a basic implementation that your implementation team may need to tweak to meet your needs. However, it's a more fully defined starting point than is available with any other e-commerce platform.

Framework vs. platform

Before digging into what AEM's e-commerce framework offers, I want to look at the difference between the terms "framework" and "platform." This is an important distinction that explains exactly what you get and don't get in the e-commerce *framework*. It might sound like language nuance, but when you go into discussions with a development team, it'll serve you well to understand the difference.

Simply put, a platform can stand on its own. Adobe Experience Manager is a platform. Often, web content management is called a "system," but "platform" is valid as well. A platform is a piece of software that, on its own, doesn't necessarily create much business value. However, it includes a set of tools and a "way to do it" that allow organizations to build an application that does create business value. If implemented well, a platform can create *a lot* of value.

On the other hand, a framework cannot stand on its own. It's generally a library of code and a set of practices that enable you to build a specific function into an application. Generally speaking, a platform is made up of multiple frameworks. In AEM's case, Apache Sling is a RESTful web framework, ExtJS is a user interface framework, and the e-commerce framework is (you guessed it) a framework. On its own, a framework does very little, but when faceted onto a software platform, it significantly extends the value of that platform.

In other words, the e-commerce framework is an add-on to Adobe Experience Manager. It requires special implementation, but it unlocks additional features that you otherwise wouldn't have.

Vocabulary

Before evaluating AEM's e-commerce framework, and definitely before implementing it, you should understand its basic vocabulary. The e-commerce API abstracts basic e-commerce functions into this vocabulary, so the marketer on the AEM side of the table has to understand only one set of terms. Let's look at those terms at a high level.

Product information management system

A product information management (PIM) system is a broad term used to describe a system that performs the basic functions of e-commerce. Generally speaking, the PIM isn't what displays a website on which people buy products; it's the backbone of the entire system. It enables you to accept payments, manage inventory, and so on. Sound familiar? If you take some slight liberties with the term, PIM is effectively synonymous with "e-commerce platform." Those who are deep into this specialized domain may argue semantics, but for the purposes of this book and what you need to understand as a marketer, consider them about the same.

Catalog

A catalog is the set of products available via your e-commerce platform. It's the part of e-commerce that you manage as a digital marketer. The catalog consists of pages as part of your website. But there's an important difference between an e-commerce product catalog and a bunch of basic product pages. A catalog's data is synchronized using the e-commerce platform so that its data is accurate. If these were just basic AEM pages, the content authors would have to constantly update information such as price and availability (which can change by the minute). You can imagine how difficult and inaccurate that could be.

Product

A product is a *thing* you sell online. The product is the building unit of a product catalog and appears as a webpage in that catalog. That unit will include specific metadata about that product—price, sizes, availability, and so on. They are also synchronized with the e-commerce platform via the framework, so the information needn't be managed manually. The key value-added is that, because the product is represented as an AEM page, you get access to all the cool features of AEM. You can create targeted content, integrate with Scene7 for dynamic images, and manage multiple language versions of the product page. You can use AEM to make your customer's online product shopping as engaging as possible.

Variant

A variant is effectively a variation of a product. Think about men's suits. The same suit can come in many varieties: regular and short, blue or black, slim cut or standard. The suit may have only one SKU (stock-keeping unit), but has a variety of forms. In the AEM e-commerce framework, variations of a product are not viewed as separate products. They are viewed as variants. This can be important to the digital marketer, because a customer's variant selection may tell you something specific about him. That knowledge enables opportunities for improving his online experience, which can create more revenue.

Promotions and vouchers

Promotions and vouchers should get marketers excited. Promotions are campaigns designed to encourage conversions (sales). They are tied into the marketing campaign management functionality (described in Chapter 14). A promotion has a start and end date and presents a specific, dynamic experience to customers.

Vouchers are synonymous with coupons, and they are used in conjunction with promotions to help sell products. The voucher has a page of its own, a bit like an advertising landing page. It also includes a voucher code that customers can enter to receive a discount. Vouchers are related to promotions, because the promotion defines the campaign, or period of time, during which the voucher is active and applicable.

Shopping cart

If you've ever bought anything online, you're familiar with the digital shopping cart. This is the container page to which a customer can add products as she shops on your website. If the customer is authenticated into a registered account, the shopping cart and its contents are associated with that customer's account. Then any time she logs in, the contents are still there. If the customer is an anonymous user (not registered with an account), the shopping cart is usually assigned to that customer using a browser cookie, so that she can return to the site and still see the contents of her cart. The shopping cart makes it easier to shop and encourages customers to buy more products during a site visit.

In AEM, the shopping cart is especially powerful because of its integration into the rest of the personalization framework. AEM stores "what's in the customer's shopping cart" in the same way it collects data to identify the user as specifically as possible. AEM tracks what physical location visitors are coming from (as closely as possible), what content they've viewed, and possibly, whatever information is in their Facebook profile. Alongside all of that information is the list of what's in their shopping carts. So, if you want to show a specific upsell banner to people from Ohio who are about to buy a certain variant of a dog toy, you can.

AEM components

The Adobe Experience Manager e-commerce framework includes some components that help make it easier to sell online. Some of the vocabulary terms I already touched on describe components as well (such as "product"), so I won't go over them again. The components covered in this section add a few more pieces to the e-commerce puzzle. You will probably want to evaluate customizing them, but they do provide a solid starting point as is.

Landing page

A landing page is a static welcome page that describes the content that lives below it in the page hierarchy. For example, consider the following site structure for a pet supplies store:

- Pet Store Home
  - Dogs
    - Bone
    - Frisbee
    - Food
  - Cats
    - Catnip
    - Food

The store doesn't sell dogs or cats; they sell only products for dogs and cats. In this example, those products are bones, frisbees, catnip, and dog and cat food. You would likely create a landing page for "Dogs" that advertises the items for dogs. It may be targeted by a promotion. It may be time relevant (during the holidays). AEM provides landing page components for building and targeting such pages, making it easier than building normal pages.

Product search

A common (even expected) feature of any online store is a product search. Some people like to click through product categories or otherwise use navigation to browse for products. Others like to search specifically for what they're seeking. What's great about the product search is that, when using an analytics platform for tracking, you can gain insight about the items customers are looking for and what they are having a hard time finding. AEM provides the necessary components to build an effective, faceted product search. The Search Results component is the cornerstone of that function.

Customer profile

If you provide an online store, you will probably maintain accounts for your customers. It helps to build brand loyalty, upsell products, and create convenience for the customer. Customers often want a personal profile that tracks past purchases, shipping information, and personal information. Adobe Experience Manager provides the components to implement a customer profile using the standard user profile and form components. Depending on your needs, implementing a customer profile will require varying levels of customization.

Checkout

If you are trying to sell things online, you're not going to get far if people cannot buy your products. The Checkout component provides the appropriate functions for enabling customers to buy their products. Like other components, this one may need some styling and slight customization to match the rest of your site. But the functions needed to "check out" are ubiquitous. Using this component as a starting point will make it easier to implement your online store.

Summary

In this chapter, we took a mile-high view of the Adobe Experience Manager e-commerce framework. If it's something you will seriously consider using, you should have more detailed discussions with your solution implementation partner. The e-commerce framework is a foundation on top of which you and your implementation team can build a fully functional online store. You will have to integrate with an e-commerce platform, but the framework provides a common interface that masks the specific e-commerce implementation from the marketer. To the marketer, what's on the backend shouldn't matter. All you have to worry about is how to distribute content about products and help sell them.

Review questions

1. Why is e-commerce and web content management integration challenging?

2. Can you build an online store using just the AEM e-commerce framework?

3. What is a product information management (PIM) system?

Review answers

1. To sell products online, digital marketers need the appropriate access to product information so that they can distribute it to site visitors as necessary. If all that data resides in a completely separate e-commerce platform, it is difficult for marketers to use the information. A better solution provides marketers with information about products within the technology platform they are familiar with.

2. No. The AEM e-commerce framework is a starting point. It's a set of components and an API that require additional implementation to create a store. The value proposition is the fact that Adobe has already built out the foundation of the ubiquitous basics of e-commerce.

3. A product information management system is a technology platform used to manage product information such as price, variations, stock information, and other types of information an organization needs to distribute their products. The term is basically synonymous with "e-commerce platform."

10 MOBILE FOR MARKETERS

Figuring out what to do about the mobile phenomenon is probably one of your top priorities as a marketer. In this chapter, we'll discuss some of the considerations raised by today's mobile lifestyle:

- How Adobe Experience Manager enables marketers to manage their websites on mobile devices

- How Adobe Experience Manager helps marketers author mobile-optimized websites

- Exploring and choosing strategies for delivering websites to mobile devices

This chapter is a catch-all for the mobile concepts that you should care about as a marketer. Some of them are related to site visitors using mobile devices. Others address how marketers can use mobile devices. We'll also touch briefly on considerations that programmers have to understand related to mobile strategy.

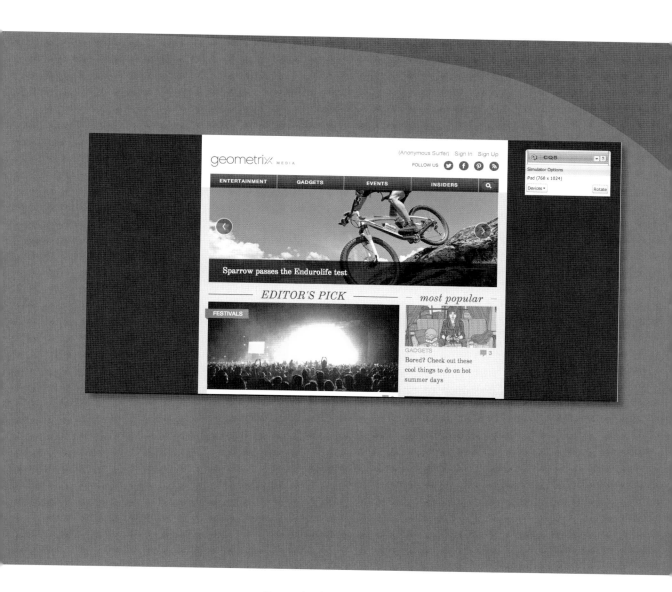

Responsive design authoring

Authoring on mobile

"Mobile" might be the buzzword of the century, but the attention it receives is not without justification. The way people use computers (not just for Internet access) has completely changed. Previously, personal computing revolved around the desktop computer. Today, you can pick from an array of computing devices from small mobile phones to large touch-screen personal computers. Generically, the term "mobile" describes this device explosion.

The new normal

The way we work is changing. It's no longer valid to assume that all knowledge workers will be using a mouse and a keyboard. Touch-screen tablets and mobile phones have revolutionized the consumer electronics market, and now workers are also also using them on the job. Unfortunately, traditional enterprise software is *not* built to support touch screens. Therein lies one of the biggest challenges faced by companies like Adobe that build enterprise technology.

You may or may not have authored content in Adobe Experience Manager. If you have, then you understand how "mouse and keyboard" oriented it is. Many of the core authoring functions are dependent on cursor hovering, right-clicking, and dragging components. These functions are difficult (if not impossible) on a touch-screen device.

Adobe Experience Manager has begun a metamorphosis that is driven by the "mobile first" design philosophy. This newer way of thinking about user experience suggests that you should design software for mobile devices first and then make adjustments for desktop platforms. Traditionally, software design has been the other way around. Adobe bought into this newer philosophy completely and encourages AEM users to adopt it as well.

We'll discuss the "mobile first" philosophy and its impact on user experience design a bit more in Chapter 19. Until then, remember that Adobe now sees their products through the mobile first lens. When you start to use AEM's newer features, you'll see how that philosophy is transforming the platform.

AEM in transition

Adobe Experience Manager 5.6 (the most recent major release) introduces a completely new user interface specifically designed for touch-screen devices. It replaces the mouse-specific functions (such as right-clicking) with gestures that are more natural for a touch screen. Adobe has also reengineered the user experience of some of its authoring interfaces so that they are easier to read and navigate using a touch-screen device.

The new touch-optimized authoring interface is still considered transitional. Adobe hasn't completely adapted the entire platform, nor has it completely committed to this new authoring interface. In fact, in AEM 5.6 you can choose which interfaces you want to use: traditional or touch screen. The strategy is that Adobe wants to gradually evolve the platform toward what marketers really need. By not immediately committing to a completely new user interface, Adobe can collaborate with the organizations that implement AEM to create the best possible authoring experience. This agile approach based directly on customer feedback is an impressive, modern way to ensure that the authoring experience becomes exactly what AEM users need in the future.

Depending on which service packs you may have implemented, different parts of the authoring interfaces may not have touch-enabled versions. Completely revamping the authoring experience is a complicated technical issue, so not surprisingly, it isn't happening all at once. You'll start to notice that documentation is leaning toward a touch-UI context. This will gradually continue until the pieces of the old interfaces are eventually deprecated. Just work with your solution partner and documentation to keep things straight.

● **Note:** Remember that most of the screenshots in this book show the traditional interface, not the touch interface.

Touch-enabled authoring

To support the proliferation of touch-screen devices, Adobe is implementing a new touch screen–optimized interface for Adobe Experience Manager. Although this interface is still incomplete, when finished it will make the platform flexible and device agnostic. It'll also help ensure that AEM is visually compatible with the other Adobe Marketing Cloud products.

The touch-enabled authoring interface contains a few key features that you will need to understand. Obviously, the easiest way to learn them is to use Adobe Experience Manager (training helps, too). But I want to describe some of the key touch interface concepts and explain why they are important.

The new gray and black interface is based on a new UI framework called Coral UI. Although marketers don't specifically need to understand how to implement Coral UI, you should know that it is a replacement for ExtJS, the framework used to create the traditional authoring interface. The most important part of Coral UI is that it is being implemented across the different Adobe Marketing Cloud platforms. Eventually, all of these products will become a holistic digital marketing suite tied together by Coral UI to produce a consistent user experience.

In addition to providing visual options such as a row view and a Pinterest-like card view, the new user interface uses infinite scrolling instead of pagination—a key difference from the traditional AEM UI. Sometimes you have a *lot* of pages or tags (or whatever) to manage, and infinite scrolling makes it much easier to move through them by swiping, rather than flipping from page to page.

The new interface offers more consistency than the old one. The content area always works the same; it just adapts slightly to the *kind* of content you are viewing. There's always a breadcrumb-style header at the top, which helps keeps you aware of where you are in the platform, and a consistent context menu is always present on the left. The options may change depending on where you are in the platform, but it's a pretty consistent experience overall.

Finally, the interface uses responsive design, which means that the interface adapts to any size screen. Whether you are working on a small tablet or a large touch-screen monitor, the authoring experience remains effective and intuitive.

Authoring for mobile

If you are a marketer who has to author a mobile site, you have the same needs as you would have when authoring a desktop site. You need maximum content-editing flexibility but structured within a framework that ensures you won't violate the brand. You also need the basic functions such as digital asset management and workflow, and an intuitive way to manage large hierarchies of content. In addition, you will face some issues that are unique to the mobile domain:

- How do you author a site that will be effective when viewed on devices of all different shapes and sizes?

- How do you implement the necesssary functionality in a way that is usable (and user-friendly) on a small screen?

- How do you ensure that mobile visitors generally have the same quality web experience as visitors using desktop or laptop computers?

AEM functionality specifically addresses these problems. This empowers you to build impressive mobile websites, using device-specific contextual authoring and the Multi Site Manager.

Device context authoring

Despite the continuing AEM interface evolution, you will often author your website on a desktop or laptop computer, at least for the present. That means you probably have at least 15 inches or more of screen real estate. You may be lucky enough to have one or two of those 32-inch flat-screen monitors. But the point is that your screen is big and bright and easy to see.

Adobe Experience Manager's authoring paradigm is all about putting you in front of your site visitor's computer screen. In-context editing is valuable, because it lets you see what the site visitor will see *while* you are creating the content. This outside-in approach is a big advantage that Adobe Experience Manager offers.

But if you are building a site for mobile phones, what do you do? Who can say that he's "put himself in front of the site visitor's screen" when yours is 32 inches in size and the visitor's mobile phone display is 4 inches? The answer is that you can't.

So, to help you see your mobile visitor's point of view, Adobe Experience Manager includes an authoring feature that lets you create content within the visual context of multiple mobile devices.

You can enable this feature (with help from your solution implementation provider) to author webpages as they will be viewed on various mobile screens. Your layout is limited to the screen resolution of the device, and to make the experience a little nicer, AEM surrounds that small "screen" with a picture of the device. Other than working within the smaller viewing area, all the same authoring rules apply. You have the Sidekick. You have the Content Finder. You can drag and drop all day. The mobile authoring interface also includes a handy QR code that links you to the public version of your page in case you want to double-check your authoring on an actual smartphone.

Figure 10.1
AEM's mobile authoring interface

This mobile authoring interface is convenient and very effective, but let me take some wind from your sails. Even though each of the mobile phone-simulating features is called an "emulator," they are not full-featured emulators. When you are building a website for mobile, you need to be aware of the functional differences among mobile browsers. They don't all necessarily support the same modern features. Older mobile browsers may not support features such as cookies or JavaScript (that, frankly, aren't even new). Mobile browsers support gestures like swiping, but may not have an equivalent to a "right-click" function.

AEM's mobile emulators do not re-create any of those realities for you. The mobile authoring interface is an aid to help you visualize your content experience on phones and tablets. It's a "quick and dirty" preview, but it's not a replacement for legitimate cross-browser, cross-device testing. The mobile emulator will not change the behavior of your desktop browser.

Device detection and targeting

The proliferation of mobile has made it extremely difficult to keep up with all the devices that your site visitors may be using. The AEM mobile authoring interface is great, but can you imagine if you had to apply it for every possible mobile phone out there? You'd be nuts to try it, and go nuts doing it.

You probably don't need to do this, because most mobile phones aren't all that different from one another. Their screen resolutions may vary a bit, but their basic functions are similar. The same is true for most other categories of mobile devices such as tablets. Instead of expecting you to build a website that is customized for myriad devices, Adobe Experience Manager provides a feature for generalizing device requirements into device groups.

Device groups

Adobe Experience Manager allows authors (with the help of administrators) to configure device groups, which are categories of mobile devices that are grouped by their basic functionality. The basic features used to define device groups are:

- CSS support
- Device rotation support
- Image loading support
- JavaScript support
- Minimum screen size (you set minimum height and width thresholds)
- User-agent (you provide a regular expression that looks for specifics from the user-agent string)

Using the first four of those features, you can generally build a set of criteria that accurately groups most mobile devices. If you add in the minimum screen size, you make it easier to distinguish an iPhone from an iPad, for example.

The user-agent string is less often used, but it's there in case you need it. A user-agent string is a stream of text sent by every web browser (mobile or not) that provides information about what software and hardware is making the request. User-agents are somewhat cryptic and not as accurate as you would hope; an awful lot of browsers claim they are "Mozilla" in their user-agent strings. But you *can* use them (sometimes) to gain some insights about specific devices.

If you implement device groups on your site, Adobe Experience Manager will inspect every page request to determine which group the requesting device falls into. It'll start with the group that offers the most functionality and work its way down. If properly configured, AEM can determine which device made the request with reasonable accuracy, and then forward the user to the version of your site built for that device. The solution implementation team that develops your website can develop the code to deliver functionality appropriate to the device group of the requester. So if a mobile phone that doesn't support JavaScript requests a page that uses a lot of JavaScript, AEM can deliver an alternate experience that may be less flashy but will function correctly.

Device groups help you deliver a web experience that is optimized for a mobile device. Device groups are not the only way to do that, but as part of AEM, they are one valid approach.

WURFL

You might be wondering what voodoo AEM uses to determine that one phone doesn't support JavaScript and another supports everything. Adobe Experience Manager's mobile device targeting is powered by WURFL (WERR-full), the Wireless Universal Resource FiLe. WURFL is a product maintained by Scientia Solutions that is intended to provide a single point of reference for identifying what every mobile device can do. When a request comes into AEM from a mobile device, AEM uses the WURFL database to determine which device group the requesting device falls into.

WURFL is a basically big XML file that is updated with nearly every mobile device and includes more detail than you'll ever need to use regarding the features supported by the device. WURFL is a licensed product, and you must pay to update its database on a regular basis. You get a snapshot of the WURFL database within your AEM instance, but the older your instance, the more out of date your WURFL file will be.

Other device detection strategies

Device groups and WURFL make device detection and targeting a little simpler because Adobe Experience Manager does a lot of the legwork for you. But using that functionality is not the only method for targeting specific mobile devices. The following are also valid solutions:

- Determine device details and make appropriate changes to the page using JavaScript (a developer will have to do this)

- Perform device detection based on the user-agent at the web server level; then direct the user to the most appropriate of multiple sites

- Use responsive web design to create a fluid design that can reorient itself to fit any screen (more on that later)

Mobile is a fast-moving domain, so you may be aware of additional strategies for managing mobile sites. Maybe you've come up with your own strategic approach. Just understand that no broadly defined best practice exists for addressing mobile issues. You should consider all options with your solution implementation partner.

Responsive design testing

If you elect to implement a responsive website (one that adapts to your screen size), AEM provides a tool for testing your layout. It works similar to device targeting but is focused only on screen resolution, not device groups. When in preview mode, you can change the relative screen resolution within the Sidekick. AEM provides device-specific options so you don't necessarily have to remember the screen resolutions for various phones.

This may seem like a duplicate feature, because it overlaps with the device group emulator. Remember that when you are implementing a dedicated mobile site using device groups, you'll use the first approach we discussed. (It applies a slightly older feature set that has been around since CQ5.4.) If you are implementing a responsive website, you should use this responsive feature. Work with your solution partner to keep the strategies straight.

Figure 10.2
AEM's responsive design simulation

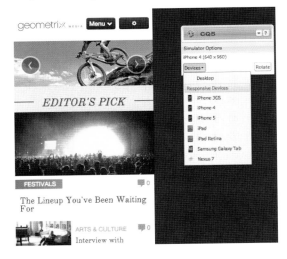

Multi Site Manager

Another powerful feature for creating mobile web experiences is the Multi Site Manager. Yes, this is the same Multi Site Manager function within AEM that allows you to make live copies of websites. These copies maintain a reference to the original content so that any updates to the original content can be automatically or manually synchronized to all its copies. The feature is great for rolling out a consistent web experience in multiple languages. It's also great for rolling out a consistent experience for multiple mobile devices.

Let's assume you elect to build specific tablet and mobile phone websites. You also decide not to build one fluid website that adapts to the screens. You may not want to include all of the desktop site content on your tablet site. You may include even less for your mobile phone. But you will use some content across two or all three sites; that is, the important content such as your key product descriptions, your home page copy, or your employment information. It's challenging enough to manage the content on a single website, but trying to manage and manually synchronize content across three is a nightmare. That's where the Multi Site Manager comes in.

You can use MSM to synchronize different pieces of content from your desktop site to your mobile site(s). But you'll have to do a different kind of translation when synchronizing for a mobile site compared to a multilingual site. To build a significantly different mobile web experience, with special attention paid to "look and feel," you'll have to implement a separate set of page and content components. You'll also need to synchronize content between some of those components.

Let's review how MSM helps you create multilingual sites and discuss how it helps with mobile sites.

When using MSM for a multilingual site, your live copies used the same components, but you replaced the content (the copy) with a translation in a different language. The look and feel and the overall web experience remained the same. The content changed once you translated it to another language.

If you use MSM to roll out mobile sites, it is just the opposite. You keep the content (the copy) the same, but when copying from one site to another, AEM changes the components used to deliver that content. The content stays consistent, but the look and feel (established by components) changes.

You would use a Rollout Config to define mappings that specify which components translate to other components. When you create a live copy using the Multi Site Manager—as you would to create a mobile site—AEM asks you to select one or more Rollout Configs. It's literally a map that says "if you see this component, turn it into this one." You won't be building the Rollout Config yourself. This is something that you'll create with your solution implementation team and information architect.

Working with an information architect will be important if you plan to use MSM to roll out one or more mobile versions of your site. The directives specified in the Rollout Config will hinge on defining the parts of your information architecture that will transfer to your mobile site. You can probably make some good guesses about which content is important enough to be prominent on mobile. It gets a little trickier when you leave out content, which you probably will have to do.

You should also be aware of the context for a piece of copy. If you have a chunk of text that makes sense only next to a large video, synching that text to the mobile site (without the video) will diminish its value. Again, these are the problems that an information architect should be in the discussion to help solve.

PhoneGap

After reading about some of the mobile authoring features, you might be asking, "What about mobile apps? Anything in there for those?" Adobe Experience Manager does have a solution for implementing mobile apps, such as those you download from the iTunes store or Google Play. It's called PhoneGap, and it's a platform that enables you to build mobile applications in HTML5 and then compile them into native mobile application code.

In less technical terms, it means you build your mobile app almost as you would a website. Then PhoneGap turns your website code into a program that iOS or Android devices can execute natively (without a web browser). The value in the platform is that you can write a mobile app one time and then deploy it to multiple mobile platforms. You don't have to write separate iOS and Android applications, which can be expensive.

PhoneGap is a pretty cool feature, but building mobile applications is a very different process than building web experiences. For that reason, I'm not going to get any deeper into it. For now, just know that PhoneGap is there if you want to consider using it. Who knows? Maybe your CTO will be tearing his hair out one day trying to figure out a mobile strategy, and you could suggest he use PhoneGap to build his mobile apps. You might just save the day...again.

Mobile strategy

So far this chapter has been all about features. Adobe Experience Manager does have some nice ones to help manage your mobile sites using desktop and mobile devices. But they are just features and by themselves are not enough to realize success with mobile. Most mobile website implementations succeed or fail before a single line of code is written, before a single component is dropped into a paragraph system. A mobile strategy ultimately defines the success of a mobile project, and the strategy is what organizations get wrong more often than not.

The rest of this chapter is dedicated to starting you down the path of building an effective, appropriately prioritized mobile strategy. It's just as important to understand what you should be doing as it is to understand how to do it. Although this is a topic that deserves an entire book on its own, I want to help you get started. At the end of the day, you can do the wrong things really well and not get anywhere, or you can do the right things early on. Organizations often have a difficult time with strategy when it comes to the mobile web. My hope is that this section will give you enough awareness of the difficulties to set you down the path of correctly answering the tough questions for yourself.

Do you need a mobile site?

This seems like an obvious question, but you'd be surprised how often organizations don't have a good answer: Do you *need* a mobile site? Maybe the better way to ask this question is: What do you want from a mobile site? If the answer is "everyone but us has a mobile site, so we're getting on board," then you're missing the point. Yes, if you don't have a mobile site, you are potentially delivering a poor user experience to anyone accessing your site on a mobile device. But doing it just to do it is not the right answer.

Maybe you already have some kind of mobile site, maybe you don't. Regardless, you inevitably have some mobile traffic coming to your site. If you have a web analytics platform wired up to your site (hint: you should), you can perform some analysis to determine how people use your site for mobile. Consider the following:

* How many people are coming to your site on mobile devices?

* How are they getting there?

* What devices are they using?

* What are they doing when they get there?

* Do you have noticably high bounce rates or lower funnel conversion rates with mobile visitors? Maybe the other way around?

* For all of these questions, how do the answers compare to non-mobile site visitors?

Asking these questions, which should lead to more secondary conversations, will help you identify how customers are interacting or attempting to interact with you on mobile devices. They may be doing the same things they do with their desktop computers, but they may be doing something completely different.

Let's say, for example, you work for a fast-food company (in digital marketing, not working the fryers), and are considering building a mobile website. You work with your analytics team to analyze past traffic and note that mobile visitors are most often viewing the Location Search page. In contrast, desktop visitors are typically viewing nutrition facts or the employment information pages. This is important insight that helps you understand why people view your website on a phone. Obviously, you would want to feature your location search on the mobile site more prominently than on the desktop site. You may even consider excluding some desktop features, such as the employment pages, if you determine that few mobile visitors are viewing them.

Another version of "Do you need a mobile site?" is "Do you need a tablet site?" Maybe you've determined a need for a specifically designed mobile web presence, but what about tablets? Tablets are interesting because they support technical features similar to mobile phones, including the same gestures. Their operating systems are generally more like those of phones. But they are different because they are too big to be with you *all the time*. They are more portable than desktop PCs and laptops but less portable than phones.

Trying to determine whether you should design a site for tablets is an even more difficult question because it deals with the gray area between phones and desktops. But you can apply the same decision process as with mobile phones. Work through the same questions and answers and determine whether you have a legitimate need. Consider that you may be able to tweak your desktop site to make it more tablet-friendly. Screen resolution tends to be less of a challenge with tablets, so you may just be concerned about usability. Again, these are all questions that must be asked, and that only you can answer.

Does this sound complicated and difficult? It should. It is difficult. That's why if you watch Twitter, you'll see hundreds of blog posts on this topic. Websites like Mashable and Smashing Magazine are all over it. It's one of the most talked about challenges of many of our careers. The mobile web is changing business and changing the world. There is no best practice, silver bullet approach, or defined structure for dealing with these problems, because the challenge is just too new. The most you can do is take the time to be deliberate in why you are building a mobile web presence and to understand the tools that are at your disposal.

Design approaches

After you decide that you do need some kind of mobile web presence, you must determine which design approach to apply to create it. Different groups advocate different approaches, sometimes with great intensity. There is no "best" approach, so you should understand them all. The optimal approach for you will be based on your circumstances and requirements. That may prove to be a mix of multiple strategies. In this section, I'll briefly describe the most often advocated strategies and how to evaluate those options.

Mobile website

If you determine that people are visiting your site on mobile for very different reasons than your desktop site, you might consider developing a dedicated mobile site. With a separate mobile site, you don't have to worry as much about transforming content, translating functionality, or designing for the least common denominator. You can let your desktop site be as complex and dynamic as you want, and worry about your mobile site in relative isolation. This approach affords you the most freedom but requires the most development and maintenance.

Fluid design

Maybe your mobile traffic isn't that significant or that different from your desktop traffic in terms of site use. In that case, your best approach may be to tweak your current website to give it a more fluid design. That just means that you don't specifically hardcode your site to be (for example) 950 pixels wide. You can set maximum and minimum sizes for some elements combined with a fluid design that expands, and more important, contracts as a device's screen resolution allows. Implementing a fluid design isn't a common strategy, especially if you have the resources (and the usage justification) to build a new mobile web presence from the ground up. But if you're looking for a relatively simple or stopgap solution, this might be a good one to consider.

Responsive design

One of the popular, newer approaches for designing a website is using *responsive design*. In a responsive website, the CSS uses a feature called "media queries" to restyle various aspects of the site based on the screen resolution. If you build a responsive website, you need only one website that will adapt itself to the device that requests it. If done well, the layout can even change in ways that are optimal for the device. For example, you could collapse your navigation component down to an accordion, which is more common and usable on a mobile phone.

Responsive design is different from fluid design, though they may sound similar. With fluid design, only the size of containers adapts. Containers become bigger and smaller as content fills them. With responsive design, you set "breakpoints" that define the sizes your site layout can be. The browser will display the appropriate layout, based on the device's screen resolution. Responsive design allows you to make any kind of style changes—not just dynamically-sizing containers.

Responsive sites are great, but there are some drawbacks to consider. Responsive design uses modern CSS and HTML standards that older browsers and more primitive mobile browsers may not support. It's also more complicated to design and implement a responsive site, so you must consider whether you have the organizational competency and staffing to take on such a task.

Finally, responsive sites can be pretty heavy if not designed correctly. That means the site may look nice on a mobile phone but will require downloading images that are bigger than necessary or text that ends up hidden. On mobile phones, file size is a concern, because mobile Internet is typically much slower than the broadband access of desktop PCs. Scene7's dynamic digital asset features can help you answer some of these questions.

Although responsive design is tough, it has distinct advantages. If it's something you want to consider, I urge you to investigate further. This section may be an introduction to the topic, but it's not enough to completely inform you of the advantages and disadvantages.

Evaluating the options

The three strategies I mentioned (and any additional ones out there) all have upsides and downsides. Trying to determine which one is best for you probably sounds daunting. Join the club. Many organizations are grappling with this question as a top digital strategy issue. You'll have to determine which issues are your highest priority to dictate what approach you'll select. Here are a few more pertinent questions:

- How much is performance an issue? Are most of your mobile viewers from the U.S. cities where 4G mobile Internet is abundant or from developing nations where slower access speeds prevail?

- How modern are the mobile devices used to access your site? Is most of your traffic from iPhones and Android phones or from older "feature" phones that support only limited Internet functionality?

- Do you have a specific user experience you want to build for mobile, or would you prefer an adaptation of the desktop site experience?

- Do you have the internal design and development competency to implement and support the kind of mobile presence you are considering?

The discussion should be deeper than these four questions, but those are good to start with. You should also consider combining approaches. For example, you could build a specific desktop site with mobile phone access in mind, and then implement some responsive design so that the mobile site will look optimal regardless of tablet or mobile phone. Sometimes the best approach is to pick and choose from the array of available options.

If you'd like to dig into more options for mobile designs, there's a website that helps to explain some of them. Visit liquidapsive.com, which displays a basic website with a drop-down that lets you select adaptive (a variant of responsive), responsive, fluid, and static (normal site) strategies. It offers some additional definitions of each approach, and you can resize the browser window to simulate various screen resolutions and see how each approach responds. If you learn by seeing, this might be a good place to start understanding these mobile solutions.

Considering authors

Most of what we've so far explored about mobile design has been from the perspective of the end user's experience. This should always be your highest priority, because user experience is what builds brand and revenue. However, you will also want to consider your content authors' experience in managing the site. After all, they are the ones who will be responsible for making your site valuable to customers. You want to try your best to avoid design decisions—especially when dealing with mobile access—that make it difficult for authors to add content to the site.

Remember how the authoring experience works. There is a lot of dragging and dropping and clicking on the components you want to configure. When you have a large desktop screen, you've got plenty of room to do those things. But when you're trying to author via mobile access, you face the same screen-size limitations experienced by your end users. In one regard, that's good, because it steers your authors away from big images and huge chunks of text. On the other hand, you still have to design the authors' user experience so that they can effectively and efficiently use the authoring components.

Your authors' experience should be a secondary consideration, but it's one that is often not brought into the conversation. If you make it difficult to author content, you're fighting against Adobe Experience Manager's fundamental content flexibility. I'm guessing after all this time and money, you don't want that.

Summary

The proliferation of mobile devices has changed the way people use the Internet. Customers have ubiquitous digital access to your brand, but they will have to access it using a device that is quite different from the PCs considered in classic web design. In light of this shift, AEM has begun a transition to a new user interface that enables marketers to manage websites with tablet devices such as iPads.

Adobe Experience Manager provides some tools to help make that mobile implementation easier. These tools allow you to target specific content or functionality to devices with different technical limitations. You can consider those tools, as well as additional strategies such as fluid or responsive design, to build an effective overall mobile web presence. Remember, this is a difficult challenge that everyone is currently struggling to address.

Review questions

1. What is Coral UI and why is it important?

2. How does AEM make it easier to author a mobile content experience for different devices?

3. How can the Multi Site Manager be used to help marketers manage a mobile site?

4. What is one of the most important tools that you should use to make design decisions about your mobile site?

5. What is responsive design?

Review answers

1. Coral UI is the name of a new user interface framework for Adobe Experience Manager. In AEM 5.6, the newest version, the platform has begun to transition to this new interface. It is designed to allow marketers to use tablets and mobile devices to perform authoring tasks.

2. AEM provides device in-context authoring, which allows authors to view the site as if viewing it using various mobile devices. It allows authors to immediately see how changes will appear in an iPhone, Galaxy S, or any of many other devices and screen resolutions.

3. Multi Site Manager can be used to roll out a mobile version of your site. Unlike the way MSM manages multilingual sites, the live copy version will have the same content. For mobile, the MSM will change the necessary components and render that content to components that are mobile specific.

4. Web analytics can provide you with insight into who your site visitors are, where they are coming from, and what they are doing. Most important (for this chapter), it can tell you what devices your visitors are using to access your site.

5. Responsive design is an approach to building a website that can dynamically adapt its "look and feel" and basic layout to accommodate any screen size.

11 ARCHITECTURE BASICS

As a marketer, your primary concern is not going to be server architecture. Those problems are typically reserved for the tech folks. However, you should know how some of this backend tech works, so you can speak intelligently with your solution partner and support team. In this chapter you'll discover:

- The difference between an "author" and a "publish" instance of AEM

- How you make your content public

- What server clustering is and why you would use it

- What the Dispatcher is and why it is used

- Some common server architectures used in AEM implementations

By the end of this chapter, you should understand the basics of AEM architecture. You won't be a system administrator, but you'll be able to talk shop better than many digital marketers.

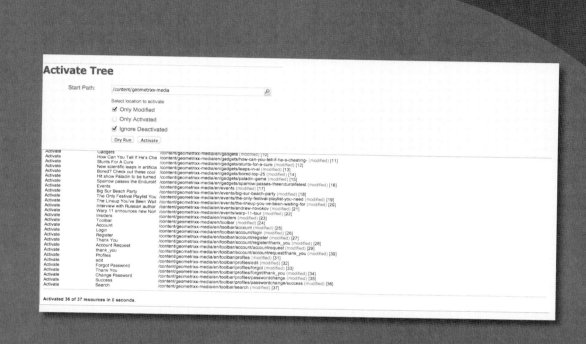

AEM's bulk activation tool

AEM instances

The term "instance" is important when discussing Adobe Experience Manager architecture. An instance is a single, running installation of the AEM platform. Every instance is fully functional, even though you may not necessarily use every feature in every instance. Without specific configuration, each instance runs in complete isolation from every other instance (though we'll discuss how to change that behavior throughout this chapter). Even though AEM is fully contained within a single instance, one instance is not enough.

AEM implementations often run many instances, each serving a different purpose. At the very least you must have two instances: one for authoring content and one for serving that content to the public. This pair is the bare minimum required to make AEM function as intended.

In practice, you will have more instances than a single author and publish. Here are some reasons why:

- You'll probably use two or more publish instances to "share" the load of your public traffic and to provide redundancy.

- You'll have multiple environments or sets of author and publish instances: one for testing, one for integrating code, and so on.

- Programmers on your implementation team will have instances installed on their development laptops.

You may be wondering how this is possible, considering that AEM is enterprise software. Most people who have worked with enterprise software know that it is huge, sucks up hardware resources, and is difficult to install.

But that doesn't describe Adobe Experience Manager. It has a unique, lightweight architecture that can even run on a personal computer. Though you still want to dedicate appropriate hardware to production instances that are delivering content, the lack of bulk in AEM becomes obvious when you perform authoring tasks on a simple laptop. Try to do that with most enterprise software and your laptop will melt.

Run modes

Every instance will have at least one run mode assigned to it. A run mode is a label, set by the system administrator, that describes the purpose of that instance in some way. These are typically just one word, such as "testing," to describe an instance in your testing environment. An instance can have multiple run modes (to describe it in multiple ways), but it must have at least one. Marketers won't have to set run modes, so don't worry about the details too much.

However, marketers should be aware of two special run modes: author and publish. Every AEM instance must be established as either an author instance or a publish instance. Author instances are those on which content authors build pages. Publish instances are those on which the "public" pages are hosted. Authors push their content from author to publish when it is ready for the world.

Author and publish are special run modes because, out of the box, they affect the behavior of the AEM instance. The biggest difference between the two is that the publish server is more locked down for security. You cannot access the authoring interfaces that you can access on the author instance. Those interfaces are there but hidden from the average user. Any run modes that you use other than author and publish will affect only the behavior of your system unless the implementation team builds an appropriate customization.

For a marketer, the most important thing to remember about run modes is that author is for creating content and publish is for distributing it to site visitors. Your solution partner will help you understand other run modes that you may use.

Quickstart JAR

Usually AEM installation is a system administrator's job, although you may hear one term that is related to AEM installation: *quickstart JAR*. It raises a technical issue, but it's a selling point of the software that you should understand. If you're familiar with enterprise software, this feature definitely stands out as unique.

The quickstart JAR is the installer for Adobe Experience Manager. The reason it's unique is because to install AEM, you merely have to run the installer—no wizards, no configuration settings, no restarting. You double-click the file, wait for the progress bar to finish, and AEM starts up in front of your eyes. It's extremely simple.

Seeing enterprise software as powerful as AEM installed with one click is impressive. The quickstart JAR is the magic that allows that to happen.

Replication

We've established that you author your content on the author instance, and then when it's ready, you put it on the publish instance. When site visitors go to your site, they are retrieving pages from the publish instance (or instances). That means you need some kind of mechanism to transfer the content you create on your author instance to the publish instance(s) where people will view it. That mechanism is replication.

The replication function pushes content from one instance to another. It's *usually* used to push from an author instance to a publish instance to make that content public. You will probably encounter a few different terms that sound like they mean the same thing. Generally speaking, they do mean the same thing, but let's examine the nuances among them:

- Replication describes the AEM function that allows you to move content from one instance to another.

- Activate (or deactivate) describes the action a content author will take to invoke replication. When you want to make content public, you "activate" it.

- Publish (as a verb) doesn't technically mean anything in AEM, but it is commonly used as a synonym to "activate," because you typically "activate" to a "publish" instance.

Effectively all three of these terms are related to moving content from author to publish, so don't get too hung up on their slight differences.

Replication should be used only to move authored content across environments. As a general rule of thumb, content authors should only activate things that you can see in the site administration UI (where you view your pages) or in the DAM. Administrators will activate some things in the "tools" UI. They also may instruct you to do so. Otherwise, limit activations to DAM assets and pages. Your system administrator should implement the appropriate user permissions to prevent anyone from doing wrong.

Figure 11.1
Basic replication

The power of replication

Replication is a powerful function, which means it's also dangerous. When you control which content is made public, you hold the digital brand in your hands. That should not be taken lightly. Most teams who have more than a few content authors put specific approval workflows in front of the "activate" feature so that content authors can merely request it. Content is then activated only when a content approver validates that it is appropriate.

In almost every AEM interface that makes the Activate button available to you, AEM allows you to activate only one page at a time. This is to keep you from accidentally publishing incomplete or incorrect content. The activation action will also prompt you to activate any references. For example, if you create a page with a newly uploaded DAM asset, you'll need to activate that asset, too. When you activate the page, AEM will ask if you'd like to activate the DAM asset.

You can imagine that having to activate every page individually might get a little tedious. In the general workflow of content creation, one page at a time is probably fine. But there are perfectly valid scenarios for activating lots of content at once. AEM provides a Bulk Activation tool that allows you to activate an entire tree of content. Do not give everyone access to this tool. You should probably limit access to administrators and managing content authors. It's a simple tool, but it makes it easy to activate a lot of content that you might not want public. Be careful with it.

Reverse replication

So far, all of the replication we've talked about has been activating content from author to publish. However, you sometimes need to go the other way. User-generated content (see Chapter 8), for example, is created on the publish instance. When a user leaves a comment on a page, that comment is saved to a publish instance. (Remember, public users don't have access to the author instance.) To trigger the UGC moderation workflow on your author instance or to ensure that the comment is copied to all of the multiple publish instances, you need a mechanism that can copy the user-generated content back to the author instance.

Reverse replication is the function for copying content from a publish to an author instance. For security reasons, it works a little differently than standard replication.

Your publish instance is available to the public. System administrators keep publicly accessible servers isolated from the rest of the IT infrastructure to prevent hackers from breaking into the entire IT system through those public servers. An internal author instance must be able to talk to the publish instance, but—because of this security safeguard—a publish instance generally cannot talk directly to an author instance. Furthermore, you wouldn't want to configure replication on your publish instances, because there isn't a good way to log into them.

The author instance dictates the reverse replication on the publish instance. The author instance polls the publish instances for new content every few seconds, and when new content is available, the publish instance responds to the polling request with that content. Every AEM instance has already set up a listener for a reverse replication request (called the "outbox"), so you don't have to configure anything special in your publish instances.

If an author instance polls a publish instance and receives some content, it then can push it back out to any other publish instances. In this way your content, even user-generated content, is always synchronized across publish instances even though publish instances don't communicate with one another. The author instance is the hub of it all.

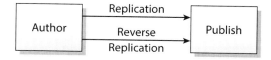

Figure 11.2
Reverse replication

Replication agents

In the Tools interface in Adobe Experience Manager, you can configure replication agents, the configuration entities for a single instance of replication. If you want to activate content from one author instance to one publish instance, you need a replication agent. When you want to add a second publish instance, you need a second replication agent. When you want to configure reverse replication for both of those publish instances, you need two more (reverse) replication agents. This configuration can be a little redundant, but it is flexible.

As a marketer, you probably won't be in charge of setting up replication agents, but you may have to understand how they work. You will likely have access to the replication agent configuration, especially if you are an adminstrative user or a managing content author. You also may need to debug replication issues someday, so it pays to know basically how replication agents function.

Clustering

Most of the time each instance is isolated from the others, though they may communicate through replication. Clustering creates an exception to that rule as a mechanism that allows multiple AEM instances (probably on different hardware) to act as a single instance. By clustering instances, you increase overall capacity by distributing work across multiple servers.

The strategies for distributing computing power are generally different between author and publish instances. Multiple publish instances live in isolation from one another. You use replication (and reverse replication, as necessary) to keep them synchronized. The web server, which accepts page requests before distributing them to a publish instance, can be configured to load balance the publish instances and evenly spread web traffic across these isolated publish instances. Replication that synchronizes publish instances can take a few seconds, but that's okay.

Author instances, on the other hand, are typically distributed with clustering. Because the author instance is the hub of everything, you *do not* want multiple, out-of-sync author instances (even for a few seconds). Users will get lost in process changes and overwrite one another's content. Therefore, when you need to spread your authoring across multiple servers, you should use clustering so the servers act as one.

Figure 11.3
Clustering

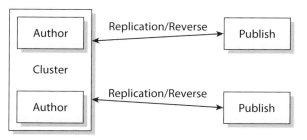

Behind the scenes, clustering works similarly to replication, but at a much lower technology level. One instance becomes the master instance that organizes the entire clustering process. The others are slave instances. The master orchestrates constant synchronization of state so that your author instances all behave as one. You still need to set up load balancing to distribute across all your clustered instances and keep traffic even.

There are a few reasons you might want to implement clustering for your author instance:

- **Increased availability**—If one instance goes down, you've still got another.
- **Performance**—The load is shared by multiple instances.
- **Backup**—You could cluster to a slave instance to create a warm backup that is always updated but not used unless needed.

Clustering is not something you'll need to use unless you have a lot of authors. Work with your solution implementation partner to determine whether it's necessary for you. You can technically cluster publish instances, too, though this is rarely done. Again, your implementation partner can help you work through this.

The Dispatcher

When an end user makes a request for a webpage that you have hosted in Adobe Experience Manager, he is routed to a publish instance. But most of the time, the request doesn't even make it to the publish instance itself. As the request is processed in the web server, it is intercepted by a module called the Dispatcher. The Dispatcher is a tool that manages requests that come to an AEM implementation, providing content caching, load balancing, and additional security. It cannot be used alone, but in conjunction with an enterprise-grade web server (like Apache HTTP Server or Microsoft IIS), it's one of the most important pieces of AEM server architecture.

As with most of the topics in this chapter, as a marketer you should never have to worry about setting up or configuring the Dispatcher. During the implementation process, though, you will end up in discussions with your implementation team where the topic comes up. My goal for this section is to make sure you understand at a high level what the Dispatcher and web server do, to equip you for those inevitable conversations.

The web server

When an Internet user seeks a URL in his browser, a bunch of things happen that lead the browser's request to your web server. We won't open up that can of worms right now, but you should know that a number of mechanisms are in place so that a given URL will go to the same place regardless of the requester and his location. When the request reaches the web server, its job is to read the request and return the requested resource (usually a webpage). In a web server's most basic form, the website is nothing but a bunch of files sitting in a file system. So if

I request www.adobe.com/aem.html, the web server returns a file called aem.html that sits at the root folder of the server.

But no one's website is that static anymore. Today, we make requests to servlets, which are URLs that dynamically build HTML pages on the fly, or to platforms like web content management systems. The same concept applies, though. A request comes into the web server, and the server knows where to get that page, whether it's sitting on a file system or is pulled out of Adobe Experience Manager. In the case of AEM, the Dispatcher allows the web server to talk to AEM, an entity it would otherwise know nothing about.

The Dispatcher is a module that your system administrator will install into whichever of the supported web servers you are using. The Dispatcher extends the functionality of the web server so that it can handle specific AEM tasks. The most important file is dispatcher.any, which is the configuration file that dictates how each Dispatcher feature will function.

The three main features the Dispatcher provides are:

- AEM-specific security
- Content caching
- Load balancing

These three things are all done in the context of AEM, making them very compatible with the platform. It is possible to elect to replace the Dispatcher with alternative technologies, but that creates a much more complex setup. Again, you'll probably never have to set up the Dispatcher, but let's look at what it gets you.

Security

Without any restrictions, AEM is a *very* open platform. When you have a basic instance set up on your own computer and you have administrative access to that computer, you can basically do anything you want within AEM. You can make requests for the source code. You can delete critical folders in the system. You can read user information. Of course, you have to know how to do these things, but if you do, you can be dangerous.

The best practice for protecting that openness from the public is to use the Dispatcher for security. Every public request to your server will *have* to go through the Dispatcher, which is installed as a module on your web server. There is no way around the Dispatcher unless someone hacks into your network. If that's the case, you've got bigger problems, Dispatcher or no Dispatcher.

The Dispatcher configuration includes a list of the kinds of requests you are allowed and not allowed to make to the AEM instance. It restricts end users from making requests that query for your entire content tree. It restricts people from pushing invalid data or malicious code to your AEM server. It also prevents denial-of-service attacks. Generally speaking, your system administrator will make these "Dispatcher rules" as restrictive as possible without negatively affecting the user experience. This keeps the bad people out and lets only the good people in.

Page caching

Without the Dispatcher, every time a page request is made to AEM, the instance re-renders that page. That's okay on your own personal instance, installed on your laptop, because you can't make that many requests at once. Even if you try your hardest, you probably can't overload AEM manually. But think about how much traffic a public-facing instance could receive. Imagine thousands or millions of hits an hour, all coming to the same AEM instance. Adobe Experience Manager is an effective, well-built platform, but it cannot handle that kind of simultaneous load without some help.

To relieve the strain on AEM servers, the Dispatcher will cache pages created in AEM. Caching the page means that after AEM renders the page the first time, it stores that HTML file on the web server file system. Any subsequent request for that page will be served that copy. At that point it acts again like a basic web server. It makes sense to cache pages, because how often does a page receiving thousands of requests change? Once a week? Once a month? Never? Why would you want to waste AEM's processing resources re-rendering the same page over and over?

The Dispatcher cache allows AEM to worry about generating pieces of dynamic content that *do* need to be redrawn on every page request. The content that stays the same is cached and retrieved later. But pages do change. In the simplest configuration, whenever a content author activates a page the action "invalidates" the cache. That just means that every page request will be rebuilt once. Cache invalidation keeps your pages up-to-date, while still minimizing the number of requests that make it all the way to the AEM instance.

Caching will be covered in more detail in Chapter 17.

Load balancing

The point of implementing multiple publish instances is to distribute the load across them, making them all more performant. This doesn't just magically happen, though, so the Dispatcher also includes a load balancing feature. The Dispatcher configuration lists all of the publish instances that are available so that as people make page requests, the Dispatcher can distribute those requests to all the available instances. It helps to make sure no single one gets overloaded.

Despite the load balancing feature, the Dispatcher also tracks user sessions appropriately. Let's say your user makes a request to your home page and is directed to publish A (instead of B or C). The user then logs into her account so she can have personalized content. A user session is maintained on server A. If she is then routed to publish instance B, her browser would lose that user session and she'd appear logged off. To avoid losing the user in this way, the Dispatcher manages "sticky sessions" to ensure that authenticated users are always directed to the same publish instance. This is an important feature for enabling load balancing.

Figure 11.4
Dispatcher-configured load balancing

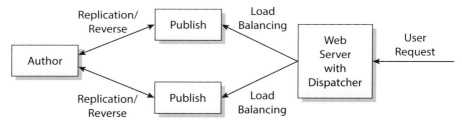

Server architecture

AEM has an extremely flexible architecture, so there are a lot of possibilities to consider when deciding how to set up your instances. I'll describe four basic architectures, but these are far from the only ones. It will help to have a basic idea about your server architecture. It will likely be some variation or combination of the four presented in this section.

Basic author-publish

The most fundamental server architecture possible with Adobe Experience Manager is a basic author-publish model. You have one author instance talking to one publish instance. It's the easiest to set up, so anyone who has a local setup will use it. It's also the simplest to configure. However, it is not commonly used for production setups because of the lack of redundancy. With this model, if your publish instance goes down, your website goes down. For most organizations that means dollars out the door.

Figure 11.5
Basic author-publish architecture

Multiple publish

To create some redundancy with your public site, you can implement multiple publish instances with a single author instance. This is still a fairly simple architecture, but it allows you to lose a publish instance without bringing down your site. You can also distribute computing power across multiple servers, making them more performant. Obviously, you would want to make sure every publish instance is running on a different physical server. Otherwise the redundancy is worthless. Though a bit more complicated to configure, this setup is still pretty simple. However, you will want to configure Dispatcher load balancing and you'll need multiple sets of replication (and reverse replication) agents.

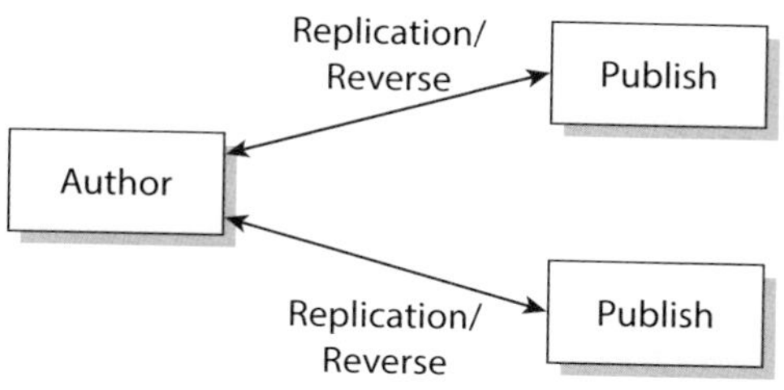

Figure 11.6
Multiple publish instances

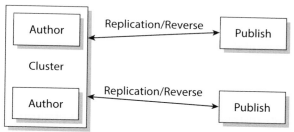

Clustered author with multiple publish

Sometimes you need to beef up your author instance, too. If you've got extremely large teams of content authors working on many websites at a time, one author instance can get bogged down. In those cases, you can use a clustered author and multiple publish architecture. Technically you cluster author instances and have a single publish. But if your sites are complex enough that you need to cluster authors, you'll also need at least a few publish instances.

Adding clustering into the mix makes the configuration quite a bit more complicated, because clustering configuration is different from replication. This architecture requires a system administrator and significant testing/monitoring to keep it functioning correctly.

Figure 11.7
Multiple publish instances with clustered author instances

Relayed replication

Adobe Experience Manager is enterprise-grade software, so sometimes it's used to host *really* huge, high-traffic sites. Some unusually large architectures may require as many as fifty or one hundred publish instances to handle the load. This is extremely rare, so don't assume you are even close to this until an expert tells you otherwise.

If this is the case, however, configuring hundreds of replication agents on your author instance is cumbersome, error-prone, and just plain difficult. You would also require your author instance to spend a *lot* of time just activating content, because it has to activate every page a hundred times. To alleviate this problem, you can set up "relayed" replication.

Let me preface this by saying that this is not a supported or advertised feature with AEM. You won't find it in the documentation. However, it's absolutely possible to do. With relayed replication, you create a middle tier, between author and publish, of "relay" instances. Their job is to do nothing more than listen for content updates and immediately replicate them to the publish instances.

The idea is that you can break up, say, one hundred publish instances into groups of ten relay instances. In so doing, your author instance needs replication configuration for only those ten relay instances. Then each relay instance needs replication configuration for only their ten publish instances.

On the author side, you can have a single author or clustered author instances. I'm guessing that if you have the kind of traffic that requires fifty or one hundred publish instances, you probably have a big enough content team to justify clustering author instances.

As you can imagine, this is a complicated architecture. You need to set up a lot of coordinated replication. On the relay instances, you must set up listeners that automatically reactivate any content pushed to them. Configuring reverse replication for user-generated content also becomes quite a bit more challenging. This architecture requires extra testing and monitoring, because it is not a supported feature. *Do not* start with this setup as your plan. Only attempt this architecture with the recommendation and guidance of an experienced implementation partner.

Figure 11.8
Relayed replication
architecture

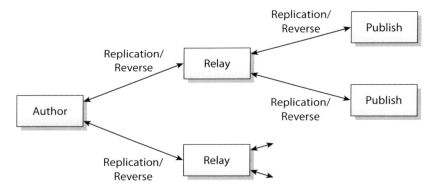

Summary

Server architecture and configuration are typically not the tasks of a marketer, so kudos if you made it through this rather technical chapter. Although you probably won't have to implement these concepts personally, you're now in a better position to discuss these technologies with your implementation partner. The features described in this chapter are designed to improve your life and the lives of your site visitors. When executed correctly, they increase performance, security, and flexibility. Architecture is something of an art form, so consider this chapter your Art 101.

Review questions

1. What is the primary purpose of an author instance? A publish instance?
2. What is the difference between replication and activation?
3. Why would you cluster AEM instances?
4. What are the three basic functions performed by the Dispatcher?
5. What is wrong with the basic author-publish architecture?

Review answers

1. An author instance is accessible to internal users and is the primary place for building pages and authoring content. The publish instance is publicly accessible, and its sole purpose is delivering the authored content to external users.
2. There is no difference. They are synonyms representing the ability to push content from one instance to another.
3. Clustering AEM instances enables them to use multiple hardware resources (servers) while still appearing as a single instance. It is most commonly used to increase the performance of author instances.
4. Security, content caching, and load balancing
5. The drawback to the basic author-publish architecture is that with only one publish instance, your public site has no redundancy. If you lose your only publish instance to an outage (it happens), your entire website goes down.

12 ADMINISTRATION BASICS

Depending on your team's makeup, you may have to take on some administration tasks in Adobe Experience Manager. If you have a large team with specialized roles, these tasks can probably be assigned to a specific system administrator. But if you work on a smaller content team, many administration tasks are commonly passed on to the marketers. That's okay, though. In this chapter we'll go over some of the administration tasks available in AEM:

- How to migrate content from one environment to another
- How to manage users and permissions
- Which reports are available in Adobe Experience Manager and how they can help you
- Other available administrative features

By the end of this chapter, you'll have knowledge that will be valuable if you need to take full or partial responsibility for administrative tasks.

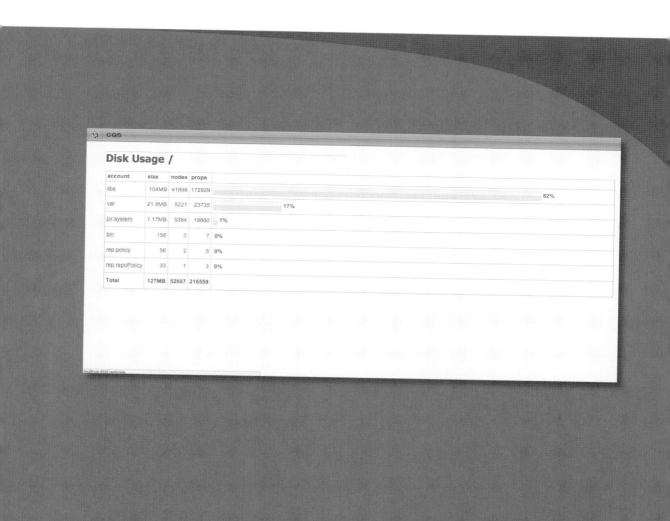

The disk usage report

Package management

In a previous chapter, I discussed replication, a feature for transferring content from one AEM instance to another. This function works well as a safe, author-oriented way to make content public. The problem is that it requires some technical overhead because all your replication agents must be configured correctly. You're also limited in what it allows you to do. When you click to activate, you just issue a request to push content to whomever is listening. This works great for activating public content, but what about the other reasons that you may need to transfer content across environments? Think about replication and consider the following questions:

- What if you need to transfer content from environment A to B, but A cannot talk directly to B?

- What if you need to distribute the content to multiple employees managing their own environments?

- What if you want to archive snapshots of content for backup purposes?

- What if you want to transfer data that resides in AEM but isn't the kind of content that is appropriate to replicate (such as source code)?

Replication doesn't support any of these needs, although they are all very real, very common activities that you'll perform in Adobe Experience Manager. Instead of using replication, you address them with a different administrative feature called package management.

Package management is a set of features that allows you to transfer packages of content from one environment to another. A package is simply a ZIP file that includes a binary representation of whichever part of your content hierarchy you've configured. In fact, if you look inside that ZIP file, you can browse through a file structure that matches your content tree. Packages can be exported from one environment and imported into others, without those environments being aware of one another. It's simply a way to export AEM data into a file that can be archived or shared with others, and it's a flexible way to move data across environments.

So far in this book, I've used the term "content" to refer to the copy, media files, and webpages that a marketer or content author creates in Adobe Experience Manager. However, when I talk about packages, I'm going to broaden that term.

Technically speaking, *everything* in AEM is content. This is one of the unique architectural concepts of the platform. AEM content includes the code that implements your site, the configuration that defines parts of it, and even the source code that is Adobe Experience Manager. It's *all* content, in addition to the content that you author. Any and all of this broadly defined content technically can be packaged and transferred. For the rest of the book, we'll retain my original definition of "content," but in the context of package management, keep in mind that the content in your packages can be anything in AEM.

The following are some cases for which you would want to use a package:

- Transferring authored content from a test environment to a production environment (or vice versa)—you only want to use replication within a single environment (such as test author to test publish)

- Deploying your website's code. As a marketer, you won't do this, but your implementation team will deploy a code package.

- Installing add-ons or service packs to Adobe Experience Manager.

- Sharing your content with Adobe support so that they can bootstrap a duplicate of your environment for debugging.

- Performing content backups that are saved *outside* of the AEM application to ensure that an unexpected repository corruption won't nuke your backups.

Generally speaking, any content packaging you may perform should be at the guidance of your implementation team. Depending on your team's circumstances, though, you may be asked to participate in some aspect of packaging. If you do work with packages, you'll do it within the Package Manager interface.

Package Manager

Package Manager is the interface that allows you to create, install, and manage packages. It's something that you'll want to limit access to, because it's possible to destroy an AEM instance from within this interface.

Package lifecycle

There are a number of steps in the lifecycle of a package, all of which are managed within Package Manager. That lifecycle is as follows:

1. First, you must create a package. In doing so, you are really generating a definition of what the package will be. You select which parts of the content tree are included and specify some other descriptive metadata. Creating a package does not generate it. This action only defines the nature of the package.

2. Then, you build the package. Building a package creates a ZIP file based on the configuration you provided when you created the package. It's a snapshot in time, so if you build the package, then change some of the content, you will need to rebuild it to update its contents. AEM automatically adds a version number to the package for archival purposes. The package definition will remain in Package Manager until you delete it, which allows you to periodically build the same package with updated content. This feature is useful for archiving or migrating content regularly.

3. Once the package is built, you can download it to your own computer as a ZIP file. To transfer it to another AEM instance, you would upload it from that AEM

instance's Package Manager interface. It will appear just as it did in the instance in which it was created.

4. When the package is uploaded, you must install it to apply the content in the package to the new environment. Installing is very aggressive. The package contents will overwrite existing content in the same location. That's one reason you must take care when using packages. Installing is basically the inverse of building and represents the end of the basic package lifecycle.

5. You can also uninstall a package, but I don't often see this feature used. Uninstalling means that you can roll back your content to the state it was in prior to the package installation. However, this is a complicated feature. If you install and then immediately uninstall, you are probably safe. But if you install, perform several functions, then uninstall, you risk data loss. I don't recommend relying on package uninstallation as part of your process, but it's there if you need it.

Package Manager provides a number of prebuilt and installed packages. The source code that powers Adobe Experience Manager is installed as a package automatically when the platform initially boots up. Don't alter these packages unless directed to do so by Adobe. Furthermore, I would be suspicious of a solution partner who asks you to modify those packages in any way, but I won't say it's completely unreasonable. If you mess up or uninstall those packages, you risk corrupting the AEM instance. If you haven't backed up your data, it could mean unrecoverable data loss.

Package Manager is a bit scary. It can blow up your AEM instance, but it's also one of the most handy tools at your disposal. Without Package Manager, migrating content and other artifacts across environments would be quite a bit more cumbersome. If you limit your Package Manager access to system administrators or capable, responsible employees, and you follow the best practices defined by Adobe in the AEM documentation, you'll be grateful for this interface.

Figure 12.1
Package Manager

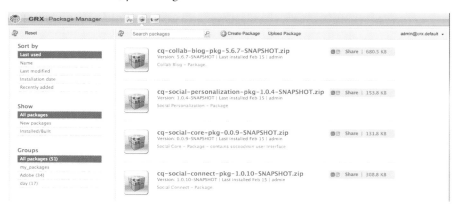

Package Share

Package Share is another AEM interface that deals with packages, but it's quite different from Package Manager. Package Share is a cloud-hosted network from which you can download packages that other parties make freely available. It was originally meant to create a social way to exchange open source community-developed add-ons, but it has succeeded in only a limited sense. (GitHub and Twitter are used more often.) However, this is the easiest place to get add-ons and service packs that are released by Adobe.

Package Share is a straightforward interface. When you open it, you'll have to log in with your Adobe ID. (You should have an Adobe ID for accessing the Adobe Support portal and various other Adobe systems.) You can then search for packages. The most common packages I see retrieved are service packs and the installer for the Dispatcher, but others are there as well. The reason the system is authenticated is because you can have something of a "private" sharing in which you make packages available to only certain parties. Occasionally Adobe, for example, may make some of their private packages available to you. Without authentication, this secured exchange wouldn't be possible.

Users and permissions

As with any enterprise technology, Adobe Experience Manager requires that you manage users and their permissions within the platform. You must authenticate into the authoring interface to access it, and therefore you must create users who have permission to do so.

If you have a small, capable content team, it's possible that you may just give everyone administrative (full) permission. But as your team gets bigger, that free access becomes exponentially riskier. Instead, you can elect to limit certain users' permission to read-only for some parts of the application, or maybe revoke their permission completely. The practices you implement will depend on your own circumstances, so in this section, I'll give a mile-high view of AEM user management.

User management in Adobe Experience Manager is complicated, and it gets trickier the more granular or specific you try to make your user permissions. AEM is based on an open source content repository called Apache Jackrabbit. When you define users and set their permissions, you are doing so at the content repository level. Since this function is such a low-level architectural concept, it's a little complicated for a nontechnical user. AEM provides a relatively intuitive user interface for defining permissions, and if you are responsible for user management, you will become quite familiar with it.

In the Security interface (the user management screen, sometimes called "User Admin"), you can define your users and their metadata, reset passwords, and grant permissions. To grant user permissions, AEM provides you with a representation of the entire content tree within AEM (not just the authored content). At each node, you can grant read, write, modify, or delete permissions. You can also define who can read or edit the ACL (access control list—the permissions) and who can replicate that node.

Permissions are inherited down the tree unless specified otherwise, so you can use these permissions for sections of the content tree. You obviously cannot customize each node individually. The challenge is that certain permissions override others, so when you try to get very specific, it's hard to keep track of which permission wins. Fortunately, the structure is straightforward. I recommend looking at the default Geometrixx users and groups to get an idea of how they are set up.

Figure 12.2
User Administration

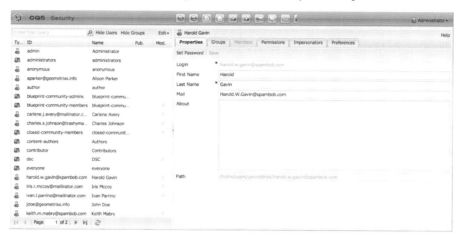

Users and groups

The two entities that you manage in the User Admin interface are users and groups, which are more or less the same thing. The only differences are that groups are collections of users, and you cannot log into the system as a group. Otherwise, they behave alike, and you define their permissions in exactly the same way.

Every user and group includes a name, email, and metadata about that user or group. The metadata isn't complicated; there are only a few configuration options per user. Most important are the permissions granted to that user or group. You can place users in groups, but you can also place groups within groups to create multiple layers of hierarchy. The interface also lets you search for, create, or delete users and groups.

The simplest way to manage users is to do so directly in Adobe Experience Manager. However, it is possible to import users from existing enterprise systems via LDAP

(Lightweight Directory Access Protocol). This is an enterprise standard for linking users and groups between technologies. For example, if your organization uses Active Directory to manage user permissions for your email, portal access, calendar, and so on, you can synchronize those accounts into AEM and create users accordingly. You can't set this up on your own; you'll need to work with your system administrators and implementation team.

You'll notice that you can activate and deactivate users. This is important if your site has authenticated functionality that is accessed through the publish instance. For example, maybe your site is an extranet or community site where internal and external users can log in to leave comments. Whether internally created or synchronized via LDAP or created by an end user's public registration, all users are stored and managed in the same way. Therefore, they must be synchronized appropriately across all AEM instances using the same kind of replication that is used to synchronize content. The users who serve as your blog-authors-to-be will need to be activated to all publish instances.

That said, if you don't have any reason to "log in" to a public website on the publish instance, just keep all your users on the author instance. It's simpler that way.

Impersonation

Adobe Experience Manager allows those with permission to impersonate other users without logging in as those users. Typically, impersonation is limited to a select few administrators, because you could do some damage in the name of another person. When impersonating another user, the system behaves as if you are logged in as that user. Impersonation is great for verifying that you've set up permissions correctly and for helping users debug problems they experience. Much of the functionality in AEM is dependent on each user possessing the appropriate permissions, so this tool is put in place to allow administrators to work through permissions issues.

Best practices

The following are some generally accepted best practices to keep in mind when managing users:

- Keep permissions as simple as possible. When you get complicated or granular with permissions, they become difficult to manage.

- Don't apply permissions directly to users. Define groups with appropriate sets of permissions, and then place users into those groups. This is a much more flexible means of distributing and changing permissions.

- Define groups that replicate how your team is organized and the tasks they perform. Doing so makes it easier to distribute permissions according to your real organizational structure.

- Minimize the use of the "deny" permission. Whenever possible, make your permissions positive, not negative. Denying permissions complicates them significantly, although it's sometimes unavoidable.

- Change the password for the "admin" user and limit its use to a single person. You can create more administrative users, but "admin" is a special account. Far too often, I see everyone using "admin," which is not secure and means you have no audit trail of who did what (because everyone will show as the same admin user).

- Don't sync using LDAP unless you really need to, because doing so can get quite complicated. If you truly have a need for LDAP sync, use it, but don't artificially create a reason.

- Keep permissions as simple as possible. Yes, I already said this. But if you remember just one of these points, remember this one.

The Adobe documentation provides additional best practices and general approaches for managing users and permissions. If it will be your responsibility to administer users, read the Adobe documentation and work with your solution partner and Adobe support to make sure you *really* understand it.

AEM reports

Adobe Experience Manager includes a default set of reporting features that allow you to gain specific knowledge about your instance. With such a big platform, it gets difficult to track macro-concepts like how much content you have, where it is, and what its status is. Some performance-related metrics are also important to monitor. Reports give you a basic way to understand your AEM instance clearly. These reports tend to straddle the line between being marketer-centric and administrator-centric, but you should understand all of them. In this section, I'll briefly describe the out-of-the-box reports and how to use them.

Page activity report

The page activity report is your window into the actions that have occurred on pages in AEM. It serves as an audit report of who did what when. Assuming you are following the previously stated best practice to *not* allow everyone to use the admin account, you'll be able to see when various users modified, created, deleted, and versioned pages. This report can also be handy when you are performing a content audit and want to know which pages haven't been updated in a long time. This report is especially useful to marketers, because it provides a broad perspective on the content that marketers manage.

Component report

The component report allows you to understand which content components are used where. It's easy to see pages in AEM, because you have a hierarchical tree view for browsing them. It's much more difficult to track down components that are embedded in pages, especially when there are potentially several layers of embedding.

In this report you can see which components are used in pages, how many times they are used, and who added them to the page. Again, when you are doing a content audit, this report can be very useful. It's also helpful when you need to replace all instances of a specific component or when you want to purge your list of components that you haven't used for a long time or don't use at all.

Disk usage

The disk usage report is definitely geared toward system administrators. It lets you identify which areas of the content hierarchy in AEM are taking up the most disk space. It's an important analysis if you find that your AEM instances are getting too large and swallowing your hardware whole. The disk usage report is a drill-down through the levels of the hierarchy. At each level it tells you what percentage of disk space is used by each node in that level of the hierarchy. To find the biggest disk space offenders, you keep drilling down into the "big" nodes until you find where the problem originates. You probably won't use this as a marketer, unless you are also responsible for system administration.

Health check

The health check report is another report primarily for administrators, but it may also be used by your implementation team. The health check analyzes your past request log files, which contain a record of every request that was made to AEM. It then reports which requests took the longest time to return.

This report helps administrators and the implementation team find inefficient pieces of code that create a suboptimal user experience. In this way, they can evaluate how to rebuild that piece of functionality to be more performant. Though the report is primarily an administrator tool, you as the marketer will be most affected by slow performance. You may notice slowdowns in your web analytics or receive customer complaints, and it's likely that slow performance will negatively affect your conversion rates. Therefore, it might be helpful if you can assist with the analysis of locating the performance issues.

User-generated content report

The user-generated content report gives you a window into all the UGC (user-generated content) created with your website. Much of the information will be duplicated in the community management interface, but this report also contains past UGC that no longer appears there. This report may be used by administrators to better understand which parts of the site are affected by UGC. It also may be useful to marketers who want a historical analysis of the customer interactions that their site creates. Because the report can also display the IP address of the UGC's creator, you can export this report and perform additional analysis, such as understanding what parts of the world produce the most UGC.

User report

The user report generates a table with data about all of the users in your system. To be clear, these are the same users that you manage in the User Admin interface. If you've got only users created for internal team members, such as content authors, this report probably isn't that valuable. However, if you allow site visitors to register, you may have hundreds or thousands of registered users, and that's a lot to keep track of in the User Admin interface. This report provides a nice printout of those users and their basic information. It can assist administrators with cleanup, but it also can be exported by marketers to be used in other marketing systems that aren't directly integrated with AEM (hint: your CRM).

Workflow reports

The workflow report and workflow instance report provide administrators with very basic information about the state of the worfklow engine. You probably won't care about this information for specific marketing purposes. Administrators can use this report to monitor how many workflow instances have been completed and how many are currently in process. Knowing this can give them insight into how the system is being used and whether any areas are candidates for workflow optimization.

Custom reports

It is possible to create custom reports in Adobe Experience Manager. In fact, there are two possible degrees of "custom reporting." The default reports are quite insightful, but organizations always seem to need something different. By building flexibility into the system, Adobe enables marketers and administrators to report on the information *they* need, not just the information Adobe assumes they need.

The first way to create a custom report is by authoring it like any other configuration page. You'll notice that when you view a report on an author instance (under Tools > Reports), you are just viewing a configuration page in author mode. You have a Sidekick that includes the components (usually table columns) that make up the report. You can modify the default reports using the WYSIWYG authoring features, but you also can create new versions by starting with the templates that define the default reports. This approach offers you some flexibility, but it is limited to the set of templates and components that Adobe provides. All you can do is tweak and organize them the way you like.

If you need to get deeper with your report customization, you'll have to work with your implementation team. Essentially, they have free rein to perform whatever customization you require. They can build additional components to add to the default reports, or they can define completely new reports for you. Ideally, they do so using the basic report framework already in place, but sometimes it's easier to create a basic configuration page that spits out textual information. That's a valid approach as well. This is an implementation concern, so we won't get any deeper into it. Just know that you *can* create custom reporting functionality and that you should work with the implementation team to define and implement your requirements.

Miscellaneous functions

This has already been kind of a miscellaneous "catch-all" chapter about different, loosely related administrative features. This section will be the ultimate "catch-all" section within this "catch-all" chapter. I want to discuss a few more features that don't fit into the previous sections. Nonetheless, they are important for you to understand at a high level. While you may not use these features without technical help, it's important to understand what they are.

CRXDE

For someone who implements WCM platforms for a living, I think CRXDE is one of the cooler features available in AEM. CRXDE is a web-based IDE (integrated development environment) for editing content nodes and some source code directly within AEM. If you are a programmer, you live in an IDE. It's the application in which you write code. However, programmers typically write the code, compile it, and then install into AEM. To change something, they have to repeat that whole process. With CRXDE, programmers can make "hot" code changes on a live AEM instance without redeploying anything. They also can directly change content in the repository, which equates to changing database data in a more traditional enterprise platform. Again, this can be done "hot" on a live instance.

There a few things I want you to understand about CRXDE:

- As a marketer, you shouldn't mess with CRXDE unless directed to do so by an administrator or member of your implementation team. You can break anything and everything. However, if you're on an instance installed locally on your computer, feel free to break whatever you want. You can just rebuild it later.

- You can't change *everything* on the fly in CRXDE. A lot of your site's implementation will be packaged up in JAR files, which must be redeployed when changed. CRXDE is best for making quick CSS, HTML, and JavaScript changes to test a fix.

- One person should have permission to access CRXDE in a production (and probably pre-production) environment. This individual should be the only one to hold that permission, and he shouldn't do *anything* with it.

- CRXDE is not suitable for full project development; it's used only for quick tweaks or testing changes. If you find your solution implementation partner is doing all development in CRXDE, that should be a big red flag about their qualifications.

- CRXDE is implemented completely with JavaScript, so it's a little finicky about browser versions. Generally speaking (and unofficially), it works best in Firefox and Chrome. Safari and Internet Explorer do okay but might exhibit some unexpected behavior. Adobe will provide official browser support information, depending on your version of AEM.

Again, marketers have little or no business using CRXDE, but you probably will hear administrators or your implementation team talking about it. It's an extremely convenient feature for developing the code that implements websites hosted by AEM.

Version purging

If you take advantage of the content versioning features in Adobe Experience Manager, you may find that past versions start to take up a lot of disk space. Maybe you found that out using the disk usage report; good thing you learned about it. If your past versions are using too much space, you can apply the "Purge Versions" feature to delete past content snapshots. There's not much to this utility, but it lets you bulk delete versions up to a certain point. You probably won't want to delete *all* previous content, but may do so up to a certain date or "number" of past versions.

You'll want to limit this tool to a few administators, especially if you are using content versioning to satisfy any regulatory auditing needs. It also may be a good idea to have a backup mechanism in place so that when you purge past versions, you have them backed up somewhere, just in case.

External link checker

Adobe Experience Manager includes a feature that checks the validity of authored links. Using it ensures that you are not linking to invalid URLs, which creates a negative user experience. You may notice that in the authoring environment, AEM will highlight bad links in context on the page. But it's difficult to use in-page information to get a holistic view of your links. The external link checker interface provides that. It's a report of all the external links (though not internal, relative links) on your site. It tells you whether they are valid URLs and how long ago they were checked.

This is another great tool to use when performing a content audit, because it helps identify links that were valid when created but are no longer functional.

Importers

Adobe Experience Manager provides a few interfaces for importing (and exporting) content. They call these "importers," and they are available in the Tools interface. They aren't used often, but I'll give a quick rundown of each one:

- **Bulk Editor**—This makes large content changes at once and exports content to CSV files. You can also use it to import content, but that's a very powerful feature. By default it is disabled and requires your implementation team to turn it on.

- **Offline Importer**—This allows you to import content from Word files into AEM pages. It's a tricky feature to use, so if you will want to apply it, tell your implementation team in advance. That way they can build pages and components in a way that is most compatible with this feature.

- **Feed Importer**—This allows you to import content via an RSS or Atom feed, which is useful when you want to import your blog into AEM from a different platform. It's also useful if you create a blog of curated content from external sources. Just don't violate anyone's intellectual property rights, please.

- **Site Importer**—Supposedly, this feature permits you to import an entire existing website into AEM. However, I've never seen this actually used.

- **Upgrade from CQ3/CQ4**—This assists when upgrading from very old versions of AEM (previously called CQ). It may be helpful, but don't try to undertake an upgrade of this magnitude without an experienced solution partner at the helm. It cannot be done with the simple click of a button.

Work with an expert to determine if any of these importers are useful to you. As I said, they aren't used often, but occasionally turn out to be a handy tool for working around a unique requirement.

Summary

We covered a lot of material in this chapter, so don't be alarmed if you feel like you've been drinking from a firehose. The features covered are generally administrative ones, but sometimes responsibility for their use passes to the marketer. Some of these are aggressive tools that should be used with care. Some of them are simple informational, reporting tools that provide better visibility into the workings of your website. The key to their use is to have a defined plan, developed with assistance from your solution implementation partner.

Review questions

1. Where can you download service packs released by Adobe?

2. How are users and groups different?

3. Which report would you use to figure out how many times the "Text and Image" component is used in your site?

4. What is the marketer's value in CRXDE?

5. Which importer allows you to pull content from an existing blog?

Review answers

1. Package Share

2. Users and groups are almost identical, with two basic exceptions: Groups act as a container for other users and groups, and you cannot log into AEM as a group.

3. Component report

4. Trick question. There is no marketer value. If you are a marketer, stay out of CRXDE unless otherwise directed by an administrator or informed member of the implementation team.

5. Feed Importer

13 WEB ANALYTICS

Web analytics are extremely important when you want to create a positive, engaging web experience. You can't personally interview the thousands (maybe millions) of visitors who see your website. But you can tally up what they did on your site. The trends of what *everyone* did on your site can provide insights into what's working and what's not. You can use this information to optimize your customers' web experience. Implementing an effective web analytics strategy is crucial to making your Adobe Experience Manager implementation successful.

In this chapter, you'll learn:

- What web analytics are and how they are used

- The features Adobe Experience Manager provides for tracking visitor behavior

- How Adobe Experience Manager can integrate with industry-leading web analytics platforms

- The best practices for implementing a web analytics strategy in Adobe Experience Manager

This chapter will by no means give you all the knowledge you need to be an expert in web analytics. But it will introduce you to the fundamental concepts so that you can work with your analytics team to make sure the effectiveness of your AEM implementation is appropriately quantified.

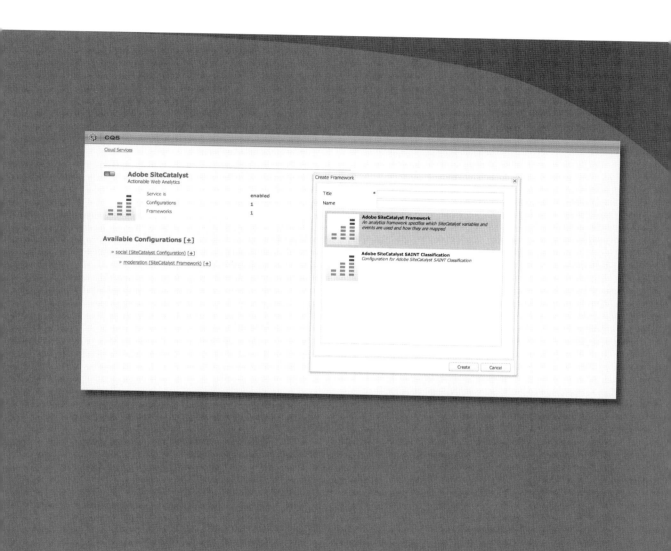

Configuring AEM to integrate with Adobe SiteCatalyst

Understanding analytics

Web analytics is the collection and reporting of data about websites, specifically about visitors' interactions with websites. By collecting web analytics data, marketers are able to understand some crucial things about their site's visitors:

- Where the website's visitors are from (search engines, links)
- What devices they used to visit your site
- Where in the world your visitors are located
- Where they enter the site
- What they do on the site
- How long they stay
- How many people return to the site multiple times
- How much money visitors are spending on the site

These are some of the fundamental facts that web analytics help you uncover, and they are far from the only ones. Modern web analytics strategy teaches marketers to slice and dice site visitor data in many different ways, always with the intent of optimizing the effectiveness of their web content.

A web analytics platform is software that collects web analytics data. The platform is designed to reduce huge datasets of site visitor behavior into reports that can be easily digested. Use of a web analytics platform is considered a best practice for managing a website, whether or not you use a web content management system. This best practice is reinforced by the fact that some analytics platforms are available for free. What's your excuse now?

Web analytics platforms come in two basic flavors: cloud-based and on-premise. Each has its own distinct advantage, but both aim to do the same thing: effectively quantify site visitor interaction in a minimally invasive way.

Cloud-based platforms such as Adobe SiteCatalyst and Google Analytics require small snippets of JavaScript that make calls to their servers to track visitor actions. Marketers can access this information from wherever the marketers may be, which is a benefit of cloud-hosted software.

On-premise platforms can use a similar JavaScript-based approach or perform analysis on web server logs to provide similar information, but without accessing an off-site, third-party server. The cloud-based approach is generally considered more modern, but in some scenarios an on-premise implementation makes sense. On-premise solutions tend to be more secure because data remains within your own network and you have full control over the technology.

Good web analysis (making sense of web analytics data) requires a mix of creativity and scientific analysis. On one hand, it demands an understanding of statistics and theoretical math to make sense of averages and build forecasting models. On the other hand, to be successful the analysis must convert those mathematical insights into marketing objectives like new content or refreshed designs for landing pages. To make all of this more complicated, the data comes at you in real time. If you aren't making the correct decisions based on that data and optimizing your site *today*, you can be sure the competition is.

Why use analytics?

If you have a website, you should be using some kind of web analytics platform. With free solutions available, you have no reason not to. Analytics represent tangible knowledge about who uses your site and why. A web analytics platform can't tell you exactly how to react to that knowledge (yet), but it can help you make educated business decisions about optimizing your website.

With the technology available to you today, you don't have to make business decisions based purely on your gut. Digital marketing is still marketing, and some part of marketing will continue to be based on intuition. But with analytics, your intuition can be backed up with data. Within days of launching a new digital marketing effort, you can see whether it is headed toward failure or success. You can test which variations of your home page lead to the most revenue or whatever other conversions are important to you. You may use intuition and knowledge to determine what you want to try, but web analytics platforms give you the data to accurately evaluate your ideas.

Typical web analytics platform features

Though web analytics software vendors have introduced some innovations over the past few years, most platforms include the same core feature set. Your choice of a web analytics platform will probably be based more on price and "bells and whistles" than these fundamental features. That doesn't mean the basics aren't important, though. In fact, if you want to get a high-level understanding of how web analytics fits into the digital marketing picture, these mostly platform-agnostic features are where you should begin.

Real-time data collection

Most modern analytics platforms capture data in real time (or close to it). Sometimes free analytics platforms will perform in near real time (within 24 hours) and charge extra for instantaneous data. Whether immediate or almost, an analytics platform empowers marketers to make quick decisions. Receiving marketing campaign feedback in hours or days, instead of weeks or months, means that marketers can assess the effectiveness of their efforts and adjust incrementally. This capability reduces risk and helps marketers more efficiently apply their budget.

Reports and dashboards

Analytics platforms would be worthless if they didn't present their data in simple, actionable ways. But there are hundreds of ways you can slice and dice site visitor data. Therefore, analytics platforms generally provide an array of reports and dashboards that show different versions of the same data. Usually the platform will provide the facilities to develop custom reports, in addition to the ready-to-go reports included to get you started. Custom reports are helpful for building executive dashboards that show managers only what is essential to them.

Visitor demographic information

Analytics platforms don't just count visits to pages, though that's a big part of it. They also track as much demographic information about those visitors as is possible. Analytics platforms use the information that each visitor's web browser sends along with every page request to determine where the user is located, what device she is using, what language preference she has set, and much more. You can use this demographic data to understand who is visiting your site and to more effectively prioritize new site features and digital marketing campaigns.

Data segmentation

In addition to providing the standard visitor demographic information, most web analytics platforms let you set up your own data segmentation. Maybe you want to slice up your analytics data according to specific sales territories. Maybe you want to pass specific data from your website into the analytics platform for data segmentation, which allows you to build on the basic analytics foundation to fully customize what you measure and how you measure it. In most platforms, both of these scenarios are possible.

Funnel conversion tracking

Generally, web analytics platforms will provide some form of funnel conversion tracking. The term "funnel" describes a sequence of steps that lead to a "conversion," a success action. An e-commerce website's checkout steps are a great example. In a four-step checkout process (step four being the confirmation after the purchase is made), you'll usually find that an increasing number of people drop out at each successive step. You can optimize that funnel by figuring out which step causes the largest percentage of drop-offs, and then test alternatives to that step. Maybe users find a form too complicated. Maybe the site doesn't look secure enough to complete the purchase. Funnel conversion tracking gives you insight into where you are losing customers who are "almost there."

E-commerce tracking

Many web analytics platforms provide e-commerce tracking for determining how site visitor actions convert to actual dollars spent. When a site visitor works through a purchase on your site, you can pass in information about that sale (such as the amount). Then you can cross-reference that data against the other analytics data such as what site the visitor came from, how many times he viewed your site before finalizing a purchase, and which pages he viewed. This functionality isn't used for accurately counting sales. You have accounting systems for that. This functionality is for analyzing the sales value of traffic-generation campaigns and your own site content. Even if your email marketing campaign brings in a ton of visitors, if none of them are making purchases, is it *really* working?

What do you do with the data?

As a marketer, you can do a lot with even the most basic web analytics data. Ultimately, you should be looking at what happened in the past to help you predict how actions will change the data trend in the future.

For example, you see that a certain landing page has a higher bounce rate than you'd like to see. Bounce rate is the percentage of people immediately leaving your site from the first page (a high rate is usually bad). You see that people are finding this landing page on Google using search terms that you know aren't relevant to your website. That's probably why people bounce. They find your site irrelevant to their search and they leave.

You create a plan to change the metadata and phrasing on your landing page so that it doesn't trigger those irrelevant keywords as easily. You predict that this will lower your bounce rate. You can make the change and see if you were right by watching the bounce rate trend after that change goes public.

This example illustrates the idea of mixing art and science. As a marketer you still need to use your artistic side to make sure the copy on the landing page reinforces your brand and encourages visitors to delve farther into the site. But you aren't relying on their intuition to know if it'll work. The availability of web analytics data enables you to perform statistical analysis on that copy. That helps you determine if and how you should change it. The availability of this data also brought this accidental anomaly to your attention. Without analytics, you may have never known that your landing page was pulling in traffic from search keywords that couldn't help you sell your products online.

One key thing to understand about web analytics data is that it isn't completely accurate. Many factors contribute to this inaccuracy. For example, a site visitor who doesn't allow browser cookies (or who clears them periodically) cannot be accurately tracked for return visits. You cannot use web analytics to track what a specific person did (and you wouldn't want to, for legal and privacy reasons).

However, knowing that all of your data has a baseline margin of error, you can focus on performing comparative analysis to gain insight. For example, if you know page views are up 50 percent from last month, that's probably a valid statistic. You can assume that you had roughly the same margin of error in both months. When using analytics data to make decisions, you should avoid looking at single data points and explore trends over time.

Your web analytics platform is there to empower you to make informed marketing decisions. It takes a lot of the guesswork out of digital marketing. You should never need to make digital marketing decisions without the data to back them up and measure their success. The web analytics platform enables you to follow that rule.

Analytics and WCMs

Most modern web analytics platforms integrate with your site via a snippet of JavaScript added to your webpages that can talk to the analytics platform. By applying the JavaScript to a page, an administrator makes the page visible to the web analytics platform so it can track how visitors got to that page, what they did on the page, and where they went as they left. If every page in your site has that JavaScript (it should), the analytics platform can report holistic user pathing and visitor action information.

When you have a static website that isn't hosted by a web content management system, a developer or administrator literally has to copy the analytics JavaScript to every individual page. But when you use a WCM, you shouldn't have to do that anymore. Ideally, applying that JavaScript to pages becomes an administrative configuration task, not a coding task. Then marketers can be responsible for the tweaks to the JavaScript that are required to implement features such as special demographics or e-commerce tracking. Again, the WCM removes the programming middleman and puts the marketer directly in control of the functionality she needs to be successful.

The marriage of analytics and content management doesn't only provide value during implementation time (when applying JavaScript snippets). It continues to provide value by allowing marketers to retrieve data about their site visitors. Marketers no longer need technical folks to build reports that present actionable data. The insight is directly in the hands of those who need to act accordingly. Since they also control a powerful content management system, they can act quickly.

Through the rest of this chapter, I'll explore how Adobe Experience Manager enables you to collect web analytics or to integrate with leading web analytics platforms.

Analytics and AEM

If you are working in Adobe Experience Manager, your primary concern is content. You are trying to build web content that engages your customers, builds your brand, and ultimately helps your organization achieve its goals. Understanding the importance of measuring your content's effectiveness, Adobe built a number of web analytics features into AEM. These features can be used to ensure the content you create with AEM is the best it can be.

Page impressions

Adobe Experience Manager includes an extremely basic web analytics function that tracks page impressions, which are just a tally of how many visitors viewed a specific page. You can liken them to the hit counters that used to show up on webpages in the '90s. Page impressions don't include any demographic information about the visitor, or where the visitor came from or where she went. They just provide the most basic of web analytics data.

The biggest advantage of using page impressions is that they are available for consumption right inside AEM. You don't have to worry about external platforms, additional logins and access rights, or setting up dashboards for your decision makers. They make it easy for a content author to see which pages receive the most hits. Page impressions are displayed in the Site Administration interface, where you create, edit, and move pages.

Page impressions do require a bit of configuration, though. Think about a scenario where you have one author instance and two publish instances. Your site visitors will be equally divided between the two publish instances because of your load balancer. Each publish instance will "count" page impressions separately because all AEM instances basically act in isolation. But you want both of those publish instances counted as impressions on the author instance. This is something your system administrator will have to set up because it can cause some complexity in a publicly accessible production environment.

● **Note:** If you need a refresher on author and publish instances, see Chapter 11.

Page impressions are fine for *very* basic, quick information, but they are far from a full-fledged analytics solution. Page impressions lack the contextual information you need to make informed business decisions. Why does one page get more impressions than another? Where are those extra visitors coming from? Are they buying more? Are they on mobile phones? None of this information can be derived from a simple page count. Therefore, even if you decide you want to use page impressions, you should still implement a dedicated web analytics platform.

Why integrate?

Part III of this book is mostly about integrating Adobe Experience Manager with peripheral marketing technologies. To generate the digital insights, you need to make your brand the best it can be, and you need to integrate best-of-breed solutions for your marketing problems. No technology can be everything to everyone, so it's important to assemble technologies to create a platform that can be everything to you.

Web analytics and content management are a perfect example. Adobe Experience Manager does provide rudimentary web analytics data (page impressions), but analytics are not AEM's bread and butter. AEM is designed to help marketers manage content, not measure your customers' engagement with it. If you try to rely on the analytics features of a platform that isn't intended to be an analytics platform, you won't get far.

The lack of functionality in AEM's built-in analytics is a good thing. You wouldn't want your content management system to also be your analytics platform. Technologies that attempt to be everything to everyone often fail to be anything to anyone. Let the analytics platforms worry about measurement, and let the content management platform worry about content. Then share data to unlock insight.

Adobe Experience Manager (and all of the solutions in the Marketing Cloud) are architected with integration in mind. You've already selected a best-of-breed content management system in Adobe Experience Manager. You should integrate it with the best-of-breed solutions for the rest of your digital marketing problems. Adobe provides many of those solutions as parts of the Marketing Cloud, but AEM is built to integrate nicely with non-Adobe products.

We'll cover strategies for integration with many technologies over the next few chapters, but for now web analytics is the topic at hand. Let's look at how AEM can integrate with different web analytics solutions.

A bit about cloud services configurations

This chapter will make reference to a concept called "cloud services configurations." It will be covered in more detail in Chapter 16, but for now, you should understand the basics. Cloud services configurations are a standardized way to integrate AEM with cloud-based technologies. Web analytics platforms are one example of a platform you can integrate with, but they aren't the only one.

Google Analytics integration

Google Analytics is one of the most popular web analytics platforms because it's good for basic web analytics and it's free. Google Analytics gives you all the basic reporting and segmentation options I've discussed so far. It's especially useful if you invest in paid search results through Google AdWords. However, Google Analytics does not always give you absolute real-time information, and the opportunities for special configuration are limited compared to a solution such as Adobe SiteCatalyst.

To integrate Adobe Experience Manager with Google Analytics, you can use the Generic Analytics Snippet cloud services configuration. Your Generic Analytics Snippet configuration has one option: a field where you enter the JavaScript snippet provided by Google Analytics. You then associate this configuration with the top-level page in your site and it is inherited down through all pages.

Generally speaking, you'll apply the same Google Analytics JavaScript snippet to every page in your site (via inheritance). But exceptions to that rule exist. For example, if you are tracking e-commerce transactions, your payment confirmation page will require a slightly modified JavaScript snippet that passes the value of the purchase to the analytics platform. You may also have multiple sites in your single AEM instance that will be tracked using different Google Analytics properties (their term for websites).

In both of these cases, you'll need to create multiple Google Analytics configurations and be diligent about how you apply them to pages. It's not much more complicated, but you do have to monitor more than one configuration. As a general best practice, however, strive to minimize the number of configurations for a single platform.

Other analytics platforms

If you guessed that the Generic Analytics Snippet configuration supports more than just Google Analytics, you guessed correctly. It also supports any other web analytics platform that requires a JavaScript snippet. The Generic Analytics Snippet just injects a bit of JavaScript that you provide into every page where it is appropriate. If you're using an analytics platform other than Adobe SiteCatalyst, and you aren't planning to develop a custom cloud configuration, this is the way to go.

Adobe SiteCatalyst integration

Naturally, the most robust AEM analytics platform integration is available for Adobe's own analytics platform: Adobe SiteCatalyst. This solution, now part of Adobe Analytics, is an industry-leading web analytics platform. It isn't free like Google Analytics, but it can give you much deeper insight into what visitors are doing on your site. Adobe has put a lot of thought into making this integration as configurable as possible so that you don't have to code anything. Furthermore, this integration improves with every new release because Adobe has prioritized the complete interoperability of their digital marketing products.

Adobe Analytics and SiteCatalyst

In Chapter 1 we discussed the five solutions that are part of the Marketing Cloud. One of them is Adobe Analytics, and SiteCatalyst is technically part of that solution. As of the writing of this book, the integration points in AEM (and other sources) still refer to "Adobe SiteCatalyst." However, Adobe will continue to develop the Marketing Cloud solutions and you'll start to see the term SiteCatalyst go away, replaced by Adobe Analytics.

With Adobe SiteCatalyst, as with Google Analytics, you get all the web analytics basics, such as user path, e-commerce, and funnel conversion tracking. SiteCatalyst also includes quite a few default report formats and enables you to design custom reports and executive dashboards. SiteCatalyst also integrates directly with other Adobe cloud offerings to make up a suite of digital analytics tools for marketers to drill deeply into customer behaviors.

For the purposes of this book, the most relevant SiteCatalyst feature is the robust integration offered in the SiteCatalyst cloud services configuration. The SiteCatalyst configuration allows you to:

- Map content and page component properties to SiteCatalyst variables (if your components are built to do so), so that you can base reports on customized data directly related to your website.

- Define multiple report suites for various run modes, so that you can distinguish traffic in your authoring instance from your publish instance.

- Map website personalization properties to SiteCatalyst variables. You can apply the same information used to target specific content to different groups of people in your SiteCatalyst reports. (We'll cover personalization in Chapter 15.)

- Set up tracking for custom events so you can build SiteCatalyst reports accordingly.

- Track analytics about videos that you host and deliver via Adobe Experience Manager. This feature enables you to measure the engagement you are creating with your videos, instead of simply tracking that someone opened a page containing a video.

This list doesn't include everything you can do when integrating AEM and SiteCatalyst, but it illustrates the significant advantages you get by going with this product combination. As a marketer, you can create an incredibly robust system that measures the effectiveness of your website in significant detail. The best part is that it's almost completely configurable without you having to worry about touching JavaScript. That experience alone is quite different from any other analytics implementation you've probably encountered.

I don't recommend you attempt this integration without support from an expert. Your solution implementation partner will help you understand the many aspects of this integration. They will help you identify which parts of it you need and those you don't. The integration workflow can seem a bit overwhelming at first glance, but with the appropriate mentoring, you can manage your own fully measured web experience. As a digital marketer, this stuff should totally geek you out. It does me.

Figure 13.1
AEM-SiteCatalyst
configuration

How do you decide?

You've already got a bunch of options, and we've just barely dipped into Adobe Experience Manager's cloud services configurations. How do you decide which web analytics solution is best for you? If you're having trouble, use the following questions to start the decision process:

- How competent is your organization in terms of analytics? Is it a functionality you have but barely look at? Or does your digital marketing team already use robust website tracking and reporting?

- What are your website's critical success factors, and what data do you need to track that map to those critical success factors? Obviously, you'll want to ensure that tracking is possible with whatever analytics platforms you consider.

- What's the long-term vision? You may be using only basic web analytics now, but do you intend to introduce multivariate testing, dynamic search, or other digital marketing capabilities in the future?

- How invested are you in the full Adobe digital marketing suite? As I continue to impress you with what it offers, how invested do you think you may become?

- What kind of budget do you have for product licensing and the professional services required to get you where you need to be?

- Which paid search and advertising services do you use? Consider how they integrate with the different analytics platform options.

Don't rule out using more than one web analytics platform. In fact, it's fairly common to use more than one. Doing so requires a bit more maintenance, but it allows you to take advantage of the upside of multiple solutions. If you go down that path, just be sure to establish up front which will be your primary point of reference and which features you are specifically planning to use in each platform.

Deciding between web analytics platforms, or any digital marketing platforms, is not easy, nor is it a decision to be taken lightly. If you take anything away from this chapter, please let it be this: Do not wait until the last minute.

Far too often, I see web analytics integration as an afterthought. When that happens, the result can become nothing more than a glorified hit counter that no one looks at. As you are building out requirements for the websites that you'll be hosting on AEM, consider what you'll want to track and why. If you place analytics in the conversation from the beginning, it'll be much easier to answer the previously listed questions and any others that come up during the implementation process. You'll be glad you gave it the appropriate attention early.

Summary

Implementing a system to collect and report web analytics data is one of the most important things you'll do when launching a website. If you don't have the quantifiable data to inform your decisions about your content, you are shooting in the dark.

With that in mind, Adobe Experience Manager includes a robust, extensible framework for integrating with leading web analytics platforms. This framework takes the coding out of web analytics platform integration and converts it into an administrative configuration task. The integration with the analytics platform Adobe SiteCatalyst is especially powerful, and it enables marketers to create a more fully end-to-end tracking solution.

Review questions

1. Explain the term "funnel."

2. Explain e-commerce tracking.

3. What are page impressions?

4. How can you configure AEM to integrate with Google Analytics?

5. What kind of data can you pass into SiteCatalyst using AEM's SiteCatalyst integration?

Review answers

1. On a website, a funnel is a series of steps in a process that ultimately leads to a conversion. The conversion represents an action that the marketing team views as a site visitor goal indicating a successful visit. A good example of a funnel is a checkout process on an e-commerce website. At each step of the checkout process, you probably lose customers who don't complete the process. Understanding where customers leave helps you make changes to reduce the number of people who abandon the process. Funnels do not necessarily have to be linear, but the simplest ones are.

2. E-commerce tracking is when your website passes financial data about site visitor actions into the analytics platform. When the platform understands the financial value of those actions, it can report on how valuable certain reporting aspects are in terms of dollars and cents. For example, you can determine how much actual revenue was generated by users who entered your site via a referral link on a partner's site.

3. Page impressions are an accounting of visits to a webpage. AEM's basic, but built-in, analytics functionality saves page impressions so that content authors can see how popular their pages are. Page impressions must be configured by a system administrator to count page views accurately.

4. You can configure AEM to integrate with Google Analytics by saving your G.A. JavaScript snippet in a Generic Analytics Snippet configuration and then applying that configuration to your webpages via the page properties dialog.

5. AEM's SiteCatalyst configuration allows you to pass data about site user interactions with components, as well as send personalization data into SiteCatalyst. That allows you to generate reports based on the same data you use to strategize a compelling web experience for your customers.

14 MARKETING CAMPAIGN MANAGEMENT

As a digital marketer, you live in a world of "campaigns." You use campaigns to draw customers into a purchase, request a consultation, or complete whatever conversion action you desire. Adobe Experience Manager enables agile marketing practices that allow you to deploy tactical marketing campaigns as needed. But AEM doesn't just allow you to move quickly; it includes a dashboard for managing content-based campaigns.

In this chapter we'll look at:

- What digital marketing campaign management is and why it is important

- What you get with the AEM Marketing Campaign Management (MCM) interface

- How MCM integrates with content targeting and personalization

- How you can use Adobe Experience Manager to perform email marketing

At the end of this chapter, you'll understand how you might manage a digital marketing campaign within AEM. You'll also know why you would choose to do so.

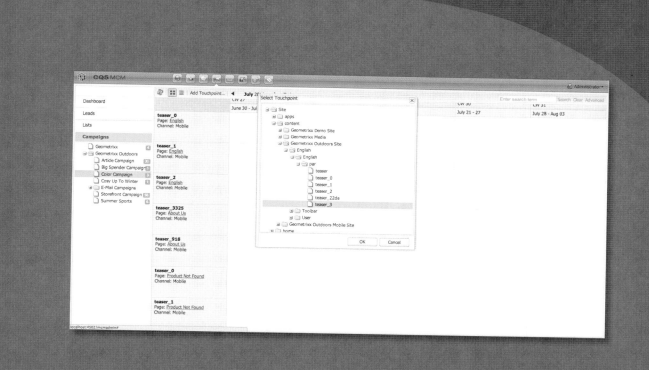

Adding touchpoints with the Marketing Campaign
Management interface

Marketing campaigns

The world of marketing is organized into campaigns. These coordinated marketing efforts go beyond the core brand to accomplish a more specific goal. Typical marketing campaigns are shorter-term endeavors than overall branding, but campaigns can sometimes last for years. They add freshness to a brand and, if executed correctly, create customer engagement through various touchpoints. Marketers have used campaigns for a long time, but as marketing becomes more digital, new challenges and opportunities are surfacing for marketers designing campaigns.

Campaigns and the brand

At a fundamental level, marketing organizations have only two goals: long-term and short-term engagement.

Long-term engagement is about building the brand. It's not about selling products; it's about building a relationship that results in selling products. Do you think many people rush out to buy a Coke every December when they see a new Coca-Cola bear commercial? Probably not. That promotion of the brand is about long-term engagement. The Coke bears represent an American tradition that gives millions a warm, fuzzy feeling every holiday season. That campaign fuels the relationship with the millions who insist that Coke is their beverage of choice. The Coke bears are about long-term engagement, not short-term gain.

On the other hand, short-term engagement is more tactical. It is intended to encourage immediate action, usually a purchase. When your local grocery store puts up a sign advertising "10 percent off all fruit, today only!" they want you inside the store buying fruit. Today. Your grocer isn't specifically doing much to build a long-term relationship with you. In six months, that sale probably won't have any bearing on your choice of grocery stores. The sale and the way it is advertised are intended to get you in the store, right now, to sell you some goods. In this case, it's creating short-term delight for customers that results in an immediate conversion.

Neither of these marketing concepts is better than the other. They are just different parts of the same marketing machine. Some organizations will tend to favor long-term engagement over short-term. Others are the opposite. Brands use campaigns to exploit both of these tactics. The Coke bears are a campaign. The grocery store sale is a campaign. Neither campaign changes the logo, product offering, or distribution channels. They are just temporary tactics that have a goal that varies from campaign to campaign. The collective equity created by an organization's campaigns over time (plus brand fundamentals such as logos and colors) build their brand and its public perception.

Modern marketing campaigns

Marketing campaigns used to be much different than they are today. In the classic "ad men" days of marketing, the choice of channel was limited, as were the means for measuring effectiveness. The opportunities for personalization were scalable only to the relatively few touchpoints you could create with salespeople.

In today's digital marketing world, you have the capability to scale completely personalized marketing to the masses. You also have the tools to measure how effective or ineffective your marketing campaigns are. You can know this in real time, long before marketers are fired for an expensive campaign that flopped. We've shifted from a marketing world controlled by creative minds to one in which the creative minds collaborate with the statistics geeks and programmers to build platforms for effective marketing.

The speed and diversity of marketing has also increased. Today's real-time feedback and highly segmented markets mean that marketing is made up of many smaller, hypertargeted campaigns, as opposed to a few large ones. Campaigns begin and end more quickly than ever before. Marketers can now stop and change directions on a dime. In fact, they are expected to. The faster you can adapt to what customers *really* want (applying strategies backed up by data), the more opportunities you create for marketing success.

Sound challenging? It is. Hundreds of tools are available to assist the digital marketer. Some of these tools are unique. Many overlap in functionality and purpose. It can be dizzying trying to build a strategy in such a fragmented, complicated technology landscape. While Adobe Experience Manager is just one of many digital marketing tools, it's a tool that seeks to end the insanity. AEM, in conjunction with the rest of the Marketing Cloud, can be your go-to platform for managing digital marketing campaigns—the epicenter of your touchpoints.

The Marketing Campaign Management interface

Adobe Experience Manager provides the Marketing Campaign Management (MCM) interface to serve as a hub for managing digital marketing campaigns that impact your web presence. The MCM interface helps you create personalized content based on the segments that you use to define your customers. This chapter will discuss the MCM interface and generally what it can do for you. We'll get into the details of how to personalize content in Chapter 15.

Leads and lists

Sometimes your digital marketing campaigns are designed for an unknown set of customers. In these campaigns, you assume as much information about a site visitor as possible and target content based on those assumptions. Of course, that process is all automated.

But sometimes you'll know who you're trying to target. The simplest example of this is when you are targeting the people who have registered with your website. They've given you their email addresses and some of their information. In so doing, they have voluntarily opted into your brand.

Leads and lists are how you manage these opted-in customers in AEM. A lead is a site visitor to whom you can specifically target an experience. A list is a group of leads that share some specific characteristic. Lists make it easier to manage leads, of which you may have many. Maybe you want to segment your email sign-up leads from your fully registered site users. Maybe you collected a bunch of email leads at a conference. I'm sure you can think of many reasons you might want to segment leads into lists.

Leads are a little more valuable when using MCM to manage email newsletters, because you know who you are targeting without requiring those individuals to do anything. However, once they enter your site from an email link, or enter your site directly as a registered (and logged-in) user, you have the ability to customize their experience. The information about the customer is managed using a browser cookie, which isn't foolproof but helps you keep a consistent context of that user over time.

Managing leads and lists is pretty simple. The MCM interface uses the same basic UI paradigm as the rest of AEM. You can create new leads one at a time by entering basic demographic information such as name, sex, and contact information. You can edit them in the same way. Just like other entities in AEM (such as pages), you'll need to activate the leads and lists to your publish instances so that when a lead visits the site, his user account is available on a public AEM instance. None of this is all that different from the way you manage pages.

Inputting leads one by one is a little tedious, especially if you've generated hundreds of them at a conference by having people sign up for a raffle. You're probably not going to open up AEM at your booth and have people register themselves. You've probably got some other system for that purpose. To allow you to transfer leads from other systems, AEM provides an "import" tool in addition to the one-off lead creation tool. The import tool allows you to ingest leads as a CSV (comma-separated value) file, which is a pretty ubiquitous format for such data. If your leads are stored in a spreadsheet, you can simply copy that data into this tool as a CSV file and pull them all into AEM with one action.

Under the hood, leads and lists are just normal AEM users and groups that don't have permission to access anything but your public websites. Obviously, you won't want to give them any kind of administrative permission, so your site remains secure. By managing your leads as AEM users, you can build components that programmatically interact with those users. You can build customer profile pages using out-of-the-box components or a totally customized solution. Work with your implementation partner to discuss the options you have available when using leads to handle different types of registration.

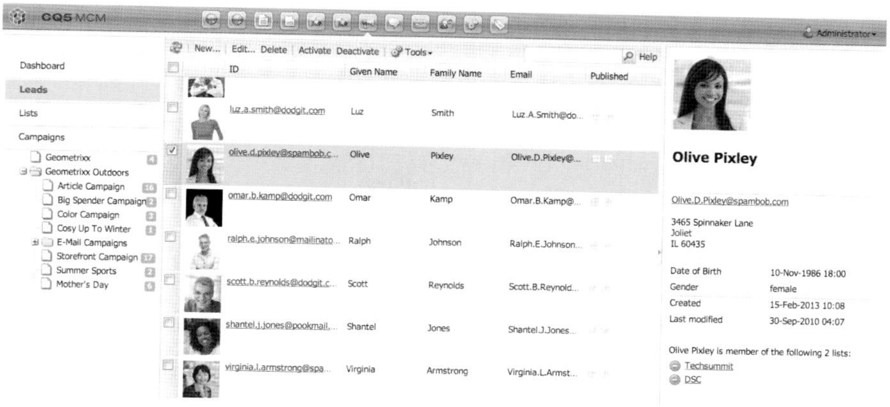

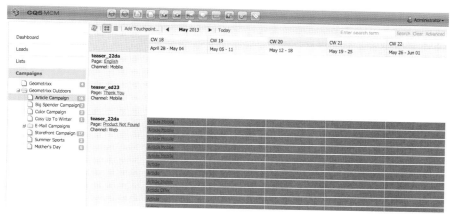

Figure 14.1
Managing leads in MCM

There's an ancillary benefit to the fact that MCM leads and lists are normal AEM users and groups. You can use the MCM "import leads" feature as a bulk (internal) user importing tool. Maybe you need to have many people use AEM but don't have the ability or desire to synchronize those users via LDAP. This feature can be a nice alternative to LDAP sync or an administrator entering each user into the User Management interface. By importing users as a list of leads, you simply move those users into groups with the desired permissions. Remember, don't give permissions to users. Give permissions to groups, and then put the users into those groups.

Campaigns

Campaigns are the scheduled executions of marketing campaigns in AEM, hence the name. In the Campaigns tab, you can create and set up when different types of campaigns will execute. You can also configure them in other ways. As of CQ5.5, this part of the MCM interface was redesigned to resemble a Gantt chart, a tabular scheduling format often used by project managers. Just know that if you are still using CQ5.4 or older, you will see a simpler interface.

Figure 14.2
Campaigns in MCM

Executing campaigns

I already mentioned that the next chapter will be totally dedicated to personalizing content with AEM. For now, you need only understand the basic concepts of managing campaigns using the MCM interface. There is some flexibility in what you can do with MCM and how you can do it, so I'm just going to define some terminology here. This section will also explore how you can use campaigns to perform email marketing—one of the most effective content marketing strategies available to you.

Campaign terminology

When Adobe revamped the MCM interface, they specified some terminology for campaign management. These terms organize your marketing campaigns into a somewhat hierarchical structure so you aren't trying to manage a disordered pile of marketing work.

Brand

A brand is the top-level unit of organization for marketing campaigns. A brand can contain multiple campaigns and is meant to align with the way your actual brands are organized. If you have a straightforward brand and are building a single website for that brand, you'll probably have only one AEM brand in MCM. However, you may have multiple websites. You may have multiple brands represented by the same website. This feature gives you the ability to break up your marketing campaigns accordingly.

The ability to separate brands in this way also makes it easier to grant AEM users the appropriate permissions to do their work. You may not want to give every user permission to work on every brand in AEM. This top level of hierarchy helps you keep those brands separate.

You should also know that the term "brand" did not exist in the platform prior to CQ5.5. Before the brand level was added to AEM/CQ5, campaigns were the top-level entity in MCM. You'll notice that the demo campaigns set up for the Geometrixx "shapes" website don't have a brand, so they all appear to be at the same level. These demos have existed in AEM since before the brand concept was introduced. To remain backward-compatible, it's still technically possible to create campaigns without a brand, but it isn't recommended. Know that an upgrade won't destroy campaigns managed in the old way, but anything you create now should be done in the new way.

Campaign

A campaign is the execution of some digital marketing tactic. It's made up of multiple experiences that are related. Maybe your campaign is to entice Christmas shoppers. Maybe it's to help your organization unload a bunch of overstock. Maybe you're an Adobe solution partner and your campaign corresponds to the upcoming

Adobe Summit. The campaign should be a set of marketing tactics with a goal in mind. Your campaign can run for as long or short a period of time as you want.

Experience

An experience is a specific piece of a site visitor's web experience that is designed to engage him in some way. These are the targeted versions of content that one visitor would see over another. Often experiences are designed to encourage conversion, whatever that means for you. Campaigns will be made up of multiple experiences. For example, in your home page's hero banner, you might display pink mittens to women and black boots to men as part of your Holiday Shopping campaign.

Experiences have a start and an end, and the collective period of active time for each experience in a campaign is what defines the length of that campaign. They also have segments associated with them that determine which experience is most relevant to the target visitors. The Gantt chart view in MCM displays the timeline of experiences per campaign so you can visually inspect how multiple experiences coordinate. Experiences are probably the most important part of Marketing Campaign Management, and we'll talk about them at length in the next chapter.

Touchpoint

A touchpoint is a piece of functionality that will deliver the targeted experience. For example, if you are targeting specific content to users on a landing page, that landing page is the touchpoint. You can think of touchpoints as micro-channels. You've got a multitude of digital marketing channels to work with: social media, digital video, your website, and so on. Then, within your website, you have different touchpoints that will engage different visitors depending on the actions they take to enter your site and the actions they take within it.

Segment

Segments are the unit used to categorize groups of site visitors, whether they are leads or anonymous site visitors. It would be a little silly to create one-off experiences for every lead in your system. Further, it would be impossible to do so for every anonymous person who might visit your site. By grouping visitors into segments, you can make assumptions that a certain group will respond more favorably to experience A and another to experience B. (Don't forget to test your assumptions.) Segments can be as broad as male or female, or as specific as brunette women between the ages of 18 and 30 living in Ohio.

Remember, though, you can only segment effectively using information that you have available. While registered site visitors may give you a lot of information, when targeting anonymous visitors you'll have to infer that information. You can infer quite a lot, but that information won't be entirely accurate. As a general best practice, don't try to get so specific right off the bat that you waste your time trying to make granular assumptions about anonymous visitors. Start with a few broad segmentation groups; then as you test and learn, work your way into a larger number of more specific segments.

Teaser

Prior to AEM 5.6 (the most recent version as of this writing), the vehicle for delivering targeted content was the teaser. A teaser is a set of configured content components that are pulled into the live site depending on the site visitor's segment. For example, you would configure different content for males and females; then the teaser component (which was added to your page) would pull in whichever content matches the site visitor.

Teaser content is created using a configuration page (appropriately called a teaser page), so it's developed outside of the context of the page on which it is displayed. On the teaser page on your site, you can include the teaser component and configure your teaser pages to be used by that component. That way, as long as the experience is active, the teaser component can display the content from your teaser page.

Email marketing

The two major types of marketing campaigns you can execute with Adobe Experience Manager's MCM features are targeted content marketing and email marketing. The next chapter is solely dedicated to the former. I'll cover the latter in this section.

Email marketing is one of the most popular and effective ways to digitally engage with customers and prospective customers. Properly conducted email marketing generally leads to higher conversion rates than other digital marketing techniques. It's unusually effective because it addresses a captive audience that you know at least *something* about, because everyone on your list has opted in voluntarily. Email is in front of people all day every day. That means at any point in the day, a succinct, attractive email can catch a customer's attention long enough to entice her into your site, where your story continues.

What is email marketing?

Email marketing is a form of direct marketing that interacts with customers and potential customers via email. It can be used for general newsletter-type emails designed to maintain an existing relationship with a customer. It can be used as a sales technique to alert potential customers about a great deal or special sale. It can be used to elicit feedback from customers or to ask them to perform some other type of action.

You can perform email marketing very well or very poorly, and a lot of that success comes down to *why* you are sending the email—whether you are delivering relevant content to your email lists. Think about cruising through your own inbox. You give each email *maybe* three seconds to grab your attention before it ends up in the trash. But when you see an email that demonstrates relevance to your immediate needs, you give it more time. It's a critical touchpoint that ideally leads to some action, like a click-through to the website or a request for more information. If your email is not relevant, it may be opened, but it won't be considered.

Email marketing is extremely efficient and inexpensive, so it can be tempting to use it to blast as many people as possible. Many like to call this wishful thinking approach "spray and pray" marketing. It involves sending as many emails as you can to maximize numbers for the low percentage number of people who typically convert. The better approach to email marketing (and all marketing, for that matter) is to target smaller segments of people by delivering extremely relevant content. Remember, you cannot be everything to everyone.

This targeted approach to marketing may sound familiar. It is! We've talked about it in this book repeatedly because it's exactly what Adobe Experience Manager is designed to help you accomplish. AEM's email marketing features are another tool for enabling you to engage with specific segments of your customer pool. AEM is not primarily an email marketing platform, so if you're used to using one of those, you may miss many of its bells and whistles. But AEM has its own bells and whistles—such as in-context content authoring—that make it an interesting addition to your email marketing toolbox.

Let's go over two approaches to email marketing in Adobe Experience Manager. The first approach is using AEM's admittedly rudimentary email tools. Their advantage, though, is that you can use them to create marketing emails using the familiar AEM authoring paradigm. Then, we'll look at another approach in which you integrate AEM with ExactTarget, a powerful inbound marketing tool that includes all those email marketing goodies.

Email marketing with AEM

Adobe Experience Manager allows you to author emails and send them to lists of leads or segments of leads. Within AEM, the feature is often called "Newsletters," but you are by no means restricted to sending news content. Email marketing is implemented as an "experience," so it's completely tied into the Marketing Campaign Management features for targeting web content. That makes sense, because your web content campaigns are likely to correspond to email *and* web content at the same time. AEM brings its in-context authoring into the mix, allowing you to author emails as they will appear in the recipients' inboxes. You can do some quick and dirty email marketing with AEM on its own, but it is not a full-featured email marketing platform.

Creating and authoring emails

You can create a new email in the MCM interface by selecting the campaign that email will be part of and creating a new experience from an email template. As with webpages, an email template is not available out of the box. You need to work with your implementation team to define the requirements for the email templates you'll need. You can probably get away with creating one email template per brand unless you are doing some serious email marketing (and if so, you should probably be using a more specialized tool anyway).

Once you've created your email (experience) with your email template, you're back in the familiar AEM authoring experience with access to the Sidekick, paragraph systems, and dialogs. But this authoring experience is a little different because it puts you in the shoes of the email recipient. Just as with the mobile module, the MCM email marketing feature incorporates a set of inboxes from which you can edit and view your emails. This way you'll know exactly how your email will look when delivered by email services such as Gmail or received into applications such as Outlook.

Figure 14.3
In-context email authoring

The general experience of authoring emails is about the same as authoring pages, but you should keep a few things in mind:

- You won't have the same opportunities to track users with cookies (which is how AEM personalization works on websites).

- Email writing is different from web writing. Don't just email out a webpage.

- Your content should be more succinct and more specific to one subject.

- SEO isn't really a concern anymore, since you can't find emails in Google.

- Metadata and tagging is only necessary for internal organization.

- Keep your pages simple. Your implementation team should help you through the specific limitations with HTML emails.

All in all, you just need to remember that, though the authoring experience is mostly the same, the content you are authoring serves a much different purpose than web content. Put yourself into an inbox state of mind and think about what would draw you in and what would make you instantly delete an email.

Sending emails

Authored emails don't do much good unless you can distribute them to your recipients. Adobe Experience Manager can send out your emails for you if you've had an administrator configure the necessary settings. This is where AEM is less functional compared to a dedicated email marketing platform. The "sending it out" part is pretty much just that. You have to rely on your own facilities for implementing analytics or making sure your email is not trapped as spam.

When you're ready to send an email, the first thing you should do is open the settings to make sure the necessary metadata is set. You'll want to specify the basics, such as the return email address and the subject. This is also where you decide what list the email will be sent to by default, though you can specify other addresses when you send it out. You can also pick the segments you want the email to target if you want to be more specific than delivering to a list. For example, if you send a "Happy Independence Day" email, you probably only want to send it to recipients who live in the United States.

After your email properties are set, you should execute a test to make sure that the email will be delivered in the way you expect. You can enter a single email address to receive the test email. When you send the test email, you'll want to pay attention to whether it makes it through your spam filter (though all spam filters are different); how quickly or slowly it loads; and of course, how it looks.

When you are happy with your email, you can send it out. You select the list to which the email will be sent and off it goes. You have the choice of sending it out from within the email itself, or in the "Lists" screen where you can send the email to a particular list. You'll likely have some bounced emails because no email list is 100 percent accurate or up-to-date. Your system administrator also can set up an importer that polls your email system for invalid email responses. That way you can always see how many of your emails are rejected.

Figure 14.4
Email settings

Integrating with ExactTarget

ExactTarget is a full-featured marketing automation platform, and one of the things it does is email marketing. It's not an Adobe product, but Adobe Experience Manager includes built-in integration with the ExactTarget platform. This integration allows you to take advantage of AEM authoring and content targeting, while using an email platform that can handle spam considerations, bounced emails, and email list analytics much better than AEM's. This integration lets you have your cake *and* eat it.

The ExactTarget integration is set up as a cloud service configuration, just the way web analytics integration is set up. ExactTarget is another example of a cloud-based SaaS platform. Once that configuration is completed, you can add components that are specific to ExactTarget. Some are required per ExactTarget standards, and others, like the email analytics functionality, are highly recommended. These features that would otherwise be added via ExactTarget have been converted into AEM content components so that the email authoring can remain in AEM.

Your process for sending out emails is a little different when integrating with Exact-Target. Instead of specifying to send the email, you tell AEM to "publish" the email to ExactTarget. It pushes email to the ExactTarget system and links you to it directly (which takes you out of AEM). From that point, the email is managed as any other email in ExactTarget. If you want to update the email and republish from AEM, you can do that as well.

ExactTarget integration is a great option if you plan to do some serious email marketing but still want to use Adobe Experience Manager to create the emails. The drawback is that it requires you to purchase and implement two completely different platforms. Since this integration requires some additional planning to establish your business processes, I wouldn't casually jump into it. If it's something you want to consider, work with your solution implementation provider to do it right.

Summary

The Marketing Campaign Management module, specifically the MCM interface, is designed as a hub for managing web content campaigns. You can establish leads (specific people you'll target) and lists (groups of leads) to which you can target campaigns or send newsletters. Marketing Campaign Management is extremely integrated with the content personalization and targeting features that will be discussed in Chapter 15. For now, know that the MCM will be the place that you can manage and see a holistic view of the targeting campaigns that you establish.

Review questions

1. What are leads and lists?

2. Why does the term "brands" have special meaning in MCM?

3. What is a segment?

4. What is the main advantage to integrating with ExactTarget?

Review answers

1. Leads are people who have registered with your website or opted into an email list. Lists are groups of leads, used to categorize where leads came from.

2. Brands are the top-level entity in Marketing Campaign Management. They are made up of multiple campaigns, which are made of multiple experiences implemented via various touchpoints. Generally you'll want AEM brands to align with the way your organization segregates its own brands. In many cases, it makes sense to use just one brand for each of your websites.

3. A segment is a grouping of site visitors based on demographic information. It is used to target campaigns to specific people you want to convert.

4. AEM can send out emails on its own, if configured to do so, but it is not a full-featured email marketing platform. By integrating with ExactTarget, which contains a rich set of email marketing functions, marketers are able to take advantage of AEM's authoring capabilities to create emails and then deliver them using ExactTarget.

15

DYNAMIC CONTENT

One of the most powerful things you can do with Adobe Experience Manager is to create dynamic content. It allows you to personalize content for specific segments of site visitors or to test variations of content to optimize the site's ability to lead visitors toward conversion.

This chapter will explain the following topics:

- The differences between dynamic and static content

- The business reasons for implementing dynamic content strategies

- How you can use dynamic content to personalize visitors' web experiences

- How to implement multiple versions of content and test which versions are most effective

- The basics of integrating AEM with Adobe Test&Target

At a high level, this chapter will inform you about two different but related concepts in AEM: personalization and optimization via dynamic content. You should then be able to talk through why you would or would not implement dynamic content and the basics of how to accomplish it.

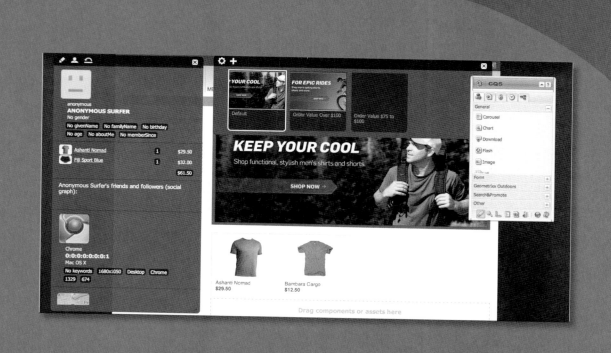

Building a dynamic content experience

Dynamic and static content

One of the fundamental differences between a web experience management platform and a web content management platform is the ability to deliver dynamic content. The WCM makes it easy to create and update pages, but those pages are generally static. They have one state. We've already discussed why single-state pages fall short in creating a rich web experience. You know that every customer is different. You know that one web experience will not be the optimal way to accomplish your digital marketing goals.

Let's go back to the hypothetical company Game Changers Sporting Goods and look at the kinds of customers who might visit that site:

- A woman in her early twenties looking to build a new wardrobe for her new running hobby

- A man in his forties seeking hockey equipment for his son

- A man looking to buy a new winter jacket for snowboarding

- A woman in her thirties with three children, looking for good deals on children's athletic clothes for the upcoming soccer season

Remember, Game Changers was our hypothetical sporting goods company. Any of these customer personas is realistic, and you could probably come up with 100 more.

Personalizing with dynamic content

Each one of these hypothetical customers shares a common goal: they are looking at Game Changers Sporting Goods to buy a product on the website. A website like this may get hundreds of thousands of visitors every day, and only a small percentage of them are likely to convert into customers. All four of these hypothetical customers are potential customers, because they've entered a site that *could* meet their needs. Your job as a marketer (once you've got them to the site) is to get them to convert—to buy.

To turn these mildly interested site visitors into purchasing customers, you need to show them content that piques their interest. If these customers were to enter the site on a landing page that was all about a big sale on golf equipment, they would probably immediately leave. Some of these customers *may* be interested in golf equipment eventually, but at the moment, the website doesn't seem to offer what they're seeking. On the other hand, if the woman looking to buy her children clothes enters a landing page advertising a sale on their athletic clothes, you've got a winner. She's going to click to browse those clothes that are on special.

There are many strategies for connecting the right people to the right content and converting those people into customers. Your paid search keywords, social media posts, and so on should pull people into relevant landing pages. Your internal site search should make it easy for people to find the information they are looking for—again, to connect the right people to the right content. These strategies can be effective and should be utilized. The fundamental challenge with these strategies is that you have to coax your site visitors to the right content. You somehow have to get them to find the right page.

Instead of just hoping you could coax your site visitors to the content that will turn them into customers, what if your content could transform itself right there? What if you could bring the relevant content to them, instead of bringing them to the relevant content? Even better, what if you were able to employ *both* strategies? Dynamically altering your content in this way based on what you can deduce about the site visitor is called personalization.

Content that is personalized can change depending on who is viewing it. The idea is that you always want to present the most relevant content possible. If you show the shopping snowboarder a pearl necklace, he'll probably move on. If you show him a new snowboarding jacket that's 25% off this weekend, you've got his attention. But you don't want to show that jacket to the woman looking for running equipment. She'll want to see running shorts and shoes. If your web content is static, you have to choose one item for the page, or create two pages and hope the right person gets to the right page. If you have dynamic content, you can personalize one page or banner so that it shows the customer exactly what they want.

Optimizing with dynamic content

You've implemented some tactics to make sure that the snowboarder gets to the page about snowboarding attire. You've personalized banners that get him to click to the page. You've set up your paid Google search keyword for "snowboarding jackets" to direct customers to the same page. You feel that you've done all you can (for now) to get the snowboarders to the snowboarding attire content. But only 3% of your visitors convert into customers, and you want to increase that number. You believe you are losing potential customers, but you're not sure why.

On a single page, so many things can affect whether a site visitor turns into a customer. One group of people don't see the "Buy Now" button. Another group doesn't like the photo of the snowboarder on the webpage because he's wearing a green jacket. Another group wasn't all that interested in the copy that described the jacket. All of these groups moved on to other pages in your site or (worse) other sites because, even though they found the relevant page, it still wasn't quite right.

As a marketer this should (and probably does) frustrate you. Even though the right person found the right page, it still didn't convert him into a customer. Why didn't he buy that snowboarding jacket? Why did he buy almost the same jacket from a competitor 15 minutes later (not that you would know that)? Wouldn't it be great if every time the right person left the right page he or she would leave a note that explains why?

Potential customers don't have time to volunteer that information. In fact, most customers would be very put off if you asked them to account for themselves. It just isn't possible to have a list of all the things that didn't work on your webpage, but it is possible to figure out which of multiple different page layouts, button colors, or paragraphs of copy convinced more people to convert. You'll never know the perfect button color, but you can know that red is more effective than blue. And by continuously testing which of two or more options works best, you can continue to hone in on a better and better content experience. It's called content testing or content optimization.

Content optimization performed by A/B or multivariate testing (we'll go over the terms later) is the other big advantage to delivering dynamic content. If you have just one static webpage, you have no opportunity to create different versions of that content to determine which is optimal. You have to run one version for a set amount of time, and then run the other for the same amount of time. Then you have to hope that no external variables affected your test results because you tested each page at a different time. It *can* work (kind of), but it's a less than ideal way to test your content.

If you can deliver dynamic content, you can randomly show every site visitor a different version. Then, over the same period of time, you can determine that the 33% of visitors who saw version A converted 1% of the time, those who saw version B converted 4% of the time, and those who saw version C converted 6% of the time. Guess which one is best? If your platform can deliver dynamic content, you can create valid tests that automatically promote the optimal content so that you can maximize conversions.

This is getting complicated!

It sure is getting complicated! But that's the nature of modern digital marketing. Everyone can deliver static content. Maybe you can write better copy, perform better search engine marketing, or run a better Facebook page. But that will only get you so far. If you've got the right person leaving the right page without making a purchase, you may be leaving money on the table. If your "right" visitors are only converting 1% of the time, you are leaving a *lot* of money on the table.

Through the rest of this chapter, you may feel overwhelmed with information. It's a big, important topic. The strategy involved with delivering dynamic content to personalize and optimize your website could fill a book all by itself. You're not going to finish this chapter and be an expert on A/B testing. However, you should be able to understand how you can start to accomplish these strategies in Adobe Experience Manager. AEM includes a robust framework for handling these marketing strategies, and that framework is part of why AEM is such a powerful platform. Start with the content in this chapter, and then work with your solution implementation partner to derive a strategy for using dynamic content targeted to your specific customer segments.

Content personalization

Think about a time when you've gone to a website and found *exactly* what you were looking for. You went to the Internet with a purpose. For example, you're going to build a dog house. You found a blog post on the website of a DIY company with well-written, feasible directions for doing so. From that blog post, you were enticed via a small banner (not an advertisement, just a small internal banner) to visit a page advertising a sale on a kit of parts you need to build the dog house you just read about. You bought all the necessary parts in one easy transaction for 10% off, and were informed that the parts would be ready for pickup at your local store.

It was perfect. It was almost as if the company knew what you were looking for, even though you gave no indication what that was. But the thing is, you did tell them what you were looking for. You just didn't realize it.

The company was able to use their digital context clues to make an educated guess about your immediate interest in their website. They knew that you were interested in a dog house project in *some* way because you were reading a blog post about how to build one. They also knew that you were within 15 minutes of one of their stores because they were able to geolocate your computer's IP address. Their web content (actually, experience) management system mathematically determined that the most relevant banner to show you was the one about the sale on the dog house kit. You never knew it, but there were 10 other versions of the same banner that advertised different items.

When another visitor views a different post about how to seed a lawn and they view it from a location that is far away from any of the company's local stores, she is given a different banner—perhaps one discussing a special on grass seed if you order online. Or maybe, because that customer purchased a power drill from this exact website three months prior, the banner contained content about a new lithium battery.

Why would you personalize?

In the scenario we just discussed, you are personalizing content to encourage the sale of products. You determined what the site visitor's interests were and you showed her products that were likely to pique that interest. But there are other reasons you would consider personalizing content.

Cross-selling and upselling

The obvious example of why you would use personalized content is to cross-sell and upsell additional products. You know that a customer has mittens in her shopping cart. You can deduce that she may be interested in the matching hat. Knowing what content a site visitor has consumed or (even better) which products she's already partially committed to buying, you can encourage her to look at related products. The dog house example I just gave would qualify. The Geometrixx Outdoors demo site that is included with Adobe Experience Manager is set up for just this kind of personalization. You can use it to experiment with some of this functionality.

Increasing site engagement

If your website's product *is* your content, website engagement is extremely important. One way to measure engagement is by tracking the "average time on site." The best way to increase the time your visitors spend on your site is to get them good content. If someone visits your site and the first page he views doesn't resonate, he'll spend a few seconds. If he reads one article, then another, and then browses products, he may spend minutes or even hours on the site. You can facilitate this engagement using personalization. Pull your site visitors into content that is specifically relevant to them.

Personalized content is why Facebook's average time on site is so ridiculously high, for example. Facebook is literally a hub for completely personalized content. You tell Facebook the movies, television shows, or anything else you like. You tell Facebook who your friends are (who create most of the content). You tell Facebook where you live and how old you are. Every single piece of content or advertisement on Facebook is completely tailored to you. Thus, Facebook's average time on site is the stuff of legends. You probably aren't going to be like Facebook. But by using content personalization, you can apply the same basic approach to increase the customer engagement you create with your website.

Delivering context-sensitive information

You can't be everything to everyone, so your content can't be relevant to everyone. If you sell dog food and toys, your content won't be relevant to someone who owns a cat. If your content is about how to implement SEO best practices, it won't be relevant to someone looking for home DIY tips. Relevance is relative. If you try to deliver one content experience to everyone, you have to do so knowing that most people who view it are probably not going to find it relevant. But if you personalize your content based on the context of each user's site visit, you significantly increase the chance that they will find it relevant.

Context is different for everyone, for every site visit, for every website. The context could be the site visitor's sex or age. It could be her geographic location. Those are easy to figure out, especially if you have a site for which people register (as is often

Your site visitor may be "anonymous," in which case the client context will not have much information. However, it'll still resolve which browser he is using, how big his screen is, and where he is located.

If your site has authenticated users, you can simulate their experience. In that case, the client context will contain quite a bit more information—virtually any information they volunteered when registering. With registered users, you can start targeting based on customer specifics.

You probably won't want to enable content authors to test targeted content using *real* registered site visitors. It would be difficult to dig through thousands of registered users to find the archetypes you're looking for. Instead, create a set of fake users that align with the basic personas you've identified as your prototypical customers. Targeted content or not, building personas is an important fundamental marketing tactic that you should have already employed. You can use those personas to create users that you will switch between when authoring dynamic content. Ideally you should create users that allow you to test every combination of campaigns and experiences you may want to implement. Needless to say, you'll need to plan this out in advance.

Figure 15.1
The client context

If you get very granular with your targeting, you'll have quite a few users to remember. That can quickly get confusing. Therefore, the client context allows you to change specific properties about a user on the fly. For example, you can drag a pin to a different location on the map to simulate the user visiting your site from a different geographic location. You can change the user's interests or browser. Doing so allows you to test how your experiences react to specific aspects of your site visitor. As you get better at content targeting, you'll use this strategy more than simply switching between the multiple test users that represent your marketing personas.

The client context is completely customizable, and you don't necessarily need a programmer to customize it. In the Tools interface, you'll find a configuration page where you can create and author custom client contexts. It uses the same drag and drop authoring paradigm as page authoring. Each piece of the client context is just a component, specifically designed to be used in the client context. Without any programming, you can add or delete the contexts available out of the box. This interface also allows you to configure client contexts for different sites or parts of your site.

The out-of-the-box client context components get you pretty far, but it's possible that you may have other ideas. You can have your implementation team build custom client context components that expose concepts specific to your organization for content targeting. You may choose to do this if you use some kind of external CRM system to manage your visitor registrations. You also may want to do this if you have a custom service for geolocation. Adobe specifically designed the client context to be customizable in this fashion, so your solution implementation team should be able to make whatever reasonable customizations you need.

Social network login

In previous chapters, we've explored AEM's social networking integration, including its ability to allow site visitors to register and log in using their social network accounts. One of the benefits to using this approach for user registration is that AEM uses those visitors' social networking data to enable you to personalize content. On social networks like Facebook, people volunteer tons of information about their own interests. You can use that information to show them dynamic content that will optimize their web experience.

The social networking integration with AEM personalization works just like any other customization to the client context. You can define visitor segments based on information shared by their social network, just as you would geolocation, for instance. Then you can target experiences for them. The result is a web experience specifically tailored to the information volunteered by the site visitor. Without social networking integration, you are making educated guesses about the site visitor. With the integration, you don't have to guess because they tell you.

Sounds great, right!? The tricky part is getting site visitors to volunteer their social network account information by logging in with Facebook. There are two parts to the solution. First, you need to give a reason to create an account and log in. Do you offer some kind of rewards program? Can you get personalized service online? You need to give each person a reason to create an account. Simply asking them to do so for no reason will probably get you very few registrations. Without visitors volunteering to sign up and giving you information about themselves, you're once again guessing about them based on limited information.

Once you've convinced visitors that it's worthwhile to create an account, you have to convince them to do so using their social network account. If you want their Facebook information, you should probably only offer them that option while also providing a normal sign-up. According to the policy of most social networks, this means you will have to request the user's permission to use their data. Some people can be skeptical of these kinds of requests and will be deterred. You have to make sure the user feels safe about providing that information, and then you *must not* abuse it. It may be a good idea to provide a policy statement describing how you will use their data.

Scene7 template components

In Chapter 4, you learned that Scene7 is a technology that allows you to take your media files to the next level. One of its capabilities is on-the-fly image and Flash file creation, which are enabled in templates (which are not the same as page templates in AEM). These media files take in data as a part of the request, and the Scene7 engine outputs a media file that is customized to those request parameters.

You can use Scene7 template components within your AEM pages. The author can configure the data that is sent to Scene7 for dynamic file creation via the component's dialog. You can use those dynamic images as targeted content by passing in different data for different segments of site visitors.

Let's say you have a big image on your home page that has a welcome message (which is part of the image, and not web text placed on top of it). The author can open the dialog for that Scene7 image component and enter the text as an authorable property. Scene7 will dynamically change the image to include the new text.

This feature becomes even more powerful when you use it for personalization. Dynamic media files make for an uncommonly engaging experience. Imagine the welcome image we just discussed. What if you could show every one of your registered users Flash video that said "Welcome Ryan!" (or their name)? Scene7 template components combined with the other personalization tools at your disposal enable you to do so.

Teasers

A teaser is the classic way to perform content targeting in AEM (and its precursor, CQ5). If you've been working with AEM for a while, you may be familiar with the feature. Teasers are intended to allow authors to create pieces of content that pull site visitors to content that matches their interests. Often, that means an internal banner ad. But teasers can be used for any kind of content targeting. They don't have to be used for internal advertising.

Teasers have three parts: the teaser component, the teaser page, and segments. The teaser component is added to or automatically included in a page component. It serves as a placeholder for dynamic content. It's also where you can specify some strategies for how the teaser will decide which content it displays. The content display options are defined in teaser pages. A teaser page is a configuration page with one parsys, in which you build out a set of content that could be delivered through a teaser component. Segments are administrator-defined user characteristics that are used for targeting ("men over 30," for instance). The teaser component executes its logic to determine from which teaser page it will show content, using the selected strategy to target a segment of users.

Using teasers has positives and negatives. On one hand, the teaser requires you to switch authoring contexts. You don't actually author the "teased" content within the page it will be displayed. You have to switch back and forth while you are testing teaser content, and that process can be cumbersome. On the other hand, you can use teasers to author "teased" content without knowing (or caring) where it will be displayed. It's possible that the content authored in teaser components could show up in any number of places on your site. In this case, it's convenient that you have to create it only once.

The other advantage to using a teaser is that your targeted content can include multiple components. The alternative to a teaser is a targeted component, which has to be configured one at a time per page. The teaser page contains a parsys, meaning you could effectively build out as many content components as you want for "teased" content. Maybe this suits your needs. Maybe it's not necessary. It all depends on your individual circumstances.

Targeted components

The newer way to target content, and an alternative to using a teaser, is the targeted component. As long as your components are built appropriately (just make sure the implementation team is on it), you can right-click any content component on a page and make it "targeted." This allows you to define different experiences for that single component based on whatever campaign you have active in the client context. This personalization feature allows you to create dynamic content without leaving the context of your page and without defining a separate entity somewhere else.

Let's say your organization is a headhunting firm that covers most of the United States. You author a paragraph of copy on your home page intended to draw potential customers further into your site. You could show one paragraph of text to everyone, or you could target that content to visitors in different parts of the U.S. After all, investment bankers seeking a job in Manhattan are different than graphic designers looking for work in San Francisco.

To target the text component that contains this introductory paragraph, you simply right-click it and select Target. You never leave the page. You don't have to create any configuration pages (unless you want to wire up to Adobe Test&Target). The entire personalization stays within the same context that you used to author the page. This is quite different from targeting with teasers.

When you decide to target a component (and test your targeting), you'll select a current campaign in the client context. The targeting you configure will then be applied as part of that campaign. You tell AEM to convert your component into a targeted component (by selecting Target), and then you can define multiple "experiences" for the various segments related to that campaign. The complexity of your experiences is limited to what the component lets you configure in its dialog. Basically, you are just providing different configurations for different segments of site visitors. These experiences can range from different copy to a different image or a different layout.

During the implementation process, you should have targeting in mind. If you know you'll want to make one of your components targeted, think through all the possible configuration options necessary to do so. That way your implementation team can define and implement those requirements up front. Otherwise, you'll go in to target a component and find out it doesn't have what you need, and then you'll have to wait until your team can implement the change. Knowing up front what you'll need saves time and money.

Figure 15.2
Configuring multiple experiences

There is one exception to the one-off nature of targeted components. AEM provides a component called the target component (not target*ed* component). It acts as a container for multiple components to be targeted in a single experience. It's useful if you are trying to target an AEM form, for instance, which consists of multiple form components. Effectively, the single component that is targeted is the target component and the content within it makes up each experience. This is another alternative to the Teaser.

Targeted components (and the target component) represent the new paradigm for authoring dynamic content in AEM. As of AEM 5.6, you should favor these features over predecessors like the Teaser. Adobe will continue to update these features via service packs and major version updates. The old features still function and remain valid approaches. But if you are starting fresh, go with targeted components for your dynamic content implementation.

Personalization with Test&Target

Adobe Test&Target, which is now part of the solution called Adobe Target, is a platform for configuring and measuring dynamic content within applications. Traditionally, you build your dynamic content experiences inside Test&Target and they are injected into your web application via containers called *MBoxes* (more on that later). But with AEM's direct integration into Test&Target, you can author the personalized content where the authoring belongs.

AEM's personalization features (targeted components especially) are designed to be used in conjunction with Test&Target. By wiring up your campaign to Test&Target using a special but straightforward configuration, you can take advantage of that platform's measurement capabilities. It allows you to understand the effectiveness of your dynamic content authoring. It also helps you plan for additional campaigns. AEM and Test&Target unlocks insights about how your customers react to your dynamic content.

Technically, you don't *have* to wire up your content personalization to Test&Target. You could use an alternative configuration called *client-side rules* that targets content without interfacing with Test&Target. You'll have dynamic content, but you won't easily be able to measure it. If you cannot measure the effectiveness of the personalized content you create, you are just firing in the dark. We'll discuss shortly how you can use a web analytics platform for measurement, but that method is difficult and limited. Test&Target is specifically designed for tracking dynamic content to help you optimize conversions. I highly recommend you use it if you will be implementing a personalization strategy.

Content testing

As we discussed in Chapter 13, measuring the effectiveness of your content, benchmarked against your goals, is an important aspect of effective digital marketing. If you aren't measuring, you are guessing. The technology available to marketers makes it possible to quantify how well or poorly your content is performing its intended function. How could that not get you excited?

I use the term "content testing" to describe a subset of the web analytics domain, more commonly called A/B or multivariate testing. Each of these represents a way to create multiple versions of your content and automatically test which one is more effective. This is not the same thing as personalization, because we aren't considering the user's context. However, I view this as a related concept, because performing content testing implies that you will be presenting dynamic content. This section will explore how AEM and Adobe Test&Target enable you to test the effectiveness of your web content.

Personalization vs. testing

When preparing this book, I had an internal debate about whether the content targeting material belonged in the chapter about dynamic content or the chapter about web analytics. The former won, but it was a photo finish. The key function of content testing is the ability to deliver different versions of content so that you can test which one is best. This means that you are delivering dynamic content, but it does not mean that you are personalizing.

The big difference between personalization and content testing is the reason for making content dynamic. With personalization, you adapt your content to what you know or deduce about your site visitor's context. The goal is to deliver a locally optimized web experience.

On the other hand, content testing is about randomly splitting *all* site visitor traffic across however many versions are part of your test. You establish a conversion goal (for example, joining an email list), and then count how many times each version of the content led to a conversion. You can assume the version that led to the most conversions was the best. Then you can come up with new alternatives to test against.

You can combine the two strategies to take advantages of both. You'd have to establish multiple versions of content per visitor segment to test how effective your content is per segmented variation. If this sounds confusing, it's because it probably will be. You will want to get very good at personalization and testing separately before you combine them. Otherwise, you run the risk of creating a heap of moving parts that cannot be measured. Remember, if you can't measure what you are doing, it's just a waste of time. You'll just be making guesses, instead of decisions based on data analysis.

Types of content testing

Content testing involves randomly displaying two or more variations of content, then counting which version leads to the most conversions. The idea is to isolate which components, colors, text, and so on influence site visitors to convert and (just as importantly) which elements don't. There are two basic strategies for content testing—A/B testing and multivariate testing, which are often confused because they are similar but not quite the same thing. Though the difference may seem subtle, the analysis involved with each is quite different.

A/B testing

When you run an A/B test, you hypothesize how one element will affect conversion. Let's say, you're testing the color of a "Click Here" button. It's currently gray, but you think a red button would lead to more conversions. Leaving all other elements constant (that's important), you create an alternative red version of the button. 50% of your traffic randomly sees the gray button and the other 50% sees the red. Then you measure if there's a statistically significant difference in the number of conversions among the visitors that saw each button.

You changed only one thing, so you can attribute any changes in conversion rate to that change. If you see roughly the same conversion rate for both buttons, you can deduce that the color of the button may not affect conversion. You could test other colors to conclusively determine whether color affects conversion. However, if you saw a significant increase in conversion rate for those who saw the red button, you can deduce that the red button is more effective and you can display that color to everyone. Or if the red button created a drop in conversion, you would know that the gray button is more effective.

There are a couple things to note about A/B testing. First, you don't have to limit yourself to two variations. Strictly speaking, you could be doing an A/B/C or A/B/C/D test for three or four variations, but this testing technique is generally just called A/B. For example, you could test your gray button, a red one, a blue one, and a green one. But if you change the button text from "Click Here" to "Click Me" in one of your tests, you've changed two variables (color and text). That's multivariate testing.

The other thing to note is that the margin that determines whether one variation has won will vary by test. In some cases a 1% increase in conversions may be significant enough to determine a winner. In other cases, it may be 10%. That margin is dependent on your specific circumstances. An expert in web analysis should be able to help you establish what that margin should be.

Multivariate testing

Multivariate testing (MVT) is similar to A/B testing, but it has one fundamental difference: the number of elements you can change (variables) will be more than one. Multivariate testing is a more advanced version of A/B testing. It allows you to be more creative and flexible with your testing, but it also requires more advanced data analysis to derive insight from your test results. The desired outcome for MVT is the same as with A/B testing: figure out what content facilitates the highest conversion rate.

Let's go back to the "Click Here" button. I mentioned that if you were to change the text of the button to "Click Me" in one of your variations, it no longer qualified as an A/B test. That's because you changed two variables (color and text), thereby making this a multivariate test. Now let's assume your green button with the new "Click Me" text drove the highest conversion rate of all variations. You could conclude that green is the optimal color. Or is it? Maybe the new text drove the higher conversion. Perhaps you should run another test.

Even in this *extremely* simple example, you can see how analyzing the results of a multivariate test are quite different from analyzing A/B tests. When you have multiple variables, you need to build statistical models that enable you to figure out which of those variables actually made a difference, without isolating the variables into A/B tests (though that's one valid approach). Challenges like this are why the data scientist is one of the hottest jobs in the market.

To work through these questions, you need someone who understands web analytics and proper statistical analysis. Statistics can be tricky, because the right answer is often counterintuitive. Don't tackle this without an expert adviser.

So which one is it?

Are you performing multivariate or A/B testing? The short answer is that it doesn't matter. As I explained, the approaches are similar and effectively used for the same goal. Trying to figure out if you are doing a multivariate or an A/B test is just a semantic argument. When it comes down to it, semantics don't make you money.

Our simple button example makes it easy to see the difference between A/B and multivariate testing. When testing gets more complex, however, it's not so straightforward.

Let's say you've set aside an area on your webpage for dynamic content and you want to test that content. In one variation, you put a button and some copy. In another, you put different copy and a clickable image. On one hand, you could make the argument that each variation had multiple elements that were different (multivariate testing). On the other hand, you could consider each variation of the entire page a single difference, knowing that you wouldn't know how the image specifically affected conversions. But instead you'll just worry about how each entire variation affected conversion. That's more like an A/B test. Confusing, right?

As long as you understand *what* you are changing and how it affected your conversion rate, you should be in good shape. Know that if you change multiple variables, additional analysis is required to determine which one specifically made the difference. Also know that it may not matter, because you've determined that one set of variables worked better than another. How detailed you get with this depends on your circumstances and, frankly, your level of curiosity.

AEM testing tools

Adobe Experience Manager and its peripheral technologies provide the tools you'll need to effectively test the content you create. It's an important part of content management, because it replaces guessing with analysis. AEM also includes built-in integration with Adobe Test&Target, a Marketing Cloud application specifically intended for content testing. Let's look at the tools that AEM offers.

MVT component

The simplest tool that AEM has for content testing is the MVT component. This component is actually left over from before Adobe acquired Day Software and built AEM (formerly CQ5) into the Marketing Cloud technology stack. This basic component allows you to create variations of linked images and test which was most effective. The component reports statistics about which variation was clicked most. That "link" would be your conversion.

The MVT component is okay for *really* basic content testing, but it won't get you far. For starters, it doesn't automatically promote the winner after it is statistically determined, as many content testing tools can. It also doesn't let you create whatever variations you want to test. You are limited to selecting variations of images. The

MVT component requires that you set up and use AEM page impressions, because without customization, it doesn't integrate into your web analytics platform. On one hand, it's nice that conversions are counted as page impressions, because it puts the results right in front of the content author. On the other hand, it isolates everything from the rest of your data.

I don't generally recommend that clients use the MVT component, but sometimes it is appropriate to do so. If your team is new to content testing, this component is a nice way to perform *very* rudimentary testing and get your feet wet. Instead of burying your team in some kind of analytics integration that adds a whole extra layer of complexity, you can experiment with using only this component. The data the component gives you is easy to understand and is shown within the component's dialog. It's easy to use. But when your team gets comfortable with content testing, the MVT component will quickly become obsolete.

Content testing with Test&Target

Adobe Experience Manager includes a cloud service configuration for integration with Adobe Test&Target (T&T), an analytics tool specifically designed for measuring the effectiveness of dynamic content and controlling delivery of the optimal content. There are a couple of ways you can use it to test dynamic content in AEM.

The classic way to use Test&Target in AEM is via an MBox. In Test&Target terms, an MBox is an area on the page that you have set aside for dynamic content. Within Test&Target, you configure multiple variations of content to be injected into the MBox at runtime to test which one is more effective. This nicely unifies the creation and analysis of tests into the Test&Target interface. On the other hand, it removes *some* power for authoring content from the content authors (unless they are the ones using T&T).

The Test&Target MBox component can be added to a page or statically included, just as any other component. It has some basic configuration to hook it up to Test&Target. You'll have to work with the person in charge of your Test&Target accounts to set this up. You'll also have to determine if this approach is right for you. But know that it has proven to be an effective way to test dynamic content.

The newer way to use Test&Target with AEM for content testing is via a Test&Target campaign. This integration enables you to combine content testing with personalization, with the ultimate goal of optimizing your site for everyone. Remember, we already noted that this method is more complicated from a practical perspective. Instead of creating normal campaigns in the MCM interface, you create a Test&Target campaign. This will be somewhat different from a normal campaign, because AEM gives you the hooks to link up your campaign to analysis in Test&Target.

When you link a campaign with Test&Target, you create it in AEM and then push it to T&T. You include a mapping of personalization properties (the information in your client context) to variables so that Test&Target will ingest the necessary information about your site visitors. This mapping works much like the mapping used for SiteCatalyst integration. Then you can create your different experiences with AEM and allow Test&Target to analyze whether your experiences are having a positive or negative impact on your site goals. As with personalization, the value is that AEM manages the content authoring and Test&Target tracks and reports on the content's effectiveness.

As you author content in a Test&Target campaign, AEM will automatically synchronize that information with the Test&Target interface. Within that interface, you can view all of the targeted content that you defined. You'll also have the tools you need to measure the effectiveness of your content experiences. Test&Target will even expose some of that measurement data back to AEM so that content authors can view it within their own tool.

Learning how to effectively create content tests and implementing them using Test&Target could fill a second book. For now, you should understand the benefit that Test&Target integration will give you compared to using the MVT component and the method we'll discuss next: using your web analytics platform to test content.

Testing with web analytics

While Test&Target is designed specifically for content testing, it is possible to use your basic web analytics platform to perform similar analysis. The approach requires more manual work and a few extra layers of data analysis, but it can definitely be effective. You just have to know what you're getting into.

To use an analytics platform (such as Adobe SiteCatalyst or Google Analytics), you'll need to map an indicator describing which content variation was presented to an analytics variable. Then when viewing your analytics data, you can filter or break down your analysis by the value of that variable. This allows you to determine how that content variation affected anything that you can measure within an analytics platform. Usually you will be tracking conversions of some kind.

The drawback to this approach is that you are limited to what your web analytics platform can do. Different platforms have limits on the number of variables you can track, so you'll need to ration them accordingly. You'll also need to plan how you'll use variables to flag site visitors as having been presented one experience over another. Then you'll have to set up the appropriate filters and reports in your analytics platform to isolate how that variable affected the actions of your site visitors.

Be careful when doing this analysis. It might be tempting to attribute far more influence to a variation of content than is appropriate. If a set of visitors sees version A, leaves the site and returns a few times, and then finally converts, you probably shouldn't conclude that the variation of content had any impact on their conversion. Technically, they were served that content and then converted, but it's a stretch to assume the two actions are related.

The long and short of it is that you can use your web analytics platform to test your content. You just have to understand what you can do to set that up with your specific platform. You also have to be careful not to be overzealous in your analysis. This approach makes a cheaper alternative or a nice complement to using a dedicated testing platform, such as Test&Target.

Summary

Implementing dynamic content is all about creating an optimized web experience for everyone who comes to your site. Personalization can be used to target specific kinds of content to specific segments of site visitors. AEM provides tools to help you deduce or collect information about your site visitors, so that you have a dataset from which to personalize. AEM also provides (with the appropriate integrations) a variety of ways to test content variations so that you can build statistical analysis into your planning. If you use AEM's integration with Adobe Test&Target, you can even combine personalization and content testing into a single campaign.

The "right" way to do it will vary from organization to organization and site to site. Understand the tools at your disposal so that you can make an educated decision about the best way to optimize your web content.

Review questions

1. What is the difference between static and dynamic content?
2. What is the difference between personalization and optimizing/testing?
3. What is a teaser?
4. What is the purpose of the client context?
5. What is the difference between A/B and multivariate testing? Why is that important?
6. In what ways can you integrate with Adobe Test&Target?

Review answers

1. Static content is one version of content that is delivered to everyone. Dynamic content can change to optimize what each visitor sees. The ability to serve dynamic content is a key function in a web experience management system, over a web content management system.

2. Personalization involves serving dynamic content based on information you've deduced or collected from site visitors. Optimization (or content testing) involves showing variations of content to visitors and counting which variation influenced the better conversion rate. These strategies can be combined for very granular insight about your content.

3. A teaser is a container in which sets of personalized content can be injected. The teaser component (the placeholder) is added to a webpage, and the variations of content are configured on teaser pages. AEM will determine which teaser page has the content to serve to different users, based on their personalization data.

4. The client context is a content author's go-to tool for testing dynamic content. It allows you to simulate different visitor personas and tweak information about an individual visitor on the fly. It shows you how your configured dynamic content will change per visitor, in real time, and from within the page context itself.

5. A/B testing involves changing one element on a page and testing which variation led to the most conversions. Multivariate testing does the same thing, but it involves multiple changes at once. The difference isn't very important in practical terms. You just need to understand that when multivariate testing, additional analysis is required to determine which of the multiple variables you change per variation actually impacted a change in conversion rate.

6. AEM can integrate with Adobe Test&Target through the use of an MBox component or the use of a Test&Target campaign that includes the use of targeted components.

16 INTEGRATING AEM

The landscape of marketing technologies is growing more diverse every day. Being a part of that landscape, your web content management system cannot live in a bubble. Modern marketing demands that your tools integrate to share data and create a streamlined customer experience. You can use a number of methods to integrate Adobe Experience Manager with other marketing technologies that are on-premise or in the cloud.

This chapter will cover:

- The realities of the current marketing technology landscape

- Models for integrating Adobe Experience Manager (simplified into marketer-friendly terms)

- The AEM cloud-based integrations available out of the box

- How and why you might create custom cloud-based integrations

This chapter will help you understand, at a high level, how you can ensure that your AEM installation integrates with the rest of your marketing technology investments.

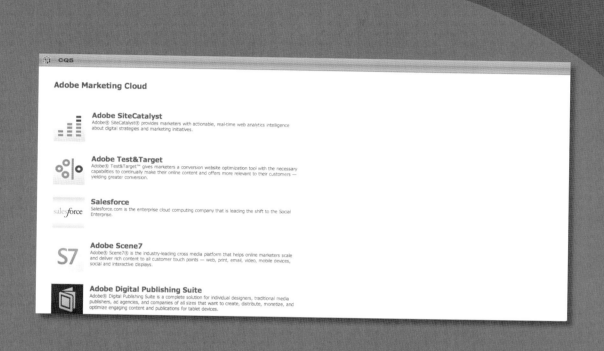

Setting up AEM's cloud-based integrations

The challenge of modern marketing

If you were looking for a fast-moving, exciting field of work, you certainly picked one in digital marketing. Marketing has proliferated into so many channels that it's hard to identify them all. Nontraditional media (mobile applications, podcasting, digital video, social media, and so on) have introduced an array of new marketing opportunities far beyond the functionality of traditional media such as print, radio, and television. It's exciting, but it's also dizzying.

Digital marketing is a systemic problem

When you're assembling a portfolio of marketing technologies, you've got hundreds to choose from. Small startups tend to build technologies that are good at solving one or two specific marketing problems. Large vendors build technologies that include a broader set of functions, but with less specialization. Then there are a number of technologies that fall somewhere in the middle of that spectrum. As a digital marketer, it's your job to establish marketing goals, and then help figure out which technologies you need to support your organization in achieving those goals.

Your first inclination may be to list every problem you have to solve, and then find a different technology to solve each one. Why not? If you've got a problem managing your social media presence, wouldn't you want to use the best-of-breed social media management tool? If you're having a hard time generating sales from email leads, wouldn't you want the best-of-breed marketing automation tool? Using a specialized technology to solve every problem you have is a form of "local optimization." That is, you optimize your solution for each problem on its own.

● **Note:** If you're interested in learning about this approach to systems theory, I recommend checking out the teachings of the late Dr. Russell Ackoff. He's considered one of the thought leaders of modern systems theory, and his views apply quite nicely to the challenges of modern digital marketing.

Many find it somewhat counterintuitive, but modern systems theory suggests that a local optimization approach is not the optimal way to solve a systemic problem. In other words, if you implement a bunch of technologies that optimally solve individual problems, the system of those combined technologies will not work as well as it could. And in case you haven't realized this already, your digital marketing technology portfolio *must* act as a holistic system. Trying to present an experience that is consistent in messaging and quality is impossible if your technologies cannot integrate and interact.

Okay, so if you shouldn't buy a technology to solve every one of your problems, should you buy one big technology that solves them all? Nope! This opposite extreme of local optimization has, not surprisingly, the opposite effect. Sure, your integration challenge is solved, because your platform is one big piece of technology. But one technology cannot possibly be best at solving the vast majority of your problems. Although it may include a solution to most of your problems, the quality of each solution will vary.

Bringing it back home

You didn't buy this book for lessons on systems theory. So, how does this theory apply to Adobe Experience Manager?

AEM solves a lot of problems in very effective ways. As an example, it's a best-of-breed solution for delivering personalized web content. But it's not going to solve every digital marketing challenge you have.

Take one problem solved by a web analytics platform, for instance: You need to understand how people are interacting with your brand via your website. Completely on its own, Adobe Experience Manager has a solution for this (page impressions), but is it the best way to solve that problem? Of course not! (See Chapter 13.)

Adobe understands that for Experience Manager to be an effective digital marketing tool, it must integrate with the rest of your digital marketing platform. AEM is far from the only digital marketing technology that Adobe offers, and the company put a lot of thought into integrating AEM with many of those other technologies. They also understand that everyone isn't going to buy an all-Adobe technology stack. Therefore, AEM provides the architecture to cleanly integrate with virtually any other marketing technology.

Many of these integration techniques involve complex technology, so we'll only spend a little bit of time on them. They are customization-based integrations that require a solution implementation partner. On the other hand, AEM has many integration resources that are completely configuration-based. Some of those integrate with other Adobe technologies, whereas others are designed to couple with other popular marketing technologies. We've touched on a few of these already (SiteCatalyst, Test&Target), so we'll review those here and also discuss the rest of AEM's out-of-the-box integrations called "cloud services configurations."

Integration models

Before digging into the technology integrations available with Adobe Experience Manager, I want to spend some time looking at basic integration patterns. The cloud-based configurations that we'll examine aren't the only ways you can integrate AEM with other systems. In fact, they aren't even always the best approach. To have a comprehensive conversation about integration would take us down a path that is too technical for this book. But I do want to introduce you to some of the basic concepts. This section will be a marketer-friendly fly-by of system integration as it relates to AEM.

There are *many* approaches to integrating information technology systems. Books upon books describe how to do it. Programmers and architects study these different patterns and build frameworks that implement them. I'm going to reduce this discussion to two approaches: cloud-based and on-premise integration. If you're a technical person, you probably just said, "But what about…?" Let me stop you right there. This is an obvious generalization. Don't expect this fly-by to make you an enterprise architect.

My goal is to make sure that you understand the advantages and disadvantages of cloud-based and on-premise integration before we discuss the cloud services configurations offered by Adobe Experience Manager.

On-premise integration

The traditional pattern for integrating enterprise software is to connect those systems within the organization's internal network, called an on-premise system. Sometimes these are called on-premise systems, even though most enterprises have many premises linked via networking technology. The concept is that all of the organization's technology is integrated behind the virtual walls of that organization.

This model grew out of necessity, the result of the limited possibilities of early information technology. Starting decades ago, organizations began building IT infrastructures. For a long time, the only way to do that was to build a mostly proprietary, internal system. Although you licensed software and purchased hardware, you then assembled it internally in whatever way best met your needs.

On-premise IT systems have their advantages. When an organization purchases and implements software internally, the organization controls it. Even if the third-party software vendor eliminates support or even goes out of business, as long as the IT organization fully understands the software, they can support it themselves. The same is true of hardware and the infrastructure required to tie it all together.

On-premise systems also put the responsibility for security with the organization potentially affected by a security breach. The IT is behind your virtual walls, so you can protect it. When your organization possesses the competence to effectively deal with security, this is a positive. If you don't possess that competency (whether you know it or not), the security benefits of an on-premise solution are merely perceived benefits.

Using an on-premise model means you can also monitor and control the bandwidth between systems. If two systems are trying to talk to one another and you find that the connection is slow, you can do something about it. It's your network, after all. You can track down and repair the bottlenecks. You can implement anything that is technically possible because you control everything.

On the other hand, on-premise IT solutions have their drawbacks.

They aren't cheap or easy to manage. It can get messy when you are tasked with maintaining (sometimes) thousands of pieces of licensed and homegrown software along with the supporting hardware and network infrastructure. Complex ecosystems of on-premise solutions are why large enterprises employ thousands of IT people. Finally, on-premise solutions require you to acquire many competencies that don't necessarily align with the core competencies of your organization.

On-premise solutions also tend to be more rigid. Some best-practice approaches to enterprise architecture mitigate that rigidity, but at a certain point, it's unavoidable.

When you build, integrate, and customize software to develop your system, you tend to build yourself into corners. It's why organizations find themselves spending millions of dollars just to maintain software that is 10 years old. At a certain point, it can become too difficult and expensive to upgrade or replace those systems.

On-premise architectures tend to grow into juggernauts. No matter how much we think we know, we are generally bad at building huge IT systems that can remain agile and flexible. Politics, time, and money always get in the way. On-premise software has gotten us to where we are today, but now we have alternatives in the form of cloud-based integrations.

Cloud-based integration

In Chapter 1 we discussed "the cloud" and different models for cloud-based systems. The proliferation of cloud-based systems is a relatively recent phenomenon, but it's changed the way organizations think about integration. Today, you must not only evaluate on-premise architectural models; you also have to consider whether a cloud-based model should be used.

Cloud-based integration means that one or more of the systems you will integrate *do not* live within the virtual walls of your organization. They might all live behind someone else's single wall. Select parts of your system might reside within the infrastructure of different vendors, while some of your IT remains behind your walls.

The biggest difference with cloud-based integrations, compared to on-premise approaches, is determining what you have to (and need to) control. When integrating with a cloud-based system, you don't have control over the infrastructure that connects the two systems. The vendors that make up "the cloud" do. On one hand, you no longer need an army of network engineers managing your connections. On the other hand, when things go bad, you are somewhat limited in what you can do to fix things.

Consider the differences between SaaS, PaaS, and IaaS models as well. Each of these approaches to cloud-based systems provides a different level of control. With an SaaS solution, you have very little control. You basically get to sign up and make some configurations. However, less control means less responsibility. With an IaaS solution, you basically have full control because you rent (not own) the infrastructure. That leaves you with a lot of responsibility to manage that rented infrastructure. PaaS solutions exist somewhere between those two approaches.

Cloud-based integration certainly has its advantages, many of which are driving the general shift to the cloud in modern IT.

- With a cloud-based integration, you only have to control what you feel you need to control. You may want the business value of a particular system but have no desire to manage that system. You can use an SaaS-based solution to accomplish that. Generally speaking, these solutions still allow those cloud services to communicate with your other systems, while putting the bulk of the responsibility for managing the solution on another party.

- Cloud-based integration tends to be quite a bit more flexible than on-premise. Don't want to use a service any more? Just cancel your subscription. You'll have to tweak your proprietary integrations to talk to whatever replacement you select, but ultimately, it's a more cost-effective and efficient solution than on-premise. You don't have to retire hardware. You don't have to bring it down slowly.

- Cloud-based integration keeps your systems modern and fresh. With an SaaS or PaaS solution, another organization can worry about improving your solution while you focus on using that system to achieve your business goals. You can always be using cutting-edge technology, even though you aren't burning resources creating it yourself.

Cloud-based integration models also have their drawbacks.

Security is the most frequently cited drawback. With a cloud-based integration, your IT is communicating over the public Internet. There are ways to do so securely, but you are still going outside the virtual walls of your organization. Some of the security concerns are perceived. Some others are real. Sometimes regulations based on security reasons (right or wrong) limit your ability to use cloud-based systems.

With a cloud-based system, you shift responsibility, but you also relinquish control to someone else. You don't have much (or any) input on new features or the direction of your software. You are simply a user. This is fine until your vendor decides to do away with something you find extremely valuable. If the system goes down completely, you depend on the vendor to restore it. The bottom line is that the functionality of your IT system rests in the hands of someone else.

Making a choice

In the preceding section, we reviewed the concepts of cloud-based IT systems and touched on how they create different integration challenges. As marketers, you should understand these fundamentals of integration because you'll discuss them with your IT department. Or maybe you'll circumvent the IT department entirely and create a completely separate cloud-based digital marketing platform. I've seen it done.

You should consider that cloud-based integration is not the only way to integrate AEM with outside technologies. In fact, many AEM implementations use both on-premise and cloud-based integrations. For example, to integrate AEM with your organization's LDAP system—to enable login using your company credentials— you'll generally use an on-premise integration. But to integrate AEM with a web analytics platform, you'll use a cloud-based one.

Any techies reading this book will roll their eyes at my gross simplifications. In technical terms, the reality is far more complicated than "cloud or no cloud." I want you to understand each strategy approach, in simple terms, so you can have real conversations with your implementation partner about what they can do versus what you need to make happen. Keep all of this in mind throughout the rest of the chapter, as we discuss the cloud-based integrations that are included with Adobe Experience Manager.

Cloud service configurations

Digital marketing software tends to work quite well when using a cloud-based model, and Adobe has invested heavily in that approach. The majority of the Marketing Cloud is made up of cloud-based technology. It includes many SaaS and PaaS solutions that integrate nicely. Adobe recently moved the Creative Suite tools to the cloud as well (the Creative Cloud). By offering a full suite of integrated solutions, Adobe allows you to pick and choose the pieces you need to meet your marketing goals.

AEM is a little bit of an outlier, because it's more like traditional enterprise software. Many people still implement AEM on-premise. Others enlist the infrastructure management services of solution partners or Adobe. AEM is absolutely cloud-friendly, but an AEM implementation requires more customization and infrastructural control than most of the rest of the Marketing Cloud. Even so, AEM is built to integrate directly with the rest of the platform and other cloud-based technolgies.

Adobe Experience Manager uses an integration concept called a cloud services configuration (CSC). We've discussed this a bit already. A CSC is a standard pattern for implementing configurable integration with a cloud-based system. In other words, as an administrator, you can configure these integrations using the same basic authoring paradigm you use in AEM. It doesn't matter which system you are integrating with or what it does.

Cloud services configurations have various options for exactly *what* you can configure. But they provide a familiar interface for doing so. It makes it easy for an administrator who already understands AEM to integrate with other systems. It also makes it easy for administrators to add or remove integrations, as necessary.

For the rest of this chapter, we'll dive into the cloud services configurations available at the time of this book's release. We'll also look at how you can work with your implementation team to build your own CSCs. Keep in mind that the list of available configurations is constantly growing. By the time you read this book, there may be more. However, the same basic concepts should apply to any new cloud services configurations.

Adobe SiteCatalyst

The SiteCatalyst CSC allows you to integrate AEM with Adobe's web analytics platform. This specific integration is extremely powerful because it links the AEM personalization functionality with SiteCatalyst variables. In other words, you can use SiteCatalyst to segment web analytics reports based on the exact datapoints used to personalize content delivered by AEM. This is the only web analytics platform that you can integrate with using a CSC that gives you an "authorable" configuration. (The Generic Analytics Snippet works a bit differently.) Chapter 13 explores this integration in more detail.

Adobe Test&Target

The Test&Target CSC enables you to integrate with Adobe's platform for measuring dynamic content and testing how effectively that content improves conversion rates. When you connect to Test&Target using the CSC, you can create Test&Target Campaigns using the marketing campaign management (MCM) features. Those campaigns include dynamic content measured and optimized via the Test&Target platform. Chapter 15 covers this in more detail.

Salesforce.com

Many organizations use Salesforce.com as their primary customer relationship management (CRM) system. For these organizations, the CRM will be their primary means of tracking, managing, and communicating with sales leads. If you've already invested in a CRM for this functionality, it doesn't make sense to utilize MCM leads (Chapter 14) as your method of lead management. You've already got a system that is intended for doing so, and it is much better at it.

That doesn't change the fact that the information in your CRM is extremely valuable if you want to create a personalized web experience for those customers. If you know (in your CRM) that someone works for a large boxed foods company, you may want to target him with specific content. But if your data about the customer isn't in AEM, that kind of content customization gets tricky.

As of AEM 5.6, you can use a cloud services configuration to enable two-way communication beween Adobe Experience Manager and Salesforce.com. This enables you to send customer personalization data from AEM to Salesforce where it can be stored with the rest of your customer data. It also enables you to pull in customer data from Salesforce to use in personalization and content targeting. This integration allows the CRM to do what it does best, lets AEM do what it does best, and enables the two to share relevant data.

Adobe Scene7

By connecting to Adobe Scene7 via a cloud services configuration, you enable AEM's digital asset management (DAM) to utilize all of the dynamic media capabilities of Scene7. This includes on-the-fly dynamic images, features like the flyout zoom, and Scene7's video streaming that can adapt automatically per device. Eventually Scene7 will not be a separate piece of software, so this CSC may go away in future releases. At present, however, it's the way you configure the powerful DAM integration features available. These features are discussed in more detail in Chapter 4.

Adobe Digital Publishing Suite

The Adobe Digital Publishing Suite (DPS) is a platform for delivering digital publications to tablet devices by helping you build electronic magazines. It's a separate product from AEM, but not a completely separate concern. Often, media companies will publish identical or similar content to their website as in their digital and/or print magazines. AEM can integrate with the Digital Publish Suite using an add-on called Media Publisher. The Digital Publishing Suite cloud services configuration connects AEM with DPS.

In Chapter 3, I described manuscripts, which is one way to author content completely independent of the delivery medium. Manuscripts are part of the Media Publisher add-on. They enable you to author what are effectively magazine articles, and deliver them through your website or your digital magazine using multiple layouts that are relevant to each display device. Again, the CSC for the Digital Publishing Suite enables your manuscripts to be linked to the platform that deploys your digital publication.

This integration also allows you share metadata with the DPS. AEM, via the DAM, is very good at managing the metadata of digital media files. Naturally, those digital media files are likely to be used in your digital publications, as well as your website. The AEM-DPS integration allows you to manage metadata in AEM but consume and use it in DPS.

Adobe TagManager

Sometimes when integrating with an external system (such as an analytics platform), you need to add chunks of code to your site. Using a CSC like the Generic Analytics Snippet or SiteCatalyst CSC is one approach to "tagging" your site with this code. Another is to use a tag management system, like Adobe TagManager. This platform is a cloud-hosted hub that you can use to centralize the many code snippets you may need to apply to various systems (not only AEM). The TagManager's cloud services configuration allows you to pull those tags into AEM so they can be applied to webpages.

Adobe TagManager also allows you to define containers of tags, grouped snippets of code that share a common subject or purpose. Grouping them in containers more efficiently organizes them and makes it easier to apply them to content. Once you wire up the TagManager CSC, you can select which containers you pull into your AEM website. Adobe Experience Manager will automatically include all the code snippets from that container into the webpage.

● **Note:** The term "tag" discussed in this context is not the same as the metatags discussed in Chapter 5. In this section, "tagging" means to tag a piece of content with special JavaScript or other code that serves as an integration hook into another system.

● **Note:** Some functionality overlaps with some of the other cloud service configurations. For example, you could use TagManager to include the SiteCatalyst JavaScript snippet, or use the SiteCatalyst cloud services configuration. It just depends on your project's requirements.

ExactTarget

Instead of using the AEM email marketing functionality, which is admittedly limited, you can integrate with ExactTarget—a full-featured marketing automation platform that includes a robust feature set for managing email marketing. By using a cloud services configuration, you can link AEM to ExactTarget, which allows you to author emails in AEM and then push them to ExactTarget for management and delivery. Details of this integration are discussed in Chapter 14.

Facebook

In Chapter 15, we talked about integrating Adobe Experience Manager with Facebook to use profile data for personalization. The AEM integration to Facebook is set up using a cloud services configuration. In fact, you'll want to set up a separate Facebook CSC for each site that you integrate with Facebook so that you can pull (and request permission to pull) only the data you need for that site.

Social networking integration is a little different from other integrations because you must request permission from your users. When you configure the Facebook CSC, you select what data you want to request permission to use. This is displayed to the user when she first elects to "log in with Facebook." If the user grants permission, AEM creates an AEM user that is linked to her Facebook account, and you'll be able to use that data to target content.

Twitter

Twitter integration works much like Facebook integration, but you can't do much with it in terms of content targeting. In Twitter, users don't provide the level of profile data that they do in Facebook, so there isn't any worthwhile data to pull in. The AEM-Twitter integration just enables you to offer a "log in with Twitter" service. Even though Twitter integration doesn't help you target content, it eliminates barriers to registration, so it does provide value.

Technically, it is possible to implement customization that would read a user's tweets and provide segmentation data, based on the content of the tweets, but it would be a custom solution. If that's something you want to do, talk to your solution implementation partner about putting it together for you.

Adobe Search&Promote

Integrating Adobe Experience Manager with Adobe Search&Promote allows you to create a more personalized, effective site search experience. Search&Promote includes functionality well beyond AEM's out-of-the-box search features. It includes better search filtering, banners that display content relevant to the search terms (good for upselling products), and other features that create an advanced site search experience.

You'll have to assess how important site search is to your web experience. If you want to build a powerful search tool, you can use Search&Promote to handle the search indexing and results filtering. Then AEM delivers that experience to site visitors. As with most of the CSC integrations, AEM lets each product do what it does best.

Adobe Creative Cloud

If you use the Adobe Creative Cloud to facilitate the creation of digital assets, there's a lot of value in being able to store those assets in the AEM DAM. Ultimately, those assets will be delivered to customers in many forms, such as your website. You can exploit AEM's full-featured DAM to also use those assets to improve your web experience. The Adobe Creative Cloud CSC enables that integration.

As Adobe continues to integrate the Creative Cloud and Marketing Cloud products, this integration may become more seamless. Therefore, this configuration-based connection may disappear in future versions, depending on the direction Adobe chooses to go with it.

Custom cloud-based integration

All these out-of-the-box cloud services configurations are great, right? But what if you don't use these particular services? What if you have other services that you want to integrate with AEM? You'll have to build custom integration with your solution partner, but it's definitely possible. Not only does Adobe provide those default CSCs, they also include a framework for building your own. This enables an implementation team to build custom integrations using the same administration-configurable paradigm as the other CSCs. AEM also provides a generic analytics CSC that allows you to integrate web analytics platforms other than SiteCatalyst.

Generic Analytics Snippet

If you want to (or have to) use a web analytics platform other than Adobe SiteCatalyst, you can use the Generic Analytics Snippet cloud services configuration. To use most analytics platforms, you need to tag every page in your site with a small piece of JavaScript that calls back to the analytics servers. A developer could build that into your pages, but that is a really inflexible way to accomplish it. When you have to make changes, you can't make them as a marketer or administrator.

The Generic Analytics Snippet provides a place to copy that JavaScript to tag pages. Then on your home page, you can use the page properties dialog to select the analytics CSC you just configured. AEM automatically applies that JavaScript to every page. If you change or remove the snippet, that is accounted for automatically. This integration is discussed in some detail in Chapter 13, where I describe how to integrate AEM with Google Analytics.

Custom configurations

If the Generic Analytics Snippet isn't enough, work with your solution implementation team to develop a custom cloud services configuration. Technically, you could build a CSC for any kind of external integration, whether it's cloud-hosted or not. CSCs give you a nice administrative configuration interface for managing that integration, so I highly consider evaluating if every integration you build can use a CSC.

Here are some reasons that you might want to consider using a custom cloud services configuration:

- You want an "authorable" configuration for your web analytics integration that is similar to what you get with SiteCatalyst.

- You want to integrate with other digital marketing technologies.

- You need to be able to add, edit, or remove integrations per each website hosted within AEM.

- You want to integrate with additional social networks. (This is the best way to do it.)

- You want to extend the functionality of any of the Adobe-provided cloud services configurations.

- You want to build an integration that is minimally affected by an upgrade to a new version of AEM.

I wouldn't start out assuming that you will build a custom CSC. In fact, if you have devoted your WCM efforts to AEM, you should strongly consider the peripheral marketing technologies with which AEM already integrates. It helps you to kill two birds with one stone. Just know that it *is* possible to create custom integrations using cloud services configurations and that you should discuss the options with your solution partner.

Summary

There's more than one way to integrate enterprise technologies. Most IT systems consist of a mix of on-premise and cloud-based integrations, especially as cloud-based technology continues to gain popularity. Both approaches have their advantages and disadvantages, but in general, cloud-based integration creates a more flexible architecture. Adobe Experience Manager includes a set of cloud-based integrations and a framework for developing additional ones. Many digital marketing technologies, including AEM (sometimes), are cloud-based systems and AEM is built to easily connect to them. Using AEM cloud services configurations, you create an administratively configurable integration that can be changed or removed as needed.

Review questions

1. Explain the theory that states it is ineffective to implement separate best-of-breed solutions for every business problem.

2. What are the primary advantages of a cloud-based integration model?

3. What must happen before you can use a site visitor's Facebook profile data to personalize content?

4. Why would you use a Generic Analytics Snippet?

Review answers

1. Modern systems theory states that implementing the best-of-breed solution to every single problem creates local optimization. However, local optimization does not create an overall efficient system, because it disregards the interactions between the parts. Digital marketing is a systemic function, so consider this theory when deciding what types of solutions you want to implement.

2. A cloud-based integration model is more flexible than an on-premise one. You can simply turn on or off integrations as you feel the need. It can also be much simpler and cheaper, because you are not required to manage the infrastructure that enables the integration. You pay for only the service with which you integrate and the labor required to set up and monitor the integration.

3. Before you can use a user's Facebook profile data, you must receive permission from that user.

4. You can use a Generic Analytics Snippet to integrate with web analytics platforms other than SiteCatalyst, while still using the cloud services configuration paradigm.

17 TECHNICAL BASICS

If you're going to invest in an Adobe Experience Manager implementation, it's helpful to have a fundamental understanding of its technical architecture. You don't need to be a programmer, but a bit of basic knowledge can help you define your requirements in terms that are technically realistic. It will make conversations with your implementation team easier and your development process more efficient.

This chapter will cover the technical basics you'll want to understand about AEM, including:

- The request-response cycle and the basics of web development
- The layers of code that will implement your website on AEM
- The basic architectural pieces of Adobe Experience Manager

This chapter will not equip you to architect solutions on your own, but it will give you the context you need to work with those who can. From personal experience, I guarantee that marketers who understand these basics will have a much smoother implementation than those who don't.

This chapter is the most technical content in this book. Hang with me, because it'll be useful information to know when starting your AEM implementation.

Java, servlets, and JavaServer Pages

Java, servlets, and JavaServer Pages (JSP) are three concepts you should understand on the server-side of the story. Together, they represent most of how an AEM
instance serves content to a requestor. Their operation is even more complicated
than the client-side concepts we just discussed, so remember that the following is a
quick fly-by. As long as you understand what each is and fundamentally what they
do, you should be good to go.

Java

Java is the object-oriented programming language used to implement Adobe
Experience Manager and any components used in the platform. It's an extremely
common programming language, so the community of people who understand it is
enormous. Java is used in many ways, from powering the software on your DVR to
software used by NASA. When we're talking about it in the context of Adobe Experience Manager, Java is used for two basic reasons: basic web server tasks (servlets
and JSP), and integration with external systems.

Java is an extremely compatible, standardized programming language, so it's easy for
your implementation team to integrate it with other systems. They'll use many techniques for doing so, but at the end of the day, this industry standard language makes
most things possible. If you're a marketer interested in learning to code, starting
with Java is probably your best bet. It's a relatively forgiving language, compared to
some others, and a *lot* of free educational content is available online.

Java is a server-side technology. The server hardware must run "application server"
software to execute Java code. This software enables the server computer to execute
code to perform a function. Most enterprise software must be deployed to an
application server. Adobe Experience Manager usually runs in its own lightweight
application server, so you don't have to install separate application server software.

The end users of a website will never know that Java is powering things behind the
scenes. Unless you learn to dig into Java and its applications, you may not ever be
aware of it. Because it is a completely server-side technology, the implementation
team is responsible for it. When the team implements your page and content
components and integrates them with other systems, they do so by writing Java,
servlets, and JavaServer Pages. Then they deploy them to the various AEM
instances.

Note: Sometimes the word "server" refers to the physical server hardware, and sometimes it refers to a type of software that runs on the server. When talking with someone about a "server," make sure you understand which type they are talking about.

Servlets

A servlet is a special piece of Java code designed to generate resources. It is the
code that spits out a webpage, an image, an XML document, or whatever else the
server needs to deliver. Everything you request from Adobe Experience Manager is
handled via a servlet.

Consider the request-response cycle we just discussed. When the web server receives a request, it has to determine how to respond and what to deliver in response. Without a content management system, your server would just pull content from the HTML files stored in folders. That's the most basic way to structure a website, but it's extremely inflexible. To change anything on your website, you have to change each HTML file directly. Doing so would be error-prone and repetitive.

When you use an application like AEM, the web server routes that webpage request to a servlet. That servlet reads the request and generates an appropriate webpage on the fly. This allows the server to create a response in real time, based on changes that content authors make on the server. Every time the request is made, the server could potentially output a different file response. This is the fundamental reason content management systems like AEM are able to let you make website changes without changing code.

JavaServer Pages

JSP is a technology that makes it easier to develop servlets to output web content. The way programmers must develop normal servlets is not optimal for outputting HTML. It can be done; it's just more difficult. JavaServer Pages combine HTML and Java development into a single file to enable the delivery of dynamic HTML content.

Let's look at a simple example. Let's say you want to develop a webpage that says "Welcome <your name>!" You can't implement that with pure HTML, because you need to dynamically look up a name. Otherwise everyone would see the same message. The HTML implementation would look like this:

```
<html>
    <body>
        <h1>Hello Ryan!</h1>
    </body>
</html>
```

Again, how would you ever change the part of the message that says "Ryan"? You wouldn't. Let's look at a JSP approach to doing so:

```
<html>
    <body>
        <h1>Hello <%= NameLookup.getName() %>!</h1>
    </body>
</html>
```

The text in blue is the HTML. The text in red is Java. The text in green is the special JSP markup that allows you to mix them. The JSP has enabled you to take advantage of the semantic descriptiveness of HTML and the dynamic functionality of Java.

When your implementation team builds page and content components, they are going to be built with JSP files. In fact, most of the AEM platform itself is implemented as JSP files, so any customizations to the platform will also be done as JSPs.

Server-side caching

If you have thousands of people a day requesting the same page from your web server, it's pretty inefficient to wait for a servlet to rebuild the page for every request. Yes, the value of using a content management system and JSPs is that you can change your content often, but does it change more frequently than every time someone requests a page? Most of the time, the answer is no. So, to use your hardware most efficiently, platforms like AEM implement server-side caching.

Adobe Experience Manager uses the Dispatcher, discussed in Chapter 11, to perform server-side caching. The first time someone requests your webpage, AEM will generate it from the JSPs. It sends that generated HTML page back as the response, but it also holds onto a copy. AEM places that HTML page in the cache. In other words, it saves a copy to the local file system (on the server). Then when anyone else requests that page, AEM responds with the already generated and saved version. This addresses the vast majority of redundant work and allows AEM to run more efficiently.

But web content does change sometimes, such as every time you activate a page that you've just modified. When that happens, Adobe Experience Manager invalidates the cache. In other words, it tells the web server to forget the cached HTML files. The next webpage request is regenerated on the server and recached. The whole cycle begins again.

Server-side caching is similar to the client-side caching that the local browser performs. Although both strategies work a bit differently and cache slightly different things, they fundamentally achieve the same thing. Caching ensures that the technology does the minimum amount of work necessary. It's also one of the most important ways to speed up your technology systems.

Caching strategy is a concern for the solution implementation team, but you should be aware of what is cached and where. It'll help you work with the implementation team to isolate bugs (which are often caused by aggressive caching) and to understand how your website really works.

AEM's architecture

Now that we've gone over the *very* basics of web development, it's time to go over the important pieces of Adobe Experience Manager that make it all happen. The rest of this chapter will cover the basic architectural layers of AEM. We'll briefly examine what each layer does, even though the full story goes far deeper.

The technologies that I'll discuss in this section are the building blocks of Adobe Experience Manager. On their own, some of them are autonomous open source projects also used in other applications. Some of them are specific to AEM. These basic pieces, along with many other smaller ones, are assembled to create AEM's compelling technical architecture. As a marketer, you probably won't fully understand its collective uniqueness, but you'll definitely experience the powerful software platform this architecture has created.

Like the rest of this chapter, this section will give you some technical context but won't make you an expert. The Adobe documentation and your solution partner can take you further into these high-tech rabbit holes if they interest you. I hope at least one does.

First, a bit about Apache

You'll notice that the Apache Software Foundation produces many of the pieces of Adobe Experience Manager. Apache is a nonprofit organization that facilitates and funds many open source development projects. The tech community develops Apache's open source technologies, although a board of domain experts leads every one of their projects. Apache software is typically openly licensed and can be used for free. This does not mean AEM is free, though.

Many Apache projects don't create a lot of business value by themselves. They typically materialize out of a development community's organic determination of need. They often solve *very* technical problems, which is natural if you consider that mostly technical people make up Apache. However, Apache projects are often assembled together and combined with proprietary technology to create a software product, such as AEM.

In life, you generally get what you pay for. The projects supervised by the Apache foundation tear down that truism. Many of them (such as the ones used in AEM) are regarded with high esteem. Thousands of organizations around the world have used Apache projects, and not just by little companies. Adobe plays a huge part in contributing to many Apache projects, including the ones that make up AEM. The philosophy behind AEM's architecture is to assemble these impressive open source technologies to power the underlying engine of AEM.

Some organizations fear this approach, but that fear is unfounded. The technologies under the hood of Adobe Experience Manager are every bit as enterprise-ready as other expensive, proprietary tech. In many cases Apache's solutions are even better.

Apache Felix

Apache Felix is an open source service platform that implements the OSGi (Open Services Gateway Initiative) specification. OSGi platforms allow you to deploy different Java libraries, called bundles, on the fly. Unlike most application servers, when you deploy Java as a bundle in OSGi, you do *not* have to restart everything. It makes for a very lightweight, agile architecture. Apache Felix manages dependencies (such as "bundle A doesn't work without bundle B"), and turns bundles on or off as dependencies to allow them to function. Apache Felix also exposes most of the low-level administrative functions needed to maintain AEM.

This is a *really* technical concept, so if you're struggling to keep up, it's okay. As a marketer you aren't going to need to worry much about Apache Felix. But you should know two things about it.

First, your system administrators (who are often part of your implementation team) may spend a lot of time configuring Apache Felix. This is done in an interface called the "Felix Console" or "system console." The implementation team will also add Felix configurations to the code, so they are automatically deployed to every AEM instance. Remember that Apache Felix is where most low-level configuration happens, and when someone refers to the "system console," they are talking about a UI for configuring Felix.

Second, know that Apache Felix is one of the biggest reasons that you can make changes quickly in Adobe Experience Manager. With a traditional application server, deploying new versions of Java code is a big task. You have to shut down the server to deploy the code, and then you have to restart it. This takes time and introduces risk. Apache Felix allows you to "hot deploy" code, so in a matter of seconds, new code can be running on a live server. This is a unique advantage provided by Adobe Experience Manager's architecture.

Apache Jackrabbit

Apache Jackrabbit is a Java Content Repository (JCR), and it's the storage mechanism used by Adobe Experience Manager. If you're familiar with enterprise technology, you know that most of the time software uses a relational database to store data. Though AEM can be configured to run on top of a database, the majority of the time you'll want to just apply the AEM default configuration using Jackrabbit. There are some notable advantages to using Apache Jackrabbit over a separate relational database:

- Those who write the code for your application can control how data is stored. In other words, you remove the need for database administrators.

- The way you store data in Jackrabbit can be changed or adapted quickly, whereas database changes can be difficult and high-risk.

- Data is stored in a hierarchical structure, much like the files on your computer. That data structure works very well for web-based projects.

- Other hierarchical data formats such as XML or JSON easily translate to and from the data in Jackrabbit.

There are many more advantages that should get the tech folks excited, too. From a marketing perspective, you should understand that the extremely hierarchical nature of AEM comes from the fact that it is implemented on Apache Jackrabbit. In fact, when you are editing pages and components, you are just editing hierarchy nodes in the repository.

Apache Sling

Apache Sling is my favorite part of Adobe Experience Manager's architecture. It's a web framework that combines the hierarchical nature of Jackrabbit with the flexibility of Felix and adapts them to building websites. With Apache Sling, everything that you pull out of AEM is a web "resource" (a *thing* you are trying to get). Sling provides you with the functions you need to "resolve" (or retrieve) those resources. It's also the reason you can resolve different versions of the same page by simply making a small change to the URL.

Apache Sling is what powers AEM page and content components. A component is just information located in a part of the content repository (Jackrabbit) that isn't visible to site visitors. It has a "resource type" that serves as a type identifier for that component. Every component you add to a page is added to the public part of the content repository. It includes a reference to that resource type and any configuration information you provide for that specific instance of the component. As a result, you don't have to duplicate the code every time you use a new component.

Sling lets you make any kind of request (via a URL) to any node in your repository. If you've included the code to handle that request, it'll output what was requested. Sling also includes the default ability to retrieve any node as HTML, XML, or JSON. For example, requesting http://server.com/my/page.html will return a normal HTML page. But requesting http://server.com/my/page.json will return the same page data as a JSON file. This means Sling is *very* open about what information you can retrieve for AEM. This is great when you need it, but it's a potential security threat when you don't. The dispatcher is generally placed in front of an AEM instance and blocks any potentially malicious requests to Apache Sling.

As an example, let's look at a way you can use Sling to power your mobile website. When you make a request to the previously mentioned server.com/my/page.html, AEM resolves to a servlet and returns the desktop version of the webpage. If you wanted to implement a mobile version of the same page without Sling, you'd have to build another page on another domain (such as m.server.com/my/page.html). But, using Sling, you can simply modify *how* you want the single resource delivered by making a semantic change to the URL—for example, server.com/my/page.mobile. html. That tells Sling "get me the page.html file, but deliver the mobile version." (This is one of many ways you can implement mobile websites with AEM.)

As a marketer, you should know how Sling makes your system flexible. You won't need to know all the details about how Sling figures out what data to present based on the URL. But you should understand that you can retrieve the same data in different forms or file types. As you work through your requirements with your solution partner, they may suggest ways to take advantage of this functionality. They'll be impressed (and excited) if you can talk intelligently about how Sling can help.

Granite

Granite is the term Adobe uses to represent the technology stack that powers Adobe Experience Manager. This includes Adobe's implementations of the Apache projects we already discussed and some other technologies such as server cluster management and information logging. As a marketer, you don't need know much about Granite unless it comes up in conversations. Just remember that it's the term that describes the grouping of the full technology stack used in Adobe Experience Manager.

AEM application

Last but not least is the Adobe Experience Manager code. On top of all the stuff we discussed so far (and many smaller technologies) sits the code that makes AEM work for you. This is the code that creates the interfaces you work in, the in-context authoring, and every other marketer-oriented feature that AEM offers.

Adobe Experience Manager is powerful because Adobe has done two things really well: it assembled and extended great open source technologies to create an underlying framework (Granite), and it built a full-featured web experience management application on top of that framework. The result? The industry-leading technology you've been reading about.

In older versions of AEM (pre–AEM 5.6), customizing the application layer could be difficult. Specifically, the JavaScript-based interfaces, such as the site administration UI, were tricky to change. It's rare that an organization *really* needs to customize them, but it's definitely not unheard of. However, Adobe's new touch UI framework makes it significantly easier to extend the AEM application. While these involve mostly technical concerns, you'll want to understand the reasons you can or cannot make a suggested customization. You'll also want to understand why you should or shouldn't make one.

A good solution partner will be able to talk you through which parts of the application are customizable and which aren't. They should also push back if you insist upon a customization that is a bad idea. Don't be mad. They just want the best for you. As a general best practice, make customizations to the platform a last resort. If you can accomplish what you need by tweaking your processes or making small concessions in your requirements, start there. Then talk with your implementation team about how to customize, if you still need to.

Putting it all together

Let's conclude this tech talk by putting all these architectural pieces back together.

As a marketer, you log into the authoring interface to create pages, put content on the pages, and do whatever else we've discussed in this book so far. All of the interfaces and functions you use are part of Adobe's proprietary layer of code. That's what unifies several open source projects into the power of Adobe Experience Manager. You then use that AEM application to make your content viewable by the public.

A site visitor makes a request for anything from Adobe Experience Manager (a page, an image, or whatever). Apache Sling reads the URL of that request and figures out what you want. It determines where the definition of what you want is—the code that implements it. Then it figures out where the content is for the specific instance of that *thing* that you want (such as the specific page of the 20 pages that are implemented by that page component).

Sling looks for all of this information inside a Java Content Repository called Apache Jackrabbit. It's the storage mechanism for all content, configuration information, and implementation code in AEM. Sling uses its rules to figure out where all that stuff lives, since it's spread throughout different parts of the repository.

Apache Felix ties all of this together: all the code libraries for the AEM code, the several open source projects that make up AEM, and any code your implementation team writes—all stored in Jackrabbit and managed by Felix. It makes sure that everything pieces together nicely and provides the administrative facilities for telling the appropriate people when it doesn't.

Summary

Congratulations! You made it through a really technical chapter.

As a marketer, you'll find it helpful to understand the technical concepts your implementation team will be wrestling with. You'll be working with them to develop a solution that meets your needs. By knowing how they make it happen, you'll be better equipped to discuss requirements in feasible terms. You'll also better understand what's under the hood of that big investment you made. Part of understanding the technical concepts is understanding the important architectural layers of AEM. They each serve a specific purpose as part of a technology platform with an architecture unique from any other. These are the things that get the tech folks excited about Adobe Experience Manager, so I hope they excite you, too.

Review questions

1. What's the relationship between the request-response cycle and client-server architecture?

2. If JavaScript isn't a *programming* language, then what is it?

3. What is JSP and what does it do?

4. What two types of caching are discussed in this chapter?

5. Why doesn't Adobe Experience Manager use a database?

Review answers

1. Client-server architecture enables the request-response cycle. The client is your local machine, and the server is a computer that hosts a website. A client makes requests to the server for information, and the server returns a response with that information or a reason why it couldn't do so.

2. JavaScript is a *scripting* language. It's a subtle difference, but it means that JavaScript doesn't need to be compiled into a special file that is run by an application server. Your browser just reads it as plain text and does what it says to do.

3. JSP (JavaServer Pages) enables developers to write Java servlets that are specifically for outputting HTML. They are often used to generate dynamic content.

4. Client-side caching occurs when your browser saves files (such as images) to your local storage, so it doesn't have to repeatedly download the same file. Server-side caching occurs when a web server saves files that are dynamically generated (such as a JSP file) so it doesn't have to rebuild the same page to respond to future requests.

5. Adobe Experience Manager uses a Java Content Repository (Apache Jackrabbit) instead of a relational database. The JCR stores data hierarchically, like the file system on your computer, instead of within a rigid structure, like a database. You can hook up the JCR to store data in databases (behind the scenes), but it's rarely the best way to go.

18 DEFINING REQUIREMENTS

I've talked quite a bit about working with your solution partner to implement the tools you'll need to author your websites. Solution partners will help you establish what you want, but at the end of the day it's up to you to decide how you're going to use AEM to accomplish your goals. You understand your brand, so you'll need to set the direction. This chapter will cover:

- How you should prepare yourself for an Adobe Experience Manager implementation

- What kinds of requirements your solution partner will need to implement what you want

- How to prioritize your requirements

- Some requirements best practices that I've compiled while working through AEM implementations

By the end of this chapter, you should be prepared to articulate what you need from Adobe Experience Manager. The more effective you are at describing your needs, the easier it is for people in my position to deliver.

Create a solid foundation for the rest of your AEM
implementation with good requirement definitions.

You are not building a website!

If you remember just one thing from reading this book, let this echo in your head through the entire implementation process:

You are not building a website!

You should read this entire chapter through the lens of the WCM implementation process: the process of working with a solution partner to build the page templates, components, and customizations you will need. This is a software development process of which you will be a critical part. This chapter is all about expressing *what* you need to achieve at the end of that process.

I'm emphatic that you are not building a website, because with any content management implementation you are actually developing a set of tools or building blocks that enable marketers to build a website. It's a difficult mindset for both software developers and marketers to accept. It's also a pretty subtle semantic difference. But it's extremely important that you understand how building a website and building a set of building blocks are, in fact, different.

To develop a normal website you need to define everything about its behavior. You need to define how everything will look. You even have to define your content, because it will not be that easy to change. It will have high tolerance for one-off exceptions in requirements, static design, and complexity. But if you build a website, you will still have significant barriers to any kind of change—especially, any change to your content.

Defining your needs for developing a website on top of a content management system means adding a layer of abstraction. You have to think about what you want your website to ultimately look like, and include all the elements you will need to implement your custom website. Then, you have to break those requirements down into a set of tools that you can use to assemble and control that website yourself. You must consider what those tools will allow content authors to do and how it will affect your static designs.

The biggest benefit of going with a WCM is that it empowers marketing people to control their digital marketing. That said, the requirements for a content management system are significantly more complex than those for a custom website. Fear not. I want this chapter to prepare you specifically for those challenges. We'll briefly review some requirements fundamentals, and then we'll talk through how you can start defining requirements to build a digital marketer's web toolbox.

Setting the stage

Maybe you've previously been part of a software development process, and maybe not. You travel a long road from signing the purchase order to getting a pat on the back for tripling online revenue. Before we venture into the requirements definition portion of that journey, it'll be helpful to set the stage by reviewing the basics of the software implementation process. This will ensure that you have a foundation for understanding the AEM-specific concepts we cover in the rest of this chapter.

Introducing the implementation process

Every software implementation process is different, but they all consist of a few common pieces. The basic phases of an implementation project are as follows:

1. Requirements definition—You've assessed a need for some software; now you have to define what you need. This includes what it looks like, what it'll do, what it won't do, and how it will deliver the intended business value. This phase is what this chapter is all about.

2. Implementation—The technical folks get their hands on the requirements and start to build what was defined. This phase is all about coding and assembling. Inevitably, some requirements will change in this phase as new discoveries are made or technical limitations emerge.

3. Testing—In this phase, the goal is to make sure that what was built aligns with the defined requirements. It also involves sniffing out any software bugs created during the development. Don't be alarmed when there are software bugs to squash. It's a part of life.

4. Deployment—This phase involves setting up and deploying the application to production (live). The first weeks that an application is live are critical. More bugs will be isolated and more things will need to be tweaked.

5. Maintenance—This is the ongoing phase of monitoring and updating the application through the rest of its life. Eventually, the application will be retired for any number of reasons.

This is a simplification of the software development process. Most projects break these steps down further. Many teams will cycle through them in small batches, instead of moving through one large, linear process. (All of these issues will be discussed in Chapter 20.) For now, this outline will enable us to talk about requirements definition.

The usual players

The requirements phase of a software implementation involves a crowd of the usual suspects who have varying levels of accountability and responsibility. Every team and situation is different, but let's look at the most common roles. As you read this section, think about which of your team members could fill these roles, while knowing that one person may fill more than one role.

Product owner

The product owner has the final say on requirements definition. This individual is responsible for setting the tone and direction of the project, and facilitates the creation of requirements to ensure they address the intended business value. This tends to be a supervisory, direction-setting role, but on smaller teams the product owner may also get down into nitty-gritty requirements details.

The product owner often has a title like "product manager" or "program manager." A product manager typically sets the direction for one application or a part of an application. A program manager oversees a collection of related products (or applications), typically called a "program." Sometimes multiple product managers exist on a project. If so, they are usually assigned to separate sections of the application. When multiple managers share responsibility for the same parts of the same project, the process easily gets messy and political.

In our discussion, we'll lump these titles together into "product owner" because at the end of the day, all of these managers do the same thing: they set the direction and high-level requirements for a software project.

Business analyst

The business analyst (B.A.) is the product owner's foot soldier. This person is responsible for defining specific requirements for every necessary part of the application. The B.A. works with the product owners to set the direction but doesn't usually make the final decisions. The B.A. conducts interviews with those who will use the application in order to assess needs, find the problems that need solved, and understand where the value should be delivered. Ultimately, this person specifies everything that will need to be built.

Typically, the B.A. will be an involved member of the development team, working closely with the programmers to ensure that requirements are communicated correctly. It is common to have multiple analysts on bigger projects. Sometimes the B.A will also be the product owner, if the project doesn't justify the need for two separate people. Business analysts have varying degrees of technical knowledge. Some used to be programmers. Some can barely start their computers. But ultimately, their job is to figure out what needs to be built and articulate it.

User experience designer

The user experience designer (sometimes just "designer") is responsible for the look and feel of the application. When thinking about web projects, I'm also lumping people such as information architects into this category. (Remember, I'm simplifying.) The business analyst can articulate business value, but that input generally doesn't translate into "what it looks like." User experience (UX) designers understand human-computer interaction, typical design paradigms, and the visual facets of the brand. They build the vision of what the business analysts and product owners define.

UX designers come in all shapes and sizes. Some of them are very technical and double as front-end web developers. (They build the client-side stuff.) Some designers focus more heavily on the *design* aspect: laying out elements, applying accurate branding, assessing human interaction, and so on. They are typically less able to program and spend most of the time mocking up application designs using tools such as those in the Adobe Creative Suite. If you have multiple designers, you may want to have a mix of technical and nontechnical designers. They'll keep one another in check.

User experience design is critical when implementing Adobe Experience Manager, so all of Chapter 19 will be dedicated to that topic.

Software developers

Software developers in your implementation team will also have their stakes in the requirements. They are likely to have considerable experience in dealing with AEM-specific requirements. Developers will also uncover gaps or contradictions in those requirements as they are building the software. No matter how hard you try, you won't be able to define everything up front. Developers will help you to uncover what you missed.

Executives

Last, there are those pesky executives. These people have titles that begin with Vice President, Director, or the letter C. They are normally the furthest away from the implementation process, but like it or not, they are a critical part of that process. Executives define the organizational direction, which eventually defines the parameters of each application that is implemented. They also control and allocate the money needed to build the software. In the end, they need to know that the money they spent on an implementation has created value for the organization.

Usually, the product owner interacts most with executives. From that conversation, organizational directives filter down to project direction. When an implementation goes really well (or really poorly), executives more closely monitor the team. Unfortunately, in so doing, some executives will micromanage or disrupt the implementation process. In my opinion, a strong executive who is on board with the application strategy but doesn't micromanage is fundamental to setting the tone for a successful implementation.

Common communication strategies

Requirements are communicated in many ways, some more effective than others. The person who sets the direction has to communicate to the person who defines the specifics. That person needs to communicate those specifics to the people who build it and test it. The people who test it need to communicate whether the requirements are, in fact, addressed. Coordinating that complex communication is usually done with a set of common strategies:

- Verbal communication—Don't forget how valuable a face-to-face or phone conversation can be. Just make sure to record any decisions made. Some team structures require verbal communication more often than others.

- Requirements specifications documents—These are documents (now usually digital) that specify everything that needs to be built. They're the classic output of a business analyst. It's not a very flexible way to manage requirements, so I see this used less all the time. The specs usually describe in great detail what must be built.

- User stories—These artifacts of agile development (covered in Chapter 20) define one single piece of business value. Everything is framed in terms of value, so the specific implementation is up to interpretation and discussion between everyone involved in building it. It's a more modern way to define requirements, but not everyone is comfortable with the initial ambiguity of this approach. User stories are often communicated using index cards on a public wall or using an online tool.

- Communication software—Today, it is rare that an entire team sits in a room together. Usually, you'll use some kind of online software to store and manage requirements, assign them to different team members, and document the decisions made. These tools include project management software, wikis, and ticketing systems.

- Wireframes and site mockups—Wireframes are unbranded designs that express the layout of an application and define the purpose of different content. Site mockups build on that with fully branded designs of how the application should eventually look. Together, these documents express how the application should look and behave.

How your team will communicate their requirements depends on a number of factors:

- Whether you are co-located

- What technology you have available to use

- How well your team generally communicates (team culture)

- Whether you have external stakeholders, such as partners or contractors, involved

Every team is different, so you'll have to assess which communication strategies work best for your team. It's also common to change those strategies as you learn which work and which don't.

Defining your needs

Every organization will use its own frameworks and practices for creating and managing development project requirements. Regardless of how you manage them, certain questions must be asked when going into an Adobe Experience Manager project. In this section, we'll discuss questions that address the needs you'll have to define. Most of these questions motivate more detailed conversations. You'll certainly have more questions to answer than the ones presented in this section, but this list should get you started.

Once again, you aren't just building a website; you're implementing a set of building blocks for marketers. Therefore, your requirements cannot be limited to what the "end user" or "site visitor" sees. Branding, site design, and information architecture are important, but they're only part of the picture. To deliver a truly successful AEM implementation, you'll need to define requirements to determine how the marketing team will use those building blocks.

Internal requirements

Internal requirements define how marketers will interact with Adobe Experience Manager. To successfully manage a web presence with AEM, your marketing team must be given freedom within the boundaries of the brand. The system is no good if it's too difficult to create the content they need or too easy to violate the brand. I find that these internal requirements tend to be overlooked, because the focus is on external ones.

Marketer-facing requirements *will* get fleshed out, whether or not you take the time to define them. However, without some foresight, the solutions to the questions in this section tend to be uncovered on the fly. The result is typically an unnecessarily complicated, frustrating implementation process and an inconsistent marketer experience within the platform. You don't need to (and shouldn't try to) set every detail in stone up front. But you should consider the answers to these high-level questions in advance.

What page templates will you need?

When evaluating *what* you need to implement within AEM, start with the pages you'll need. The branding plays a part, but your information architecture, expressed as wireframes, is more important. You'll want to think about which elements are "part of the template" and which areas of the template should be available for free-form content.

This is also where you start to define how much control you'll give your marketers. Embedded components are less flexible than free-form content areas (paragraph systems). There are tradeoffs with either approach. If you rely more heavily on embedded components, you'll control your pages more tightly, but you'll also need to define more templates to accommodate every specific use case. If you rely more heavily on free-form content, you'll loosen restrictions and you'll be able to define fewer templates because they are based on layout rather than function.

As a general best practice, I favor using fewer templates based primarily on layout. Think about defining one-, two-, and three-column layouts or similar categorizations for templates. Generally speaking, the fewer number of templates that you provide to content authors, the better their authoring experience. You'll still have some embedded components, such as logos and navigation bars, and you'll still require exceptions where a template serves only one specific purpose. But for most content entry, stick to simple, open templates.

Note: Keep in mind the relationship between the template and page component, as discussed in Chapter 3. I'm just using the term "template" to keep the wording simple.

What components will you need?

This question seems so obvious, and yet it's rarely addressed with the appropriate priority. Usually the frame of reference for requirements is branded site mockups and supplementary requirements. Mockups are pictures of pages, so they are often (and inappropriately) created to express what a *page* should be. Though that's part of the equation, it's incomplete. You need to define how the various pieces of content represented in your wireframes and mockups should break into components.

We'll dig into this a bit more in the next chapter.

How would you like to author each component?

It's not only important to understand the customer-facing business value of each component; you also need to understand (at least at a high level) how marketers will interact with a component to author it. What fields will be in the dialog? How will they link it to other components or systems, if necessary? Where can you place the component within your site? What are you going to call the component? All these issues affect how the content authors experience the platform. If their experience is optimized, your AEM implementation will be more successful.

If you are new to Adobe Experience Manager, you'll probably need your solution partner's help to define the authoring experience. After all, to do this, you must be familiar with what options are available and their tradeoffs. From your perspective, consider the following:

- Keep it simple. Don't make every little thing configurable if you don't need to. It just makes content authoring complicated.

- Don't allow content authors to configure styling changes (especially with CSS) when they author components. Some people disagree with me on this, but I find that allowing styling changes seriously diminishes the authoring experience and places design considerations where they don't belong.

- Try to be consistent. The method of configuring an image should be same on every component with an image. Your rich text editor should have the same options everywhere. There are exceptions to this rule, but the more consistent you make things, the easier you'll make it for content authors.

- Avoid the temptation to circumvent the paradigms established by AEM. Stick with familiar concepts like dialogs and configuration pages, instead of trying to define a custom content entry mechanism.

- Apply the appropriate validation. Content entry validation is often overlooked because it's a little tedious to define. However, requiring validation makes it much harder for marketers to do what they aren't supposed to do. In the end, that improves your web experience.

You need to put on content author's shoes and play dumb (not to insinuate that your content authors are dumb). Pretend you know very little about the authoring interface and imagine how an intuitive, self-explanatory system would interact with an author. This will help you understand how to define an effective authoring experience.

What AEM features do you plan to use?

As you drill down from high-level ideas about what you need to build to application specifics, consider what AEM features you plan to use (and which you don't). You'll want to define requirements in terms that are compatible with each relevant AEM feature.

For example, if you plan to implement a site blog using the Social Communities blog components, you'll need to start with the framework provided in AEM. Then work backward to what you need. It may be a reskinning of what's already there. It may be a significant customization. You *may* determine that your requirements don't align with the parameters of the blog components and elect to build something completely customized. It's important to work through this assessment early, especially if you need to license additional modules from Adobe to accomplish what you want.

Be careful with this approach, though. You don't want to *start* in terms of AEM features. Start with your business goals and what you need. Then evaluate how they align with the specific features of Adobe Experience Manager. If you start with the features, you'll end up with a cookie-cutter site, much like the Geometrixx demo that ships with the product. That's not going to impress anybody.

How will you supervise content creation?

What governance and processes will you put in place to facilitate team-based content creation? Typically, many people will be responsible for different parts of your site. The bigger your team, the riskier it becomes to give everyone full permissions. You need to define permission levels (who can do what and where) as they relate to content publishing processes. These requirements will define how user permissions are configured and enforce any approval process or other types of workflows.

You can probably get away with putting this off for some time. In fact, you may want to feel out your permissions and workflow strategies as your site is developed. But you should definitely have the appropriate governance in place when you roll out AEM to the full team in a production environment. Unfettered production allows marketers to make mistakes that end up costing money or jobs.

How many people will use the system?

How big is your team? Do you have 10 people who will be authoring content or 100? Are they sitting in the same row of cubicles or located all over the world? How much content authoring do they plan to do? All these questions help define the internal load that the system will need to support.

Hardware sizing should be done pretty early in the process, because it probably includes licensing concerns. If you have only one author instance but 100 content authors who will work concurrently, you are going to have performance issues. It's just too much load for a single author instance to handle.

On the other hand, three clustered author instances is probably overkill if you have only 10 people logging in. Work with your solution partner and Adobe early in the process to size your system. Fortunately, AEM's flexible architecture easily allows you to scale up and down (especially in the cloud), so you can adapt as needed.

What other systems will you integrate with?

If you want to use data from other systems, you should call that out early in the process. From a marketing/business perspective, you'll need to map out what data you want to gather and what you want to do with it. Think in terms of how you can use data from other systems to enhance your brand's web experience, as we discussed in Chapter 16. However, avoid the temptation to just pull in data for the sake of it.

Once you have defined your integration needs, you can work with your solution partner to determine how to address them. Your programmers may build or set up a cloud services configuration. They may build a custom integration layer. There are many ways to accomplish the same thing. Again, avoid the temptation to circumvent the authoring and configuration paradigms already established in AEM. Your solution partner should also be on board with that AEM-compatible frame of mind.

External requirements

With any website, whether or not it uses a content management system, you'll need to specify external requirements that define how the website works for those who visit it. These requirements define how the site visually represents the brand, as well as the interactivity available to site visitors. I find that these requirements are typically a bit easier for everyone to get their heads around, because you are talking about your website from the perspective of your customers. The following questions should be asked along with the internal requirements questions we just discussed.

What is your information architecture?

Before you determine how a website should be styled, it's good practice to define its information architecture—that is, what kinds of information will be delivered and how it will be organized. Effectively, this means mapping out the multiple sections of your site to determine what kinds of information goes where. The objective is to identify what method of content organization will be intuitive for your site visitors.

You may be asking, "If we are dictating where all the content goes anyway, why use a content management system?" The information architecture isn't specific enough to define every single piece of content. It's more like a roadmap that specifies where certain types of content will exist in your site hierarchy. Your information architect will generally document this information as a "site map" that shows the breakdown of content types in the same hierarchy that will become the actual site.

In other words, you don't generally give your content authors full choice about what pages are created where. Typically, your top-level pages will be predefined by the information architecture. You'll still have to author them like any other page, and they can be edited or deleted. But they are specifically defined ahead of time. The lower down in your site structure you go, the more flexible the content becomes.

Another important set of artifacts developed as part of your information architecture are wireframes. These are unbranded pictures of your site pages that define their layout and content priorities. Instead of showing sample or *Lorem Ipsum* content as in a design mockup, a wireframe explains how important different page areas are and how they may be are related. Once the wireframes are mostly agreed upon, the designers will generally use them to create styled mockups.

Your wireframes are often a good way to define which page templates you'll have to build. Remember, it's a best practice to build page templates that correspond to the various page layouts you'll want to provide to content authors. Wireframes will generally match up one-to-one with eventual page templates. Of course, you'll have your one-off templates as well.

What does the website look like?

This one is easy. What does the website look like in terms of styling, colors, fonts, and so on? A website can be one of the most important representations of your brand, so you want to ensure that its quality and branding are consistent with the rest of your organization. You'll want to be sure that logos and colors are recognizable. However, be careful not to focus *too* much on the visual styling of your website. It *is* important, but visual considerations occasionally consume more effort than they should during an implementation.

Note: Website appearance is discussed in more detail in Chapter 10.

How much traffic do you expect?

How much web traffic do you expect your site to generate? 500 hits a day? 5,000? 50,000? Having a general idea is important up front, because the volume of traffic has significant impact on how many instances of AEM you need to license. You'll always want to license at least two publish instances for redundancy, but I've worked on implementations with 40-plus publish instances. If you don't honestly assess the anticipated web traffic early in your implementation, you could find yourself later needing to license more software and increasing your capital investment.

The volume of traffic will also have a big impact on the caching strategies that your solution partner will implement. For sites that expect huge amounts of traffic, very specific caching techniques become quite a bit more important. You'll always have at least a baseline caching strategy, but for bigger sites, your solution partner will probably pull out a few extra tricks to ensure that your highly trafficked site remains highly available.

What is the point of the website?

Organizations sometimes get so caught up in the implementation process that they lose site of the purpose of the website they're building. You should be able to define the "mission" (so to speak) of the site in a clear, concise manner. That mission statement should be the guiding principle for every development or content creation decision you make. You can be assured that if you cannot clearly communicate what you want visitors to do on your site, then your visitors won't be able to figure it out.

Determining the mission of the website (or websites) is the job of the product manager, along with the executives. This should be the first, most high-level requirement defined for the project. For every requirement defined thereafter, you should be able to explain *why* it supports the overall mission of the site. Otherwise, you will waste time and/or confuse content authors and site visitors.

What actions will constitute a conversion?

Although you need to define the purpose of your website, that mission statement *should* be too broad and abstract to specifically measure. If you can measure it, then you missed the point. Once you define the mission, you should detail the various actions that you want your site visitors to take within the site. These actions confirm that site visitors did what you intended them to do. The term "conversion" is usually used to describe the actions that "convert" site visitors.

Every tactic you use to improve your site, such as building new components or authoring pages, should drive site visitors toward conversion. If you can't explain how a page or a component contributes to conversion, that's a sign that it's not very important. Generally, you will implement dynamic content, using personalization or A/B testing, to optimize your conversion rate. Your web analytics platform will also measure all of your content in terms of how it contributed to conversion rate. Conversions are important. They are the tangible, measurable actions that fulfill your site's mission.

How will you measure your site's effectiveness?

You can define all the conversions you want, but they won't do you any good unless you define how you'll measure them. Without real metrics about how well you are converting customers, you'll have no baseline for improving or regressing. You need to know that changes you make to your site improve or reduce your conversion rate. Those metrics will help you understand your customers and hone in on improving your content. This is called conversion optimization.

The easy answer is that your web analytics platform will measure your site conversions, and that may be sufficient. You'll want to specify what analytics tools you use so that your solution partner can assist with their integration into AEM. You'll also want to determine whether you want to use specialized analytics tools like Adobe Test&Target to put further emphasis on your conversion optimization plans.

You should also consider secondary metrics that define your site's effectiveness. Analytics platforms track a lot more than how well your content contributes to conversion. Other metrics, like percentage of traffic that is mobile or site load time, may also be important, even though they don't directly relate to conversion optimization. If you define secondary metrics that aren't tracked by your analytics tools, you'll have to work with your solution partner to define what additional technology integrations may be necessary.

What languages and geographies will you target?

If your brand is global, you'll want to think about which languages and geographies you intend to target. Your international strategies will have an impact on your site design and the processes you put in place to author content. If you are targeting any right-to-left languages such as Arabic, you'll also want to build the flexibility to reverse your site's flow into your design. Virtually every site receives traffic from all over the world, but you should try to focus on those initial locations where you *want* to target your brand. You can always expand your multicultural strategy later.

Best practices

To conclude this chapter, I want to share some best practices I've acquired through the many implementations I've worked on. Some of this content will be a rehash of ideas you've already considered in this chapter. Some will represent new insights. Take these practices for what they are worth, but know that I'm sharing them so you can learn from my experiences.

You are building a marketing toolbox

One last time: You are not building a website! You are building a set of tools to enable your digital marketing team to build a website. This frame of mind will help you realize the additional requirements you'll need to define. You have to address your site visitors' experience and also your content authors' experience. This is often overlooked, and when it is, the result is a less-than-ideal experience for the marketers who have to work in AEM every day. Ultimately, when it's easier to manage your web presence, your web presence will be better.

Keep it simple

When you begin defining requirements for your AEM implementation, you can feel a bit like a kid getting ready for Christmas. You may find yourself writing down every wonderful thing you would ever want to do. That kind of vision is helpful over the long term, but trying to bite all that off right away won't work. Always keep your requirements simple. Think in terms of what you *need* to accomplish now and what the next reasonable evolutionary step might be. If you can't express how a feature immediately contributes to your overall goal, or you can't comprehend how to get there from your current reality, then you are likely getting too complicated.

Avoid use of complex workflows

When you are trying to detail a complex data processing requirement, it can be tempting to default to "Let's just make a workflow do that." I recommend that you avoid creating complex workflows, at least in the early stages of your AEM implementation. Launch with the basic workflow functions that you need, such as a simple content approval workflow. Initially, favor manual (albeit somewhat slower) business processes to keep requirements modest. Then as you gain confidence with the platform and understand what the workflow engine can and cannot do well, start defining more complicated workflow uses.

Don't work against AEM

Adobe Experience Manager includes well-thought-out experiences for content authors. Sidekick, drag-and-drop authoring, configuration pages, and cloud services configurations are familiar paradigms for content authors and administrators who work in AEM. As you develop requirements for customization or integration, avoid working around these basic experience paradigms. You always want to try to do it "the AEM way" because when you don't, you create yet another (potentially) unintuitive procedure that people need to learn.

Think in terms of components, not pages

It's easy to think about websites in terms of pages, because that is typically how the user experience documentation presents it. It is more appropriate to think about the building blocks of your site in terms of components (and templates). Each single piece of business value in your site should be a component. Each layout should be a template (and page component). When you remember to think in terms of components, it's easier to identify opportunities for reusing functionality. It also puts you in mind of the content author, who *must* think in terms of components.

Don't dig a customized grave

Avoid making decisions that will dig you into a hole later. For example, customizations to the source code of Adobe Experience Manager can make upgrades difficult or impossible. When you define requirements that circumvent AEM paradigms, create complicated customizations, or produce an unstable architecture, you sacrifice long-term flexibility for short-term gain. If you are new to Adobe Experience Manager, you probably aren't going to be qualified to accurately assess whether decisions will dig you into a hole, which brings me to my next point...

Lean on your solution partner

Your solution partner should be just that: a partner. Do not create a relationship in which you define requirements that you throw over a wall to your solution partner. You will not be happy with the result. Involve your solution partner as early and as cooperatively as possible in your process. In fact, many partners will even get involved before you purchase AEM, assisting you in determining whether AEM is the right solution for you. Implementations based on a positive, interactive working relationship are always more successful. Be prepared to lean on your solution partner to fill in the gaps and start out on the right foot. If your partner is not ready for a close working relationship or is afraid to push back on your suggestions, find a new partner.

Everything should support your mission

You need to define the mission for your website and Adobe Experience Manager implementation. *Everything* you do should support that mission. If it does not, then you probably shouldn't be spending time or money on it. It's easy to get caught up in the day-to-day of writing code, cranking out documentation, or authoring pages. Never forget why you are doing all those things or how they are all related. Your site visitors will know instantly if you've forgotten.

Summary

Developing appropriate requirements and implementing the processes to manage those requirements are crucial first steps toward a successful Adobe Experience Manager implementation. Every team and every implementation will be different, but certain practices universally ring true.

Remember that you are building a set of tools for your marketing team to build your website. Remember also to consider both your site visitors' experience and your content authors' experience. Apply the practices described in this chapter as you work through the requirements phase of whatever software implementation process your organization uses. It'll save you money and frustration in the long run.

Review questions

1. What are you not building?

2. What is the purpose of the product owner?

3. Would consideration of the authoring experience produce internal or external requirements?

4. What is a conversion?

Review answers

1. A website. Don't you forget it. You are implementing a set of tools that allow nonprogrammers to build a website.

2. The product owner is responsible for setting the tone and direction for a software development project. The owner does not generally define specific requirements, but defines the goals that all requirements should support.

3. Consideration of the authoring experience generates internal requirements.

4. A conversion is a measurable action that a site visitor can perform on your website that supports your overall mission. It signifies a "successful" site visit because it means you got your customer to do what you wanted him to do.

19 USER EXPERIENCE DESIGN

A web experience management system like Adobe Experience Manager is designed to enable marketers to deliver an effective web experience to potential customers, readers, or anyone else you define as your site user. The platform can do all the heavy lifting, but you must first design the experience that you want the platform to deliver.

This chapter will cover:

- The fundamentals of user experience design and why they are important
- How to design for a content management system such as Adobe Experience Manager
- The "mobile-first" user experience design approach

User experience design (UXD) is one of the earliest and most critical phases in an AEM implementation. A poorly architected design can derail your project before anyone writes any code. This chapter will point you in the right direction.

UXD: The art of designing user interaction

What is UXD?

User experience design is the practice of defining the visual elements of software to optimize it for human interaction. In layman's terms, UXD shapes your website visuals so that people will intuitively know how to use it. Modern web technology enables you to implement powerful user experiences. As a result, the relevance of UXD has skyrocketed over the last decade.

To successfully market to current and potential customers via the web, you need to understand the basics of user experience design. You should consult an expert who can architect your user experience. Losing conversions because visitors are lost, confused, or just plain annoyed leaves money on the table. But before we dive into the design issues, let's talk about user experience.

What is user experience?

The user experience is the interaction a site visitor has with your website (or any piece of software, for that matter). It encompasses the appearance of your site, how visitors interact with it, how information is organized, and other visitor-touching issues. User experience is based mostly on feeling. Such a soft concept is difficult to define, design for, or even agree on. That's why the practice of user experience design has emerged as a sexy new business arena.

Your site's user experience has a serious impact on how effectively your site meets its business goals. A good user experience will delight your visitors and make it easy for them to engage in the ways you want them to engage. A poor user experience will confuse or irritate visitors. A poor user experience is often the culprit when you find that certain pages on your site have unexpectedly high *bounce rates* (the percentage of visitors that leave after seeing one page) or low conversion rates. The UX can be a competitive advantage or a huge thorn in your side.

User experience is also extremely objective. *Everyone* thinks that they are a usability expert because everyone knows what they prefer when visiting a website. Human-computer interaction is an emerging field of study that defines user experience practices backed by quantitative analysis. But it has only begun to scratch the surface in terms of understanding what truly defines a "good" user experience.

In Chapter 15, we discussed creating dynamic content via personalization and multivariate and A/B testing. Personalization involves tailoring the user experience to the preferences of a visitor. Content testing is about randomly presenting different user experiences, and then analyzing which ones realized the most conversions. All of these activities are designed to optimize the user experience. While there's no such thing as a "perfect" user experience, you'll want to constantly inch your website toward that mythical perfection.

The practice of UXD

You might consider UXD a subset of the requirements definition processes that we discussed in Chapter 18. But don't overlook UXD as just another part of the requirements gathering. Designing an effective user experience requires specifically skilled people who can execute exact processes that hone in on the best possible design.

User experience designers generally have a skill set that sits at the intersection of technical, scientific, and artistic considerations. They often possess degrees in visual communication, human-computer interaction, or graphic design. UX designers know the technology and science well enough to understand and test their ideas. However, they also possess the creative skills to produce visually appealing presentations that practically support their scientific findings. In other words, user experience design is tough and a good UX designer is an invaluable member of your team.

Some of the topics that are generally addressed within the domain of user experience design are:

- Information architecture—How content is organized for consumption (we talked about it in the last chapter)

- Visual design—Colors, images, fonts…the pretty stuff

- Site interaction—How visitors click, drag, swipe, or flick to interact with your website

- Accessibility—Making sure that users with disabilities (such as those using screen readers) or with older web browsers can still consume content

These primary areas of focus, combined with some lesser concerns, comprise the practice of user experience design. If you can do these well, you can be an effective user experience designer.

Measuring user experience

User experience can make or break your site. If your site contributes in any way to your revenue stream (and I'm going to guess that it does), you don't want visitors leaving your site confused or annoyed. Each person should easily find their desired content on your site. You need to quantify and analyze how accessible your site is.

You can measure user experience using quantitative or hard methods. Multivariate and A/B testing allow you to test which of a set of user experiences is best. To determine "the best," you need to define your conversion criteria. In general, a higher conversion rate will be the result of a better user experience. Other quantitative measurements include measuring how much your content is shared or how long people spend on your site (which can also be considered a conversion criterion).

You should also use qualitative or soft methods for assessing user experience. Concepts such as brand loyalty or customer delight aren't measurable in dollars and cents, but they certainly reflect the effectiveness of your user experience. Customer conversations and other "soft" data collection methods can help you understand how your website makes people feel. You want to ensure that the digital representation of your brand accurately reflects the feelings you want to evoke.

Best practices

To maximize your use of a UX expert, it's important that you understand the UXD basics. The following are some general best practices related to user experience. They should give you an idea of what a user experience designer evaluates every single day:

- Design for the lowest common denominator. If you make some crazy, complicated user experience that requires modern technology, you've alienated everyone who doesn't want to or know how to upgrade their tech. Start with an experience that everyone can use, and then work up.

- Don't stray too far from the generally accepted web user experience. People expect a navigation component at the top of a webpage. They expect a breadcrumb interface to tell them where they are. They expect their cursor to turn into a pointer when hovering over a link. Like it or not, most people look for these elements on websites. Don't confuse them by insisting on something else.

- Keep your interactions simple. If someone has to press Alt+Ctrl+click on an image to perform an even remotely important task, you'll lose them. Even if you provide instructions, a complex key command (for example) like that is just confusing. Assume your users are children—maybe they are. Don't make things too hard for them.

- Don't start playing background music. Don't move things around without your user knowing. Don't start playing a video until the user requests it. Little surprises like these are annoying.

- Avoid using high-contrast colors. You'll want to accurately represent your brand, but (for instance) red text on a black background is hard to read. Just because they are "your" branding colors doesn't mean you need to apply them everywhere.

- Always focus on what you want the user to do. Everything should be designed to encourage the site visitor to perform conversion actions.

- Don't assume you know how people will perform an interaction. Some people fill out a form and press Enter. Some tab to the Submit button and press the spacebar. Some just click the button with the cursor. For common web interactions like forms, links, and so on, make sure that you allow for all possibly desired actions.

- But don't make up a bunch of interactions just to be cute.

- Test. Test. Test. If you don't, you are just assuming that you have created a decent user experience. You need quantitative support to verify that every new idea is better. When a new idea is verified as better, it should become the status quo.

Hundreds of books have been written about user experience design. Many of them are very good, and most are easy to read. I highly recommend learning about UX, even if you aren't a designer. It will only help you to better understand the science (and the art) behind it.

UX and WCM

User experience design is complicated enough when executing a piece of software or a website that remains static. Adding a web content management system into the mix complicates UXD even further. When using a WCM to manage your website, you have to sort out all the de facto UX issues. And then you also have to worry about these additional issues:

- Designing a website that can handle content of any size

- Designing the website in terms of "components" that will be reused and adapted throughout the site

- Designing the content author's user experience to be intuitive and consistent with the platform

These are not easy tasks. User experience designers who truly understand the complexities of designing for a content management system are rare. This section will dive into those complexities to give you a better idea of how to manage your UXD process through them.

Designing for fluid content

Imagine you are designing a static website that doesn't pull content from a database. You draw every single page and the content inside it. You know exactly how everything is going to look after it is coded and delivered. Building the content into the design in this way ensures that you know exactly how much space the content needs. You know on which words the lines of text break. You know how big each image is. There won't be any surprises come implementation time, unless someone changes the content or the design.

But that approach is completely unrealistic when you are using a web content management platform. (Actually, it's *never* very realistic.) Remember, you are designing (and then building) a set of tools for the digital marketers to build a website. When you design the site, you likely will not know what content goes on every page. You won't know when authors will use an image instead of a video. You won't know if the copy is 150 or 1,500 words. So you have to design accordingly.

The design process for a WCM-driven site should involve a business analyst. You should have a clear idea about what content should be editable, what content will be static, and how the authors will want to edit that content. If you know that certain areas will be dynamically authored (as most areas will be), you have to build flexibility into your layout to allow for that process.

I often see designs that include authored copy that must remain within a static height and width area. Here's the problem with that. Text needs somewhere to flow. English tends to flow downward rather than to the right, so you most likely need to allow text to push downward. If your design depends on maintaining a specific height for a component, it will complicate (and compromise) everything an author does. You will have to limit the length of what the author can enter, or you will have to build flexibility into the design.

The behavior of fluid content is often overlooked when designing a website to be implemented on a WCM. You need to anticipate those edge cases. What happens if the author copies half of *Moby Dick* into that text area? What happens if he adds a 7000px image? One concept of how a page will look is not enough, because it doesn't foresee the behavior of that content. If you neglect to anticipate these issues, your implementation team *will* raise them later, because they'll have to. Building the answers into your design reduces risk and complexity later in the project.

Designing for a component model

Adobe Experience Manager uses a component model as the basis of the authoring experience. Components are the pieces of content. They are the building blocks that marketers assemble to create a web presence. Authors create a page, configure any components that are statically included, and then add and configure any other components that are available. During the design process, you'll have to keep that workflow in mind.

Designing for a component model requires you continually ask these questions:

- What are my components?
- Where can I put components?
- How is each component visually presented?

Work with your implementation team through the design process to deliver answers to these questions. Typically a user experience designer doesn't think in terms of "components." He thinks in terms of a site visitor trying to accomplish a goal. Collaboration between UXD and implementation teams is essential to create the best outcome.

What components?

The obvious question is "*What* components are used on a page?" In other words, if you draw a picture of an entire webpage, what parts of that picture are realized with which component? It's not as simple as saying every block of text, image, and link is its own component. Different parts of that page are related and should be logically grouped. Maybe you've got a video with a block of text that describes it. Maybe you've got a list of links with a title. A component is made up of content that is logically related.

You'll want to think about what defines a component, because you'll want to reuse those components throughout the site. They may appear in different ways (we'll get to that), but if they display the same data and are authored in the same way, they should generally be the same component. Really simple components, such as a block of text, are easy to reuse. Complex components tend to be less reusable, because they are applied to a few specific use cases. You'll have a range of complexity within your component list, but try to keep in mind what defines each one. It'll help you develop an intelligently componentized design.

Where are components used?

It's important to understand what each component is, because you'll also want to think about *where* each one can be used. Your information architecture should define the purpose of different pages in your site hierarchy along with different content areas on the page. It should be the guide for choosing what types of content to use and where they are allowed. In AEM, you can limit components to certain types of pages or certain areas on a page, and you'll want to think about how your design adheres to that principle.

Thinking about where components should go improves the site visitor experience *and* the author experience. Again, a text component can probably go anywhere. Your "shopping cart" component will probably go on only one page. Site visitors won't get confused as long as they don't see certain components in places that don't make sense. Authors won't be confused because rules (enforced by the technology) will dictate what components can go where. Achieving this level of UX logic is only possible, however, when the design supports it.

How will you use components?

A component can appear differently in various places on the site, mostly through the application of CSS. You may have a title on the top of a content page and also in the sidebar of that content page. That can be the same component, even though they appear vastly different.

A title is a simple example, but you'll encounter more complex ones. Focus on *what* kind of content is being shown and where it originates. Is the content authored or pulled from some other system? Behavior trumps style when determining whether two parts of your design should be created using a single component. Try to isolate where parts of your content share behavior, and then allow yourself to design each instance differently as necessary.

Designing to the platform paradigm

With a web content management system, you aren't only required to be cognizant of the site visitor's user experience. You also have to consider the content authors and the marketers who will work inside the platform. If authors and marketers are confused or find it difficult to do what they need to, *the work isn't going to get done.* Much of the responsibility for this falls to the software company that builds the content management system (in our case, Adobe). But some of it falls on the team implementing your customizations.

When you implement a website on top of a content management platform, it's like you are extending that platform. The WCM gives you a baseline set of tools, practices, and interfaces that you'll use to build your website. Then you tell an implementation team what else you need to enable marketers to build the site.

Designing to optimize the content author's user experience means making sure you design to the paradigm of the platform. Everything your implementation team builds or customizes should feel like just another part of the system. When the content authors train on the system (probably using a Geometrixx example site), they can apply what they learned throughout the site. If you violate the platform paradigms, you'll probably confuse your authors.

For example, in Adobe Experience Manager, you edit a component by clicking it and selecting Edit. A dialog appears, which is just a tabbed form that shows all the available options for configuring that component.

If you've decided that you don't like using dialogs, you might ask your implementation team to design a completely different way to edit components. Could they do it? Probably. But if everyone working in AEM expects to edit components in a dialog, why would you force them to edit components in a different way?

In reality, the responsibility to design the content author's experience falls almost completely on the implementation team. User experience designers will typically focus on the site visitor, and then collaborate with the developers to make sure the component supports a positive authoring experience, too. When working through an implementation, the entire team should be aware of these issues, but only the implementation team will truly understand the platform. As a result, they can help you best understand, from their experience, what works and what doesn't work for content authors.

The key is to think about building an authoring experience that just seems natural. When you do that, employees will be more productive and less stressed. And don't we all want that?

Assessing tradeoffs

You may be feeling a little skeptical after reading this section. It may sound like a lot of impractical advice bellowed from a mountaintop. To a certain extent, you're right. Reality is rife with deadlines, cash flows, politics, and misunderstandings. You may want to do something "the right way," but your manager (and his budget) requires you to do it the fast way.

Use this section to assist you during the design process of your website, but don't consider it a map to the perfect site. Although you'll want to address these issues as responsibly as you can, you can't do so at the expense of getting things done. Lack of information, time, or money may prevent you from approaching perfection, and that's okay. This section is less about dictating what you *have* to do and more about explaining what you definitely shouldn't do. If you ask these questions when developing your design, then you'll be on the right track.

Mobile first: A modern approach

The proliferation of mobile Internet devices has changed the way we should approach user experience design. It's not okay to design just for 20-inch computer monitors. Now we have to support smartphones and tablets of all sizes. Internet watches might be coming. Or Internet-connected appliances! You never know where, when, or how someone is going to access your website, but you must *always* present a strong representation of your brand. Therefore, your design has to adapt to any context in which it is presented. This fairly new approach to user experience design is often called "mobile first."

Adobe's view of UXD

Mobile first is Adobe's approach to dealing with the vast array of new devices and delivering an optimal UX for them all. It's the guiding light for the features within Adobe Experience Manager that enable building mobile-friendly websites. It's the reason Adobe implemented a new touch screen–oriented user interface in AEM 5.6. Adobe believes that you must take a mobile-first approach to guarantee an experience will delight people using any device.

Adobe also endorses the mobile-first approach for those who use Adobe Experience Manager. The "CQ5 Mobile" functionality is still in the platform, and it allows you to set up device groups to respond to different requests (discussed in Chapter 10). You can still use it, provided you've licensed the platform appropriately. But Adobe recommends that moving forward, you should use a mobile-first, responsive approach to designing web experiences. (I generally do, too.) Further, they will continue to develop AEM with that priority.

The topic of "mobile" is a controversial one. You may agree with Adobe's viewpoint. You may disagree. The rest of this chapter will provide a neutral explanation of the mobile-first approach. That way you can judge for yourself and understand Adobe's path for future AEM developments.

Understanding mobile-first, responsive design

A mobile-first design philosophy suggests that you reverse the typical design process. Traditional website design begins with the desktop computer. You have at least 1,000 pixels of width. You have a mouse and a keyboard. Web development best practices have evolved assuming the computer as a base platform. The problem is that what works well on a desktop computer doesn't usually work well on a mobile phone or tablet. We started with "desktop first," and that approach kind of blew it for every device that came after the desktop.

You can find hundreds of online articles and blog posts explaining how smartphones and tablets are on the rise and the desktop computer is just barely staying steady. Internet access using mobile devices is way up. These trends have helped reinforce the mobile-first philosophy.

A mobile-first design accounts for a number of factors, including but not limited to the following:

- Some site visitors will use a keyboard and mouse, some will use a touch screen, and some will use a stylus. The interactive parts of your website should allow for them all.

- Sometimes your site will be on a huge, wide screen. Sometimes it will be on a small, narrow one. The site needs to adapt so that it's always presented in a way that properly represents the brand.

- If site visitors use a mobile phone to access your site, they may have limited bandwidth for downloading files. The site design should be conscious of when to use large images or videos.

- Different mobile devices have browsers with different capabilities, and those don't necessarily align with the capabilities of a desktop computer. For example, some mobile browsers don't support many new HTML and CSS features. Your design should have a fallback to support them all in ways appropriate to the hardware and software in use.

- Some content will be more relevant to a mobile visitor. Other content will be more relevant to an at-home desktop computer user. Your design should anticipate what your user is trying to do and how she's trying to do it. And you should be prepared to objectively measure the effectiveness of your solutions.

You start by addressing mobile solutions and then work back to serve all facets of the user experience. This ensures a consistent brand experience no matter how a person views your site.

● **Note:** The term "mobile" is a little misleading here, because it doesn't necessarily mean portable. It's the term used to encompass everything that isn't a desktop. As of this writing, that mostly includes smartphones or tablets. But a small web browser in your refrigerator door or the dashboard of your car would count, too. The mobile-first approach assumes you have little idea how your site visitors will come to your site. So you need to account for a wide range of current and future possibilities.

An important approach for implementing mobile first is responsive design (as discussed in Chapter 10). This strategy technically implements a website to adapt to many screen sizes. It has gained popularity in recent years because of new web standards that support it. If you are taking a mobile-first approach to your user experience design, you are likely going to apply responsive design.

Developing a responsive, mobile-first web experience takes more work than developing a desktop-centric website. Add in all the other complexity of designing for components and unknown content size and you've got a challenge. Remember that you won't be able to do everything perfectly, and not all the ideals expressed in this chapter will be possible. Get the basics down and work from there.

Above all else, put yourself in your site visitors' shoes. Their experience is what matters most.

Summary

User experience design is the practice of designing a person's interaction with a piece of software. Since we're talking about Adobe Experience Manager, that probably means a website. With a content management system like AEM, you will have additional considerations when designing your site visitors' user experience. You'll also have the secondary consideration of providing the best UX for your content authors.

Adobe recommends a generally accepted modern approach called "mobile first" when designing user experiences. It's the philosophy driving the design of AEM's new user interface and a philosophy encouraged by the AEM feature set. You'll have to initiate those philosophical design policies yourself, but you definitely need to make your website represent your brand consistently across any device.

Review questions

1. What is a user experience designer's main job?

2. What is challenging about designing for a component model?

3. How does Adobe recommend that you design to account for the proliferation of mobile devices?

4. What is mobile-first design?

Review answers

1. The user experience designer is tasked with developing the requirements for users' interaction with a piece of software.

2. When developing for a component model, the user experience designer must anticipate how different parts of the design will be reused as components. They must be aware of the logical groupings of functionality and content that will define components. When they are designing for a static website, these considerations are not necessary.

3. Adobe recommends and has adopted a mobile-first design approach.

4. Mobile-first design means making the assumption that you do *not* know the visual context in which visitors will access your site. Therefore, you build into your design the flexibility to display on any device.

20 THE IMPLEMENTATION PROCESS

Adobe Experience Manager is not the kind of software you can install and immediately use. You have to build the necessary page templates, components, and customizations before you can build your website. This book has been preparing you for your role in that process. But the one thing we haven't yet discussed in detail is the software implementation process and your role in it. This chapter will cover:

- The basics of software development

- Agile development and how it empowers agile marketing

- Best practices for software development

At the end of this chapter, you'll understand what you'll be getting into when working with your implementation partner. Everyone's process is a little different, but you'll be aware of the general procedures that you'll experience virtually everywhere.

Making your website a reality

Implementation phases

Everyone uses a different software implementation process. The process may take the blame for failure or be lauded for success. But at their core, all software development processes represent the same basic phases. Formalized workflows may give these phases different names. Sometimes they even reorganize when the phases are performed. Although we've previously explored some aspects of implementation, if you understand the basics behind each phase and the workflow, you'll be better prepared for any kind of software implementation process.

Requirements gathering

During the requirements gathering phase, the product owners and business analysts figure out everything that will need to be created. During this phase, end users and customers are often consulted for feedback. Then, the team translates business challenges and customer requests into executable goals and creates a formalized "wish list" of all the desired features.

Gathering requirements for an AEM implementation means understanding the digital marketers who will be using AEM to build your website and the customers (or site visitors) who will use that site. If the marketer can't build an effective website, the customer can't use it to achieve his goals. If the customer is confused or lost on your site, the marketer's goals will not be met. And who gets the blame for that? The marketer.

Most of the time, I see the majority of this phase happening before the AEM implementation partner is involved. However, I recommend involving your solution partner during requirements gathering. Typically an AEM partner has realized plenty of implementations and will be familiar with the pitfalls. They'll know what is and isn't important in terms of requirements gathering. While your organization will have final say over all requirements, it can be extremely helpful to involve the implementation partner as a requirements advisor.

Development

During the software development phase, the technical team translates the requirements wish list into technical specifications and then builds the software. This phase is usually a collaboration between the technical architect (often leading the development team) and the business analyst.

After technical specifications are defined (at least clearly enough to get started), the development team can start writing code. Throughout this process, you'll see your implementation come together. You'll have a chance to get your hands on the build in progress, and you'll have new templates and components to begin constructing your site. This is where implementation starts to get fun.

Be prepared for additional conversations about requirements during this phase. It's impossible to anticipate absolutely everything at the beginning of the process. Once you start implementing software, you'll find holes in requirements and unexpected technical challenges, and you'll have to address the ever-changing business landscape. There will be a lot of give-and-take and reprioritization during this process, and it's the product owner's job to keep the eye on the prize.

This phase is usually when your solution partner will begin heavy involvement. The translation to technical specifications is often a prerequisite to generating an accurate estimate of the implementation costs. It also reveals whether the partner understands your business needs deeply enough to continue. The solution partner will run the show during this phase, but it's important that you diligently champion the interests of your brand and your customers.

Testing

The testing phase confirms that the software achieves the business needs specified by the requirements. In this phase, you verify that the messiness, miscommunication, and give-and-take of the development phase didn't put your team off track. And if it did, you put things back on course. This phase also involves kicking the tires of the implemented software to flush out technical bugs. And there *will* be technical bugs, no matter how good your implementation team is.

You could read about various kinds of testing for days and find many opinions about which testing techniques are important. This list is a summary of the types you can expect for an AEM implementation:

- Requirements verification—Does the completed software adhere to the specified business requirements that were specified?
- Usability testing—Is the user experience design as awesome as you hoped it would be?
- Software testing—Where are the software bugs? Are there any unanticipated edge cases where things don't work correctly?
- Load testing—How does the site perform when we simulate 1,000 concurrent site visitors? 10,000? 100,000?
- Unit testing—Does each piece of the software do what it's supposed to do?
- Integration testing—Does the software integrate with other systems correctly?
- Regression testing—When you added new features, did you break any of the existing features?

Deployment

You've got the software defined, written, and tested. It's time to make it available to the world. The deployment process involves setting up the production environment that will present your application to the masses. It's a risky endeavor, because if you go live with a revenue-producing site that doesn't work, it can cost you lots of money. The deployment process is about going live while being prepared to quickly solve any problems that were not flushed out during testing.

During the first launch of a new website on Adobe Experience Manager, you'll often perform a "soft deployment." You get the entire platform operating on a production server so that you can test it one last time. You do everything except changing the setting that points your URL to that server.

In subsequent updates to your site, you won't have the luxury of a soft deployment because you'll already be live on AEM. Those changes are a little riskier, but you also won't be launching as much new functionality. Once you have the baseline pages and components developed, subsequent releases are really just the extra goodies on top.

Your implementation team will be heavily involved with this phase, because they know what it takes to manage the infrastructure that supports Adobe Experience Manager. Sometimes, partners even host the site for you as part of their services, which reduces the need for your involvement.

Maintenance

The maintenance phase is the ongoing work that follows the production launch of your site. Even after going live, you'll find bugs or discover that you have too little or too much hardware. Your web analytics will reveal that some elements aren't working as well as you'd hoped. The maintenance phase is about making those optimizing tweaks as well as monitoring the availability and performance of the platform.

The marketing team, led by the product owner, should be in charge of prioritizing and implementing bug fixes. Remember, though, there's a difference between a bug and a missed requirement. An implementation partner will typically fix bugs that involve software not working correctly or not adhering to the previously defined requirements. However, your contract with your solution partner will usually stipulate that missed (or undefined) requirements will only be implemented at additional cost.

The infrastructure team is responsible for monitoring the system for performance and availability. If your solution partner is hosting your AEM instances, they'll do the monitoring. If you are hosting your site in-house, your own information technology department will be the tech watchdogs. But in any case, you can't just turn on the site and forget about it. Ongoing maintenance will require *someone* keeping an eye on things and recommending necessary changes.

When do I build my website?

This whole process has been about developing page templates, components, and customizations to AEM. You may be asking yourself, "If we are developing the tools

I need to build my website, when do I actually build it?" Good! You've been paying attention. The process as outlined does not say when the digital marketer will use the tools being developed to build the website.

Most of the time you can start assembling your site during the development phase. During the requirement phase nothing is developed, so you can't start site building at the very beginning of our implementation. But as your solution partner moves through the process of building components and templates, and establishing the basic plumbing of your application, you'll be able to build pages. The implementation team will often start by creating the most important features, such as your basic content page templates and navigation component. If so, you can start your site as early as possible by building out your web content.

However, there is risk involved when building content during the development phase. As you use page templates and content components, their implementations can change. You can build a site with an early version of your "Contact Us" component, but that component may work differently in a month. When that happens, you may need to reexamine where the component was used in your incomplete website and ensure it still performs as you intended.

Despite the risk of change, I don't recommend waiting until everything is built to start building your website. This "on-the-fly" content creation process helps to flush out bugs and identify incomplete requirements. Finding problems early makes them less expensive to fix.

Agile processes

Up until this point our discussion of implementation phases has assumed a linear progression, one phase proceeding after another. For a long time, this was how all software was built. It's a process that's based on "locking it down" for the next phase. It tends to be heavy on documentation and sign-offs. It also tends to be micro-managed.

Frustrated with this approach, a community of software developers came up with a different way to manage software projects. *Agile* project management breaks the long, linear software process into small, rhythmic iterations (sometimes called *sprints*). Instead of moving through the entire process one phase at a time over months or years, you cycle through the phases every few weeks for a small subset of the project. It's an idea designed to reduce the inevitable cost of change and to empower the development team to build the best possible application.

It's extremely likely that your solution provider will prefer to use an agile project methodology for your AEM implementation. Maybe your in-house development already uses it. I *highly* recommend embracing the concept. If you are new to AEM or web content management, you won't be able to conceptualize everything you'll need from the get-go. You'll need to get your hands on it to learn what works for you and what doesn't. Therefore, you absolutely don't want to define and lock down all your requirements at the beginning of the process. Agile management is specifically intended to address the possibility of change and to take advantage of learning gained during development.

In this section, I'll first explain agile software development, because you'll likely be participating in the process. Then, I'll introduce agile marketing, an emerging idea that leverages the same principles. You'll see that the two enable each other in the digital marketing space. Keep in mind that this is a *very* high-level summary of agile processes. If they sound interesting, I recommend picking up one of the many great books on the topic.

Agile software development

You'll find many software developers who are passionate about agile practices, because it's a movement that grew out of their frustrations. Today, many organizations have adopted or are experimenting with adopting agile software practices. It's often considered the "modern" way to write software. If your organization hasn't considered agile software development, you are behind the curve.

Agile software development can be summed up by the *agile manifesto*, the creed that defines the core of the movement. It states that you should prioritize your values as follows:

- "Individuals and interactions over processes and tools"
- "Working software over comprehensive documentation"
- "Customer collaboration over contract negotiation"
- "Responding to change over following a plan"

The manifesto doesn't mean to say that the concepts on the right of "over" in the bullet points above are useless. It just suggests that those on the left are *more* valuable. This is the inverse of how many traditional (also known as *waterfall*) software development strategies operate.

Flavors of agile

In general, being agile simply means that you embody the principles stated in the agile manifesto. But that definition is a bit too abstract to help you understand what exactly you should be doing. Therefore, the agile movement spawned a few methodologies for "doing" agile. These are more prescriptive processes for running a software development project using agile principles. It's rare that any organization sticks to one process exclusively. More typically, organizations apply bits of many of these methodologies. Your solution partner (or your organization) is probably doing the same thing.

- Scrum—This is the most popular agile framework. It involves working in two-week to four-week *sprints*, having daily standup meetings, and iteratively presenting fully functioning software. Most organizations that are being agile follow this methodology.

- Extreme programming (XP)—This is an early agile methodology formulated by software developers. It includes practices that enable programmers to embody the spirit of agile, such as pair-programming (two developers sharing one computer) and automatically testable code. XP is a little more focused on programming practices than processes.

- Lean/kanban—Lean software development is a flavor of agile, inspired by the lean manufacturing principles of Japanese automakers. It focuses on reducing waste and increasing throughput of finished software. Lean processes are usually expressed with a kanban board.

There are certainly other adaptations of agile, but these three are the most common. You'll typically see pieces borrowed from all three of these methodologies in any given agile process.

Some agile terminology

Since you'll probably be participating in an agile process in some manner, you should also understand some of its basic terminology. These are words you'll hear project managers and software developers throw around. You'll want to know what they're talking about.

- Daily standup (a.k.a. daily scrum)—The daily standup is a practice encouraged as part of the scrum framework. It's a 15-minute meeting held the same time every day. Stakeholders in the developer process state what they did since the previous standup, and what they plan to do next. Finally, the participants identify any issues that need to be discussed after the meeting. This meeting is specifically capped at 15 minutes to prevent it from becoming burdensome to the team.

- Pigs and chickens—Two types of attendees participate in a daily standup: pigs and chickens. The terms come from an adage in which a pig and a chicken decide to open a ham and eggs restaurant. Both have a stake in the endeavor, but the pig has much more skin in the game. During a standup meeting, pigs (those who are responsible for the success of the project) are the only ones who get to talk. Chickens are welcome to attend to gather information, but are not permitted to interrupt or interject.

- Kanban board—A kanban board is a way to communicate the stage of completion of work items. Traditionally a kanban board is displayed on a wall for everyone to see. As you complete tasks, you move sticky notes representing your task to the next column, signifying its movement to the next phase (such as from "in development" to "in testing"). Because of the virtual nature of modern teams, kanban boards are often managed digitally.

- Sprint (a.k.a iteration)—A sprint is a timeframe (or *timebox*) for finishing a subset of an application's functionality. They are typically two to four weeks in length. Every team is comfortable with a different cadence. At the end of each sprint, the development team is expected to deliver fully functional code for the features agreed on for that sprint. The scrum process recommends that each sprint starts with a meeting in which stakeholders agree on the scope and ends with a demonstration of the completed functionality.

- Story point—Most agile practices identify a logical fallacy in estimating tasks in "time to complete." The idea is that humans are flat-out bad at estimating time, when estimating ambiguous or creative tasks (like software development). Instead, many agile teams estimate story points, which are number values that have no meaning other than as a size relative to other tasks. What one team calls three story points, another might call five. The key is that within a specific team, they remain consistent. Story points should not be equated to a unit of time. They are a measure of relative complexity, not length of time.

- Burn-down/burn-up charts—Burn-down and burn-up charts are used to track a team's progress through a sprint. They map the team's progress against the average trajectory required to complete the agreed-on scope before the end of the sprint.

As a marketer, you're generally not going to be working with these concepts on a day-to-day basis. However, you'll probably be invited to sprint demos. You may attend standup meetings as a chicken. You may watch the kanban board to see how the team is doing. So it's important to understand these agile concepts and why the development team uses them.

Agile marketing

As organizations continue to find success using agile practices for software development, they've begun to experiment with applying the agile spirit to other areas. Agile marketing is a concept that is starting to gain momentum. It involves applying the philosophy of agile software development to the specific tasks and challenges of marketing.

As with most agile methodologies, agile marketing embraces the fact that the world is constantly changing. As the world continues to digitize, that change is accelerating. Agile marketing suggests that it's not entirely valid to set a marketing plan in stone for an entire quarter or fiscal year. Agile marketing sets a long-term vision but plans incremental tactics for applying that vision. The agile benefits are the same as for software developers: an increased tolerance for uncontrollable change.

Agile marketing doesn't have quite the general acceptance as agile software development, and there aren't any commonly accepted frameworks for agile marketing. There is, however, a lot of good (and free!) content available on the web that applies frameworks such as Lean and Scrum to marketing challenges. I highly recommend checking out information on agile marketing and considering its potential for your organization.

Agile software development and agile marketing can combine to create a very effective digital strategy for responding to your customer. If you are executing your marketing goals iteratively, you can also coordinate iteratively with software development. Doing so avoids creating long, drawn-out plans and huge software projects to implement changes. Effectively, you have two parallel agile processes that intersect when marketing establishes the need for a technical implementation.

If you are in digital marketing, expect your world to move toward this model. Embrace it now and start to learn. The organizations that use agile to respond to customer needs will put themselves in an advantageous position. Those who aren't yet using agile marketing, probably will sooner than later.

Development concepts

There are a few development concepts that only developers worry about that will also be part of the process that you'll participate in. You should understand what the development team is doing and why, but you needn't know more than the basics presented here.

Tiered environments

As developers build the functionality of your AEM implementation (page templates, components, and customizations), they'll migrate them through an ecosystem of tiered environments. Here's how that process might look:

1. The developer writes the code for a feature and tests it on a local environment (usually an installation of AEM installed on the developer's computer). Only the developer has the code for this feature, and she tests it before anyone else sees it.

2. All developers check in their code (see "Source control repository" later in this chapter), and it is merged into an *integration environment*. This is a software environment that everyone has access to, so they can test their code alongside the code written by the rest of the team. This environment is constantly changing as developers build and check in new features.

3. At milestones throughout the project (such as the end of a sprint), the code will be migrated to a *testing* or *quality assurance environment* in which testers bang on the features without worrying about developers changing code on a regular basis. Updates to this environment are performed in a controlled manner.

4. Before pushing to the live production environment, the code may be migrated to a *staging environment*, which should be an exact replica of the production

environment. It serves as the last chance to find and fix bugs before production. It's a locked-down environment, and it's updated only following important milestones, such as the end of an entire release.

5. Finally, the code is pushed to a *production environment*. These live AEM instances are accessed by real users. Any bugs that make it into this production environment will just have to remain until the development team pushes fixes through this entire process. Production environments are highly regulated because they tend to be mission-critical systems.

6. Once you launch your site, content authors will work in the production environment. Periodically, their content (like pages they create) will be copied back to all the other environments so that they stay relatively synchronized.

Not every organization follows this process. Some use additional tiers of environments, some use fewer. Some call the tiers by different names. The important thing is that in-progress functionality will migrate through multiple tiers of environments, meeting different expectations each time, until they are finally made available to the public.

Source control repository

Have you ever collaborated on a word processing document with another person who is located elsewhere? If you have, then you know how difficult it is. You have to make changes, email the document to your coworker, and then wait for her changes. If you do any work in parallel, one of you will overwrite the other. It's complicated when two people work on one file. Imagine 5, 10, or 50 people working on thousands of files that all depend on one another. This is the reality of software development.

Obviously, manually managing this mess is impossible. Developers use a *source control repository* (SCR) to do it for them. An SCR maintains a single master copy of the code. The developer checks out all the files, makes whatever changes are necessary, and then commits the altered files back to the master copy. If the SCR sees that someone committed a file change after the developer checked it out, it asks the developer to manually merge the changes. That means they have to look at both versions and combine them into one.

Sometimes a source control repository can merge the files programmatically so that the developer doesn't have to do it. Further, the development team will implement frequent commits/checkouts in small batches and assign tasks that have logical separation to enforce version control. But sometimes version conflicts are unavoidable.

The two most popular source control repositories are Subversion (SVN) and Git. There are many others, but they all fundamentally do the same thing. They allow a team of people to work on a program made up of hundreds or thousands of files without stepping on each others' toes.

Continuous integration

Software teams often use *continuous integration* (CI) to ensure the quality of the code they write. This concept goes hand in hand with source control and tiered environments. It requires that you frequently deploy the master copy of the code so that it becomes quickly apparent if a programmer unintentionally breaks a feature. The longer something goes broken, the more expensive and difficult it becomes to fix it. CI seeks to provide instant feedback about such an event.

When a team uses CI, a new build is created as team members check in changes to code. That build process also deploys the newest code to the integration environment. Some teams write automated tests that programmatically check for bugs. (In other words, they write code that tests their code.) If any of those tests fail, the developer who checked in the new code is notified. The developer is also responsible for manually examining the integration environment to ensure he or she didn't break any functionality.

The practice of continuous integration embraces the fact that there will be bugs and that people will make mistakes. It seeks to find and fix them as quickly as possible.

Best practices

This isn't a book about software development, so I'm not going to dwell on best practices for software development. But this *is* a book about digital marketing and its intersection with software development, so you should be aware of the following best practices for how you should expect to interact with the software development process.

Embrace the process

Every solution partner is going to bring a different software development process to the table. They'll have developed that process based on their experience of what works and doesn't. But it's also part of their job to adapt their process to the specific circumstances of your implementation. You should be open and flexible while working with your solution partner to settle on a process that everyone can live with.

Explore agile marketing

The agile philosophy has created a lot of success for software developers all over the world. The risk reduction and flexibility gained by an effective agile process are undeniable. Strongly consider exploring agile marketing processes for your organization. If you work with a solution partner that uses agile software development, the synergy created between the two processes is a potential competitive advantage.

Learn. Adjust. Repeat.

Whether or not you implement an agile methodology, focus on learning and adjusting. You aren't going to get all the requirements correct at the start. You aren't going to get the process correct at the start. Forcing yourself to stick to whatever you documented on Day 1 is counterproductive. Be open to learning from mistakes and successes and adjusting your processes throughout the implementation process and beyond.

Pick the right partner

A big part of an effective AEM implementation is picking the right solution partner. You'll want a partner that embraces the same values as you. Avoid partners who want to contractually protect themselves above doing what's best for you. At the same time, your solution partner shouldn't just be a hopper into which you dump your independently defined requirements. They should become a participant in your marketing organization, and their needs should become your needs (and vice versa). To build that kind of give-and-take relationship, you need to be thorough in selecting a solution partner and then work closely and cooperatively with them.

Summary

As a marketer, you don't develop software, but you'll need to understand the software development process. The implementation that your AEM solution partner undergoes (with your guidance) is a form of software development. Programmers have a whole set of challenges to deal with that don't always align with what you as a marketer have to deal with. Success is born of both the marketers and the programmers understanding each other's needs and building processes that meet them. Without a successful AEM implementation process, you'll have a hard time justifying the cost of buying the platform. Don't overlook the importance of getting it right.

Review questions

1. What are the basic phases of software development?

2. What happens during the deployment phase of a software development project?

3. At what point during the implementation process will you likely start building your web content?

4. What is a daily standup meeting?

5. How do programmers keep from overwriting each other's code?

Review answers

1. Requirements gathering, development, testing, deployment, and maintenance.

2. The deployment phase is the point in the process where software is migrated to a live production environment. It involves "last chance" testing and all the work needed to launch the software on a secure, stable environment that is suitable for public access.

3. The marketing team will likely start building web content at some point during the development phase. As soon as enough of the templates and components are built, it's important to start using them to flush out any bugs or missed requirements as quickly as possible.

4. A daily standup meeting is a 15-minute daily gathering where all development team stakeholders share three pieces of information: what they did since the last standup meeting, what they plan to do before the next, and what issues they need to take "offline."

5. Programming teams use a source control repository system to track and manage changes that are made to code files in parallel. It keeps one master copy of the code and forces all developers to check in/out from that.

INDEX

in user experience design, 305
Information technology. *see* IT (information technology)
Infrastructure as a Service (IaaS), 8, 259
Inheritance
 content, 47–48
 of permissions, 192
Installation, AEM, 175
Installation, package, 190
Instances
 clustering, 177–178
 defining traffic expectations, 295–296
 overview of, 174
 run modes, 174–175
Integration
 with Adobe platform, 20–21
 with Adobe SiteCatalyst, 211–213
 with Akismet spam filtering, 137
 with authoring emails, 225–226
 with cloud service configurations. *see* CSCs (cloud service configurations)
 considering AEM and, 32
 continuous, 327
 custom cloud-based, 265–266
 DAM–AdobeDrive, 80
 DAM–Scene7, 78–80
 defining needs for, 294
 as digital marketing tactic in MCM, 222–223
 with e-commerce, 22–23, 145
 with ExactTarget, 228
 with Google Analytics, 210–211
 integration models, 257–261
 modern marketing challenges and, 256–257
 overview of, 254–255
 review, 266–267
 with social networks, 138–139
 testing in implementation process, 319
 with web analytics, 209–210
 WEM cross-platform, 6–7
Interaction
 mobile first design and, 312
 scripting with JavaScript, 274
 user experience best practices, 306–307
 user experience design for, 304–305
 workflow, 121–122
Internal metadata, 93–95
Internal requirements, 291–294
Internationalization. *see* multilingual content
Internet portals, AEM issues, 24–25
Intranets, AEM issues, 24–25
IT (information technology)
 choosing integration method, 260–261
 in cloud-based integration, 259–260
 considering AEM and, 30

global site design issues, 104
modern marketing challenges, 256
on-premise integration and, 258–259
Iterations, in agile processes, 321–322, 324

J

Java, 275–276
JavaScript, 274
JCR (Java Content Repository), 279–280, 282
JSP (JavaServer Pages), 276–277

K

Kanban board, agile methodology, 323
Kicking off workflows, 121–122

L

Landing page component, e-commerce, 150
Language
 creating basic pages, 50–51
 maintaining global web presence. *see* multilingual content
Language copy, 109
Launchers, workflow setup, 122
Layout, webpage, 44
LDAP (Lightweight Directory Access Protocol) syncs, 193–194
Leads, Marketing Campaign Management, 219–221
Lean software development, agile methodology, 323
Lens components, Asset Share, 77
Libraries, 86–88
Licensing considerations
 AEM, 31
 using implementation partner for, 33
 WURFL for mobile authoring, 161
Lifecycle, package, 189–190
Lightweight Directory Access Protocol (LDAP) syncs, 193–194
"Like" buttons, social web, 131
Links, external checker for, 198–199
Liquidapsive.com, 168
Lists
 in Marketing Campaign Management, 219–221
 sending marketing emails to, 227
Live copy
 creating blueprint, 109
 for multilingual content, 108–109
 in referential inheritance, 49
Load balancing, 181–182
Load testing, 319
Locking pages, 60, 108–109

Multinational sites, 108
Multiple publish model, server architecture, 182
MVT (multivariate testing)
    choosing, 249
    for content optimization, 234
    limitations of, 249–250
    measuring user experience, 305
    overview of, 248–249

N

Namespaces, tag, 96–97
Naming conventions
    renaming pages, 59
    for SEO page optimization, 60–61
    taxonomies, 97–98
News articles, 53–54

O

Offline Importer, 199
Online shopping experience, 144–145
On-premise integration systems, 258–261
On-premise platforms, web analytics, 204
Open Graph protocol, 89–90, 93
Open Services Gateway Initiative (OSGi),
    277–278
Open source software, 29, 277
Optimization
    with dynamic content, 233–234
    user experience design for. see UXD (user
        experience design)
OSGi (Open Services Gateway Initiative),
    277–278
Outputting web content, with JSP, 276–277
Outsourcing, drawbacks for marketing, 30

P

PaaS (Platform as a Service)
    as cloud application, 8–9
    cloud-based integration with, 259–260
    outsourcing marketing technology, 30
Package management, 188–191
Package Manager, 189–190
Package Share, 191
Page components
    Blog component as, 134
    configuring using dialogs, 45–46
    content components vs., 45
    creating in DAM Asset Editor, 78
    creating in DAM Asset Share, 77
    defined, 43
    paragraph system using, 46
    powered by Apache Sling, 280–281
    relationship of templates to, 47

understanding, 43–46
Page impressions, 209, 250
Page Properties dialog, 45
Page-centric content system, AEM as, 41
Pages
    activation/deactivation of, 58
    activity reports for, 194
    creating content for. see content creation
    defining information architecture
        requirements, 295
    defining needs for AEM implementation,
        291–292
    Dispatcher-configured caching of, 181
    moving/copying/deleting, 59
    page-centric content and, 41
    properties, 93–95
    renaming, 59
    when to start building, 321
Paragraph system (parsys), 46
Parallel process flow, workflow, 118
Passwords, admin user, 194
Payload, AEM workflow, 121
Performance
    DAM optimizing, 70
    DAM workflows impacting, 124
    measuring marketing campaign, 219
    monitoring in maintenance phase of
        implementation, 320
Permissions
    accessing CRXDE via, 198
    best practices for, 193–194
    managing users and, 191–193
    role of administrator in, 39
    viewing/editing workflow models, 120
Personalization
    Adobe SiteCatalyst for, 212
    of campaigns and experiences, 238–240
    with client context, 240–242
    of content, 20
    content testing. see content testing
    defined, 233
    with dynamic content, 232–233
    of e-commerce customer profiles, 150
    of e-commerce shopping carts, 149
    of e-commerce sites, 23
    features for, 20
    how it works, 235
    of marketing campaigns, 219
    overview of, 238
    reasons for, 235–237
    review, 252–253
    with Scene7 template for, 243
    of social network login, 242–243
    strategies for, 237–238
    targeted components for, 244–245
    teasers for, 243–244